D0090369

SHADOW
CULTURE

SHADOW CULTURE

Eugene Taylor

Psychology and
Spirituality in
America

COUNTERPOINT
WASHINGTON, D.C.

Library of Congree Cataloging-in-Publication Data
Taylor, Eugene.
    Shadow culture : psychology and spirituality in America from the
Great Awakening to the New Age / Eugene Taylor.
        p.   cm.
    Includes bibliographical references and index.
    ISBN 1-887178-80-5 (alk. paper)
        1. United States—Religion.   2. Spirituality—United States—
History.   3. Psychology, Religious—United States—History.
I. Title.
BL2525.T39   1999
200'.973—dc21   99-17527
                                                                            CIP

FIRST PRINTING

Jacket and text design by Guenet Abraham

Printed in the United States of America on acid-free paper that meets the
American National Standards Institute Z39-48 Standard.

COUNTERPOINT
P. O. Box 65793
Washington, D.C. 20035-5793

Counterpoint is a member of the Perseus Books Group

10   9   8   7   6   5   4   3   2   1

For Lily

Contents

Preface and Acknowledgments

THIS PROJECT BEGAN IN 1977 WITH THE DISCOVERY OF A VAST reprint collection of ephemera on spiritualism, mental healing, demonology, witchcraft, multiple personality, and other topics that had been originally brought together by the American philosopher-psychologist William James and deposited by his heirs in the Harvard College Library in 1923. Dubbed by his son, Henry James Jr., the lawyer and Harvard overseer, as probably the largest collection of crank literature from turn-of-the-century New England ever assembled, the material formed an important part of my reconstruction of James's previously unpublished Lowell Lectures of 1896, titled *Exceptional Mental States,* and led to the subsequent reconstruction of the so-called Boston School of Psychopathology, which flourished between 1880 and 1920 before the advent of psychoanalysis—the topic of my own Lowell lectures, originally delivered in 1982.

As a historian of psychology and psychiatry at Harvard University for the past twenty years, I have been privileged to have access to an unprecedented cache of materials in both the university and Medical School archives. At the same time, I have been an occasional procurer of such materials for the university libraries when I happened to discover them in some barn or attic. From this vantage point, it soon became readily apparent to me that, whereas E. G. Boring's monumental *History of Experimental Psychology* (1929, 1950) has yet to be surpassed as the seminal text defining the history of the field, it is now generally recognized that there is more than one interpretation of the history of American psychology. I would carry this argument one step further, however, to suggest that history shows us there is, in fact, more than one definition of psychology in common currency.

Although these ideas are being more fully developed elsewhere, in my view, American psychology can be seen as a torrent of at least three separate streams. The first is the history of American academic laboratory psychology, which is comprised of a vast literature on the institutionalization of psychology as a scientific discipline within the university curriculum. The second is the history of clinical psychology, referring generally to the history of the assessment and treatment of persons, such as job candidates or student applicants, or the delivery of therapeutic services to patients with mental problems, but referring more specifically to the practice and theory of psychotherapy, that ubiquitous activity of psychologists, psychiatrists, pastoral counselors, and other mental health care workers that is a continual subject of controversy. To date, there is no definitive history of clinical psychology, although certain attempts have been made in that direction. The third stream is the history of folk psychology, referring to a psychospiritual tradition of character development that appears to have been endemic to the American scene ever since the founding of the American colonies and that now appears to be driving a significant revolution in American popular culture focused on an experiential interpretation of higher consciousness. Literally, it has moved out of the shadow into the light. The present text represents a historical sketch of this third stream and is offered as both a commentary on American social history and a definition of an altogether new addition to our concept of what constitutes the scope of psychology in modern culture.

I am indebted to numerous individuals and institutions for assistance over the past twenty years in the construction of this statement: trustees of the Wesley N. Gray Fund; Raphael Guiu and Michelle Gargiari of the Swedenborg Library; the late Marian Kirven, librarian at the Swedenborg School of Religion in Newton, Massachusetts; Barbara Moss, archivist at the Concord Public Library in Concord, Massachusetts; trustees of the Thoreau Lyceum in Lincoln, Massachusetts; Bay James Baker of Newburyport, Massachusetts, literary executor of the estate of William James; Richard Wolfe, former Garland Librarian in the Boston Medical Library and archivist at Harvard Medical School; the staff at the Houghton Rare Manuscript Library at Harvard University and the staff at the Harvard University Archives in Pusey Library; and ministers and members of the congregation at the Spiritual Fraternity in Brookline, Massachusetts. Professor Emeritus Jacques Barzun of Columbia, the late Henry A. Murray of Harvard, and the late Francis O. Schmitt of MIT, all served as my most important literary critics; while the late John Adams Abbott of Lincoln, Massachusetts, and the Massachusetts General Hospital, who for many years was my guide to historic Boston psychiatry. I am particularly indebted to Elizabeth Erihig and staff at the Bakkan Library of Electricity in Life in Minneapolis; trustees of the Museum of our National Heritage, in Lexington, Massachusetts; officers and trustees of the American Society for Psychical Research; and especially Lisette Coly, Eileen Coly, and Joanne MacMahon of the Parapsychology Foundation in New York City. Ellen Ratner of Washington, D.C., proved to be a fellow spiritual traveler through the literature on mental healing of the nineteenth century, as did the Shaker scholar Larry Myers of Lincoln, Massachusetts, while Sonu Shamdasani, formerly of the Wellcome Institute for the History of Medicine in London, played a key role in providing invaluable material on Carl Jung.

Hara Marano, editor at *Psychology Today,* greatly facilitated the dissemination of my ideas by inviting me to write a summary of the contemporary spiritual scene, a statement that turned out to be so suggestive that it was scooped by *Newsweek* without attribution. Tom Hurley, Barbara McNeal, and Wink Franklin were responsible for adopting my work on the American visionary tradition as the theme of the twentieth anniversary of the Institute of Noetic Sciences; they were responsible for the creation of both National Public Radio and Public Broadcasting Service interviews on my work, especially through the two series titled *Thinking Allowed,* with Jeffrey Mishlove, and *New Dimensions Radio,* with Michael and Justine Toms. Miles Vich, editor of the *Journal of Transpersonal Psychology,* and Tom Greening, editor of the *Journal of Humanistic Psychology,* were instrumental on many occasions in providing crucial historical information. Michael Murphy and George Leonard of Esalen Institute were periodic confidants to the project, as was the late Rollo May. Saybrook Graduate School and Research Institute, under the skillful leadership of President Gerald Bush and Dean Maureen O'Hara, supplied continual support, as did numerous faculty there, including Stanley Krippner, Jeanne Achterberg, David Lukoff, Ian Wickram, and a variety of students, among them Paul Shane, Thomas J. Martinez, Janet Piedilato, and Richard Hartman. I thank them for important material resources and intellectual discussions.

I am also particularly indebted to Jenny Bent for introducing me to Jack Shoemaker and the staff at Counterpoint, with whom I am most pleased to at last publish this work. Finally, because of her keen and long-standing interest in spirituality and my studies on the American variety of it throughout the course of her entire young life, I dedicate this book to my beloved daughter, Lily Augusta Taylor.

Eugene Taylor, Ph.D.
Cambridge, Massachusetts
August 13, 1998

Chapter One

Folk Psychology and the American Visionary Tradition

THE PHRASE "RELIGION IN MODERN AMERICAN CULTURE" often conjures up images of a church or synagogue. We may think of scriptural texts, particularly the Bible or the Torah, and the rituals surrounding birth, marriage, death, or the High Holidays. Or we may think of weekly worship services, with someone always in charge, usually a kindly older gentleman dressed in the vestments of priestly office. Yet an extraordinary amount of evidence suggests that our conception of spirituality is undergoing enormous change. Consider the following examples:

When Mary Fisk was near death, she felt herself going down a long tunnel and entering a domain of extraordinarily bright light. On the way, she met those whom she had known but were now long dead, and she claims she encountered numerous beings whom she could only describe as angels, who wrapped her in an ever-increasing, loving presence. She later reported hearing a voice tell her that she should go back, that it was not her time yet, that there was still work for her to do in the world. She awakened from her coma in a hospital room. After her recovery, she went back to school and became a social worker in a hospice environment, helping others in their transition between life and death.[1]

Rita McClain, an Iowa farm girl, was brought up in the Pentecostal Church. To escape from the heavy sense of guilt, she tried a less rigid form of Protestantism, but by the age of twenty-seven, she rejected all organized religion. For the next eighteen years, she stuck to rock climbing and hiking as her source for peace of mind. After the trauma of a divorce, she suddenly experienced a spiritual awakening once she became involved with the Unity School of Christianity, a modern-day version of the New Thought movement from the nineteenth century. From there, she developed an intense interest in Native American religions, and her spiritual practice now focuses on Buddhist meditation.[2]

Jack Huber, a clinical psychologist, became interested in Zen and went to Japan to attend a one-week intensive training session for beginners. He was guided by a Zen Roshi through the initial stages of practice, and near the end his teacher affirmed that he had experienced *kensho,* or satori—that is, he had glimpsed what the teacher called "one's own true nature." He reported that his personality changed completely thereafter. Stressful events did not bother him anymore. He met whatever happened to him with an even-mindedness that he found surprising. He also felt more free from the constraints of time, not harried or pressed. And he felt that he now chose what was going to affect him and what was not. He also reported that he was able to keep in touch with his original experience through daily Zen sitting by himself once he had returned home.[3]

Then there is China Galland, a working mother with two children. In her recent book, *Longing for Darkness: Tara and the Black Madonna,* she recounted how she left the sterile patriarchy of Catholicism by going into Zen, before discovering Tibetan Buddhism. Within Buddhism, she discovered a lineage of goddesses whose identity she began to explore intensely. When her spiritual search widened to the feminine aspect of God in other religions, she rediscovered her roots in Catholicism through the

Polish icon of the Black Madonna. Enriched by her spiritual journey, now deeply contemplative, she is once again a practicing Catholic, but now, she believes, on her own terms.

Such examples can be endlessly reproduced. Personal testimonies to belief in a higher power are now regularly proclaimed not from the church pews, but in Alcoholics Anonymous meetings and in other twelve-step programs. In books, in magazine articles, at weekend retreats, and in hotel seminar rooms, spiritual enlightenment, communication with angels, and talks with God before returning from the dead are now in vogue. Discussion of women's rights has given way to examination of women's spirituality. As one woman from a small Midwestern town put the situation after reading *The Feminine Face of God,* "Before you couldn't find this anywhere; now it's even playing in Peoria." Meanwhile, interest in men's spirituality has been spawned by the popular works of Robert Bly, James Hillman, and others, so that we now have Harvard psychiatrists who specialize in the topic. Such scholars are also looking at religion along the life span. Robert Coles, for instance, has recently presented his research on the spiritual life of children. Indeed, a quarter of the titles on the *New York Times* best-seller list are on spiritual subjects, one of which, Scott Peck's *The Road Less Traveled,* a book on spirituality by a psychiatrist, was there for almost 600 weeks. The top best-seller at one point was none other than *Crossing the Threshold of Hope,* by Pope John Paul II.[4]

Religious consciousness is now penetrating into the most secular corners of popular culture. The Benedictine monks of Santo Domingo de Silos had a new album of Gregorian chants that soared past Gershwin and Pavarotti on the popularity charts in the classical category. One of the top five best-sellers of all time, the monks' album outsold music's top secular stars such as Bonnie Raitt, Nirvana, and Snoop Doggy Dogg. Not to be outdone, the Beastie Boys produced an album that contained a Buddhist rap. In the world of sports, Phil Jackson, a Buddhist practitioner for twenty years, revolutionized basketball coaching by leading the Chicago Bulls to three consecutive NBA championships with Zen training he had learned under Jon Kabat-Zinn. Jackson's approach is to emphasize awareness, selfless teamwork, and aggressiveness without anger. Although we would normally expect to see his face in one of the big national magazines such as *Sports Illustrated,* the new popular journal reviewing Buddhism in America, *Tricycle,* has also featured him.

Scholars confirm that we are in the midst of an unprecedented period of spiritual activity. Pentecostalism has increased significantly, according to Harvey Cox, professor of pastoral theology at Harvard Divinity School. Martin Marty, professor of religion at the University of Chicago, has published a series of volumes on the widespread renewal of fundamentalism. At the same time, Timothy Miller, professor of religion at the University of Kansas, has released the most recent evaluation of America's new alternative religions, showing that what was originally thought to be a passing fad of the 1960s has now matured into a collection of altogether new and well-secured faith communities.[5]

Scientists have also shown an interest in the subject. At meetings of the American Association for the Advancement of Science, symposia on religion and science draw standing-room-only crowds. The Boston Theological Institute, a consortium of divinity schools in the New England area, has launched the Center for Faith and Science Exchange, which invites distinguished scientists to speak on religious themes. This center is part of a much larger network of institutes and organizations interested in the dialogue between science and religion. Some of these include the Center for Contemporary Science and Christian Theology, the Institute on Religion in an Age of Science, and the John Templeton Foundation, which annually awards distinguished scientists for contributions to religious subjects. One of the foundation's programs entailed a major symposium on religion and genetics, in which the implications of the Human Genome Project were considered by scientists who were also theologians. Another institute held summer courses on the relationship between Christianity and scientific theories about the origin of the universe, while yet another launched conferences on the religious and ethical implications of brain neuroscience. And what does neuroscience have to do with religion?

Interdisciplinary communication in the neurosciences is now taking place at an astronomical rate among investigators in molecular genetics, immunology, endocrinology, neurology, and psychiatry. The subject of their discussions is the biology of consciousness. While scientists have long been able to study the physical world with confidence in their methods, they have had to deal with questions of ethics and the essential relation of human beings to the animal kingdom once they moved into the domain of biology. Now, however, the new domain is the brain, and the questions that naturally arise are all about the relation of the physical organ to our experience of the world. What is the essential relation of the brain to the mind? Paradoxically, this is the kind of philosophical question long banned from purely scientific discussions but one that has now returned with new urgency because it has become the central problem in the study of consciousness. And with such questions has also come increased dialogue about whether or not beliefs and values play a role in such scientific activities as the construction of an experiment, the interpretation of data, the framing of a diagnosis, or even the determination of outcomes of a medical procedure. Such discussions are not far away from the more basic issue concerning the dialogue between science and religion.

One of the great pioneers in the neuroscience revolution, the late Francis O. Schmitt, addressed this issue in his memoirs before he died. His autobiography, *The Never-Ceasing Search,* was based on the successful history of the Neurosciences Research Program (NRP). Launched under his directorship, the NRP carried on research activities over a twenty-year period and later formed the nucleus of the present-day 18,000-member Society for Neuroscience. Because he believed that the new revolution in consciousness is even bigger than the Copernican revolution that preceded it, in a surprise ending to a long litany of scientific accomplishments, Schmitt's final chapter, which he also delivered as one of the prestigious Templeton Lectures, called for the adoption of his strategy for launching the neurosciences as a blueprint to foster a similar revolution in the dialogue between science and religion.[6]

Psychiatry, as well, is reflecting the new awakening. The category of "spiritual emergencies" is now recognized in the most recent edition of the *Diagnostic and Statistical Manual (DSM-IV),* the listing standard that psychiatrists and insurance companies use to diagnose and calculate the cost of treating major mental disorders. Before now, psychiatrists acknowledged behavior as being only normal or abnormal. All experiences that deviated from normal everyday functioning were considered abnormal and treated accordingly with various regimes of drugs and psychotherapy. Now, however, recognition of spiritual emergencies, empirically defined by clinical psychologists David Lukoff, Robert Turner, and Francis Lu, alerts psychiatrists to patients who might be going through a nonpsychotic spiritual crisis.[7] These people, instead of being misdiagnosed, medicated, and confined to a hospital, need only to be assisted with philosophical problems of meaning and identity. When this happens, evidence shows that they achieve a full and rapid recovery of the presenting symptoms.

The American philosopher-psychologist William James referred to such examples as an awakening to a new sense of the mystical. He believed that, although mystical experiences are transient and cannot always be brought on at will, they carry a sense of knowledge deeper and more significant than that of the rational intellect. The motivational psychologist Abraham Maslow referred to them in terms of both peak and plateau experiences and associated them with the emergence of the self-actualizing aspect of personality. And the Swiss psychiatrist Carl Jung described them as an integral part of the process of individuation, which he said was a movement away from egotism toward autonomous selfhood.[8]

In short, hardly anyone in popular culture still seems to be chanting the guiding pronouncements of the past century that began with Nietszche, who proclaimed that God was dead. Marx followed by announcing that religion was the opium of the masses, and Freud finished by establishing, in the name of science, that religion was nothing more than the redirection of repressed sexual impulses toward more socially acceptable ends. Indeed, a spate of T-shirts and bumper stickers has dismissed the entire century of philosophic controversy on the subject by proclaiming instead that "Nietszche is dead."

The Character of an Unprecedented Movement

THIS WIDESPREAD FLOURISHING of spirituality appears to have a number of defining characteristics, the primary one being that the motivating power behind it is not originating in mainstream institutionalized science, religion, or education. Rather, we are witnessing a popular phenomenon of epic proportions that is at once profoundly personal, experiential, and transcendent. Expressed in a psychological language, I would say that the new awakening is directed toward an opening of the inward doors of perception and is perceptually grounded in what the experiencer believes is a deeper level of the immediate moment.

On this point hangs an important distinction between religion and spirituality that also characterizes this apparently new movement. The denominational churches are not the ones that are leading the current awakening. This is not the elevation of one catechism over another or the rise of a some new organized religion that everyone must follow. Instead, the revolution is occurring in the minds and hearts of millions of individual people whose biographies cut across all categories of type and culture. It is a revolution based on the expression of a new breadth and depth to contemporary experience that goes far beyond the ability of traditional institutions to address.

Today, numerous individuals report having such experiences. As a result, there has been a veritable explosion of interest in esoteric and mystical traditions. Paganism, Gnosticism, and Neoplatonism are reappearing in the form of contemporary adherents. Such medieval mystics as St. John of the Cross, St. Teresa of Avila, and Meister Eckehart are being more widely read through such efforts as those of the Paulist Press, which has produced a monumental series entitled Classics in Western Spirituality. Even the more esoteric teachings of such modern mystics as Swami Vivekananda, Paramahansa Yogananda, Sri Aurobindo, and now Mother Meera are familiar to entire communities of meditators.

Another feature of the new awakening is its eclecticism. As the 1993 World's Parliament of Religions in Chicago demonstrated, whereas there are still many denominational adherents who affiliate with only one church and one set of teachings, many people who appear to be deeply interested in spiritual subjects by no means confine themselves to a single tradition. The basic truths of spiritual life can be found for these eclectics as much in the Christian Bible as in the Torah, the Koran, the Tao-te Ching, the Heart Sutra, or the Bhagavad Gita.

A century ago, it was expected that people would live out their lives within the confines of the religious tradition into which they were born, yet it is not unusual today for someone to have been brought up in a family where the mother might have been a Catholic, the father a Lutheran, and the children attendees of the Episcopal Church. These same children today could just as easily be agnostics as Unitarians, Swedenborgians, or practicing Buddhists. Likewise, a middle-aged American Jewish professional can still attend a synagogue, follow the teachings of the Tibetan Buddhist Sogyal Rimpoche, and practice meditation with the Vietnamese Buddhist teacher Thich Nhat Hanh, while in the past having been a transcendental meditation initiator.

Yet another feature of the new awakening is its inherently psychological character. Its content has to do with the alteration of consciousness, with the integration of the mind and body, and with the connection between physical and mental health. Originally an outgrowth of the counterculture psychotherapeutic movement, which dealt with problems of adjustment and identity, paying someone to talk about oneself outside a traditional institutional setting has now become more overtly psychospiritual and holistic. According to Philip Reiff, author of *The Therapeutic Revolution,* psychotherapy, particularly its psychoanalytic branch, has become the new sacrament in the modern world. But Freudian psychoanalysis dominated the American scene only until the 1960s, after which a completely deregulated atmosphere developed in which radically different systems appeared. There was a veritable explosion of new psychotherapeutic regimes, chiefly due to the widespread use of psychedelic drugs in the American counterculture and to the so-called expansion of consciousness. Jungian analytic psychology became much more popular than Freudian analysis, precisely because it acknowledged such a transcendent dimension of personality functioning.

But Jungian psychology turned out to be only one development among many. On one end was somatic therapy, the use of bodywork in conjunction with psychotherapy. The most intense of these therapists were involved in the politics of sexuality, such as the followers of Wilhelm Reich, who employed nude therapy sessions focused on developing the potency of the orgasm. In the middle were the sensitivity training groups and experiential encounter techniques of the human potential movement. At the other pole were meditation and psychotherapy, practitioners of which blended Asian meditation techniques, such as exercises in one-pointed concentration and breathing regimes from yoga, with the more traditional verbal exchange of psychotherapy.

In this environment, forms of psychotherapy dedicated to intensive spiritual practice were able to emerge. Since the 1960s, they have matured in their own right and show no signs of diminishing. These include such regimes as Stanislav Grof's holotropic breathwork, Roberto Assagioli's psychosynthesis, and Jack Kornfeld's Buddhist insight meditation techniques. As well, shamanic practices from various non-Western cultures, which involve drumming, singing, and dancing, have also emerged as popular psychotherapeutic tools for inducing what are believed to be healing states of ecstatic trance.

An American Shadow Culture

ONE OF THE MOST DISTINGUISHING MARKS of the new awakening is that it appears primarily to be a shadow culture of Judeo-Christian Protestantism. By this I mean we have all the elements of the mainstream before us—our great universities, a science establishment, the organized churches and synagogues, the military, the federal government, and industrial and corporate culture, all largely created and driven by the male psyche. There is then the media in all its various dimensions that reports on the general and specific content of these great cultural institutions. Then there is the shadow culture—a vast unorganized array of discrete individuals who live and think differently from the mainstream but who participate in its daily activities. When these are people from other countries, we call them "unassimilated." When these are people of minority extraction, we have tended to call them "subcultures," because they pass back and forth between the dominant white middle-class culture and their separate but organized and identifiable enclave. Native Americans are a special case of the shadow culture, since they have always been here but have never been integrated into the mainstream. Furthermore, children, the elderly, and prisoners tend to fall easily into the shadow culture, because, collectively, they are captive populations manipulated and controlled by the system.

At the same time, the shadow culture is also made up of individuals who simply cannot function in normal society: the homeless, the mentally ill, the destitute, and even the sociopathic—those who cannot adjust to any culture. Recovering patients also fall into this category, since, identity-wise, the road back to health is a transitory, intermediate state.

There is a special category of person to whom the present volume is referring, however, that also populates the shadow culture—a kind of spiritual pilgrim. This is the person who has awakened to his own self-nature; the entrepreneurial genius who has broken the mold in his particular niche; the creative artist who has adopted a visionary view of the cosmos; the mendicant who has taken a voluntarily accepted vow of poverty; or the person who simply thinks differently. In other words, the spiritual pilgrim is an otherwise healthy personality who, for one reason or another, has willfully chosen to disengage from culture, either permanently or temporarily, and who has, as a result, adopted a different way of seeing daily events.

If the interpreters of modern culture wonder what the current revolution in spirituality is all about, they have only to recognize a widespread emphasis on the transcendent by those of the largely white middle-class generation who left the institutional church, altered the course of their studies in the university, postponed having families, or turned to new and unexpected forms of vocation. Put another way, the American counterculture movement of the latter half of the twentieth century has been and continues to be a profoundly Caucasian phenomenon.

Meanwhile, people from Asian cultures are already steeped in alternative views of transcendent reality, although many have set aside their indigenous outlook after passing through the Western educational system. Latinos have long hidden their deep native spirituality behind the symbols of traditional Christianity. African Americans have an ethnic religious tradition that has remained intact and has helped them endure and then emerge from centuries of servitude, while at the same time they have created their own uniquely American churches. And Native Americans already have an integrated view of the physical and spiritual world. Consequently, all these communities are hardly surprised when white authors on the *New York Times* best-seller list proclaim that there is, in fact, a spiritual world!

This list, it should be noted, contains books predominantly for the educated white middle class, which represents the liberal Judeo-Christian roots of American culture and which is collectively searching for universal truth, largely according to the dictates of the Western rationalist tradition. But the list is becoming more and more populated by visionaries from the shadow culture, who are now more than ever assisting pilgrims from the mainstream in discovering that the most important and vital elements related to meaning turn out to be the repressed aspects of one's own unconscious. These hidden aspects, the folk tradition tells us, when bathed in the light of contemplative consciousness, lead to the spiritual awakening of personality.

It is quite important to realize, however, that the shadow culture to which I am referring remains radically different from the general audience of the mass media and should not be confused with popular consciousness. Mass media is the primary theater in which the shadow culture finds its most overt and immediate expression, but the shadow culture is not exactly identical to the level of social consciousness which is captivated and therefore manipulated and shaped by that means. The shadow culture tends to be derived from the reigning Judeo-Christian and Anglo-American definition of reality, but it also behaves as a subculture distinct from its parental roots. It is still largely white, middle class, and slightly overeducated. It probably is made up more of women than of men and contains more artists and writers than engineers and scientists, but these proportions are also rapidly changing.

Finally, in the larger view, while the Judeo-Christian, Greco-Roman, Western European, and Anglo-American definition of reality continues to dominate Western civilization, throughout its history the West has, nevertheless, also fostered a shadow culture that is distinctly visionary in character.[9] Beyond the religious law of the Jewish Pharisees, the mystical Essenes flourished. Beside Aristotle's logic was Plato's analogy of the cave. Alongside early Christianity were Gnosticism and Neoplatonism. Behind the Talmud was the Kabbalah. As a counterpoint to the religion of the Mullahs was Sufism. In the shadow of Catholicism and the Protestant Reformation were the Rosicrucians and the Freemasons. Next to astronomy was astrology; alongside chemistry was alchemy; and beside mathematics was numerology.[10]

The contemporary philosopher of religion Robert Ellwood has called this shadow culture the "alternative reality tradition" in the West.[11] Numerous authors before him have written about this hidden tradition, and many have tried to show that there is a continuous thread that links the different schools and periods, making it appear that there is a defined path of the great masters, a secret brotherhood, or a single underlying catechism of mystical teachings. Rosicrucianism drew on the sacred texts of the East and the Hermetic tradition. Masonry, which had links to Rosicrucianism, was also related to the Templars. All of these drew their inspiration from Gnosticism. Likewise, Ralph Waldo Emerson has been compared to the Neoplatonists, and so on.

I believe that, although such a grand scheme may exist, it is neither as clear-cut nor so vastly interconnected as it may first appear. Rather, it may be more of a concatenation of synchronous expressions, many of which arose by themselves, only some of which may be connected at different historical points. All, however, seem to be suggestive of an interior vision that has been discovered and rediscovered over and over again as individuals, groups, and sometimes whole cultures turned inward. The one thing that may be said is that, as opposed to the dominant culture, which has been outward, rational, reductionistic, dominated by the senses, and driven by the letter of the law, this alternative reality tradition has been inner, contemplative, ascetic, and mystical, believing itself to be the true aristocracy of the spirit from which the letter of the law was derived.

The American shadow culture is the most significant contribution of American culture to the larger alternative reality tradition in the West. At the same time, it functions as the unconscious equivalent, or the repressed antithesis, of the larger and more visible collective consciousness of Judeo-Christian culture. In this way, the shadow culture holds exactly the opposite prejudices of the dominant culture. Where the dominant culture tends to overemphasize its Judeo-Christian and Anglo-European roots, the shadow culture embraces world cultures rather than defining itself as separate from them. These are the white men and women who have lived successfully among Native American Indians, the Christian and Jewish practitioners of Hindu yoga and meditation, the Caucasian musicians who have mastered the African drums, the Jewish psychology professors who have attained the rank of Moslem Sufi masters, and the American women who have become Buddhist nuns.

This syncretism is extraordinarily important because it occurs in two ways: first, in the manner in which ethnic subcultures assimilate to what they perceive as the American way of life and yet still retain strands of their individual identity; and second, in the way visionaries of the American shadow culture, in turn, absorb the identity of ethnic subcultures and yet remain within the iconography and mythology of the dominant culture.

The psychological mechanism at work here is a profound, persistent, and continuous alteration in consciousness that allows the person to, in effect, live in two cultures at once—one, the dominant culture of normative science and mainstream religion; the other, a shadow culture of mythic and visionary proportions.[12]

A Visionary Folk Psychology

THERE ARE, OF COURSE, many different kinds of psychology, although the definition of the field gets more and more restrictive the closer one gets to the university departments that purport to teach it, government funding agencies that sponsor only certain kinds of research, and clinical settings that allow only certain kinds of tests and therapeutic techniques to be employed. To understand the way the word "psychology" is used here, however, one must think in terms of the idiosyncratic subjective life of the individual. Think of poetry; think of visionary experience; think of psychology as focused on the experience of consciousness in the immediate moment that flows forward in a stream. One of the ways I have tried to reorient the reader's attention to this new definition is to collectively refer to the history of all idiosyncratic and personal attempts to define experience as a form of folk psychology.

The term "folk psychology" has its own particular history.[13] It first came into use in the mid-nineteenth century in German-speaking countries under the rubric of *voelkerpsychologie.* There it meant, first, an investigation into the intellectual and moral life and other mental characteristics of people in relation to one another, as well as into the influence of these characteristics on the spirit of politics, art, and literature. Specifically, it was wielded as a conceptual tool for the fomenting of a Pan-Germanic nationalism among German-speaking populations scattered in different countries throughout Europe.

However, around the same time, *voelkerpsychologie* also came to mean the study of the whole of mankind—the history of the mental development of the human race, viewed from the various perspectives of language, religion, philosophy, and custom, something akin to what we might call today "social psychology." Folk psychology, in this higher intellectual sense, informs the content of all the mental sciences as creations of a social community, inexplicable in terms merely of individual consciousness. "Folk," here, embraces families, classes, clans, and groups, but it is qualified in terms specific to psychological investigation.

The noted German experimental psychologist Wilhelm Wundt wrote five volumes on the content, meaning, and methods of folk psychology.[14] This involved the historical study of the religious, social, and mythic dimensions of mental phenomena that could not be explained by a strictly experimental laboratory approach. Unfortunately, his definition of psychology as an experimental laboratory science was widely read in English at the turn of the last century, while his ideas on the other half of psychology—its historical, religious, and social side—have yet to be translated.

The term folk psychology has again come back into vogue in the late twentieth century with the development of the cognitive neurosciences. The cognitive neurosciences in psychology represent a domain largely populated with cognitive scientists—in other words, statisticians, behaviorists, and computer programmers who have adopted a mentalistic language to describe the behavior of thought processes and whose training in philosophy is generally limited to the Western analytic tradition. Before, Aristotle, Descartes, Kant, and Hegel were out of fashion because they were philosophers, not scientists; now, they are back in, being discussed along with Bertrand Russell, Ludwig Wittgenstein, and Willard Quine, because the neuroscience revolution, essentially about the biology of consciousness, has created a host of philosophical problems about how science can study itself. Meanwhile, the most vocal protagonists of the cognitive neurosciences take the old presuppositions of positivistic science as a given, while trying to analyze the upheaval of that very system with the same analytic tools used to create it in the first place.

The main premise of the neuroscience community is that neuroscience is superior to folk psychology.[15] Here, neuroscience means the rational ordering of sensory data, gleaned from a computer or a magnetic image of the brain, or a paper and pencil test, that has been translated into explanatory theories that can be debated among scientists. The only sentences worth analyzing, Professor Quine says, are the logical ones. This, they claim, is the only real and legitimate source of knowledge about reality. Folk psychology, conversely, is now defined broadly by the neuroscientists as the commonsense language of everyday experience that attributes feelings, motives, and intentions to human action. Neuroscientists, touting their own line, maintain that they have clearly shown the fallacy of everyday thinking about the world. Their alternative is that one does not need to know what people say about their own experience to understand the new science of how we think. The arguments of these not-quite-philosophers/not-quite-scientists are very technical, but they can be boiled down to the general realization that what they are really carrying on is an insiders' debate on why the old theories in psychology of how we think should be displaced with the new theories of these authors.

My version of folk psychology is radically different. I take it as a mythic and visionary language of immediate experience—a spontaneously generated language of interior life, the function of which is self-realization. This language is simultaneously psychological and spiritual in character. It is psychological insofar as it pertains to the various ways in which a person navigates different states of interior consciousness and has self-consciously adopted a metaphorical language for doing so; in the American cultural setting, this is usually some form of depth psychology related to psychotherapy. It is spiritual insofar as its function is the evolution and transformation of personality; that is to say, it encompasses those themes that a person takes to be of deepest, highest, and ultimate concern, and it expresses these concerns in images that transcend language by their numinous, mythic, and visionary character.

Such a psychology is characterized by its emphasis on multiple realities, by its view that personality is shaped by dynamic forces of the unconscious, and by its aim toward an understanding of extraordinary states of consciousness and expanded human potential. It is also known by its intense attraction to the natural environment and by its hint that there is some fundamental relationship between a return to nature and the recovery of basic values. It can be identified by its millennial vision of world peace. In its search for parity between science and spirituality, it rests on the assumption that mental healing is an essential part of physical health and that there is healing in community. It promotes the paranormal as an integral part of human functioning, and it takes seriously accounts of spirit communication on the after-death plane, dream images, personal symbols of one's destiny, and religious visions. One can see from this that, above all, the most important element of this psychology is its emphasis on the possibility of the transcendent—that consciousness can be molded into something higher, purer, better.

I have also mentioned that the American shadow culture tends to have closer affinities with non-Western and even nontechnological cultures than with the institutions of the dominant mainstream. As a result, regarding discussions about the more general dialogue between science and religion, the visionary ideas inherent in the shadow culture tend to be oriented more toward the phenomena of depth psychology and comparative religions than to the more limited dialogue between physics and Christianity now going on in conservative religious and scientific circles. A key reason for this difference is that broad-minded conservative Christians genuinely interested in the resolution of the conflict between science and religion have tended to interpret this integration as the application of scientific method to prove the truths of Christianity. The shadow culture, on the other hand, has tended to radically transform the definition of psychology, moving it away from being just another category in the domain of the social sciences and placing it more in the center of phenomenological awareness, thus equating psychology with the immediate experience of personal consciousness. This is also the central orientation of the better-developed "inner sciences" of Asian cultures, such as the philosophy of yoga in Hinduism or the articulation of stages of meditation in various Buddhist schools.

This is to say that folk psychology has a history and, within the American shadow culture, even a direction; but more often than not, these elements have remained diffuse and peripheralized. Their effects, however, are now becoming more visible to the collective waking consciousness of the dominant culture. In its present form, the tradition of American folk psychology remains elusive precisely because it has no leader, no center, no fixed teachings and because it is concretely centered in the experiential life of the individual, ungeneralizable from one person to the next, yet perpetually there making its mark.

The Great Awakening

THE IDEA THAT THERE MIGHT BE SOME KIND of collective new awakening is also not new. There is, first of all, a vast literature on the millennialists and utopian visionaries of different eras who have forecast some apocalyptic change or end or beginning.

There are also numerous works on the day after. I remember one such book, *When Prophecy Fails,* by Leon Fesdinger, which first came out in 1956; it was a study of what happened to a group that had predicted the end of the world on the day after they had given everything away and gone to the mountaintops dressed in white, only to discover the next day that nothing happened and that now they had nowhere to go. Afterward, they held a press conference and proclaimed that they were embarking on a crusade for new members because their efforts had obviously saved the world.

The apocalyptic sense that a great change is imminent is nevertheless an important psychological phenomenon at the level of personal transformation. More often than not, it hints at a cataclysmic change in personal consciousness rather than some world conflagration, although for the person going through such a change, the universe for all intents and purposes is changed forever.

There is also a large scholarly literature on the kinds of awakenings that have shaped American culture from its inception.[16] The period formally called the "First Great Awakening" occurred from about 1720 to 1750 in the American colonies and was a part of a much wider movement throughout Western European culture, spearheaded by the Pietism in Germany, called "Quietism" in England. It was as much a reaction against the formalism of established churches as it was a statement about the encroachment of science into one's definition of personal reality. In the Calvinist attitude that predominated in New England, only the elect could be saved, and they were the senior families in the community. The large majority of the congregation was not saved but was nevertheless permitted church membership. Everyone else was required to go to church by law, even though they were not formal church members. Everywhere throughout the colonies, the church was intertwined with the local government, and the seat of power ultimately governing this arrangement was the English Crown on the other side of the ocean.

In the fledging domain of American science, meanwhile, the new teachings relied solely on sensation and reason alone as the only legitimate avenues for accruing knowledge about reality, and the sterile picture that the logic of science painted of the universe met with a variety of reactions.[17] On the one hand, the most pious recoiled in disgust because the new science undermined the miracles of Christianity, upon which the power of individual belief, as well as church membership, depended; on the other, especially in America, many welcomed the voice of reason as the only effective weapon against the pretensions of the corrupt church and believed that science and spirituality were not incompatible. Indeed, the earliest American definitions of social science leaned heavily toward the interpretation that science would at last reveal God's true plan for man while at the same time debunking the superstitions of the formal denominations.

The essence of the First Great Awakening was that it elevated emotional experience and mystical revelation to the level of public consciousness. Trance states, ecstatic whirling, automatic utterances, falling down in the spirit, joyful exuberance, and spiritual happiness were all common occurrences, and all were fully sanctioned by the very governing church bodies that had forbade such behavior in public in the past. And the fervor was by no means confined to New England. Samuel Davies in the Southern states, William Tennent in the middle colonies, and David Brainerd out on the frontier were all figures associated with the new religious revival. Its ultimate effect was the liberalization of religious expression and the permission to dissent, which contributed significantly to the emergence of the ideals that led to the American Revolution.

In the decades after the American Revolution, beginning in the 1820s, a second era of religious revivalism occurred that was associated with the dramatic westward expansion of the country. This was the era of frontier camp meetings, some of which involved tens of thousands of people and went on for months at a time; it was the era of an enormous number of utopian experiments in Christian socialism; and it was the era of wide experimentation with every form of religious expression, from the ultraconservative to the ultraliberal. During this time, for instance, the ranks of the mainstream denominations, such as the Presbyterians, the Baptists, and the Methodists, swelled to great numbers in the Midwest, and transcendentalism overtook New England. In this seething cauldron, what it meant to be an American, and what the manifest destiny of the new nation was to be, found definition. This era came to an end with the Civil War.

One could also say that after the Civil War had cemented our sense of the Union, yet another kind of great awakening took place in which we were confronted with evolutionary science and industrial progress. The reaction of American society to these changes led to the secularization of the religious impulse and the concomitant rise of techniques in scientific psychotherapy, pastoral counseling, and self-help. These helped deal with the psychological and spiritual crises in people's individual lives that always take the form of the common psychoneuroses of civilized culture.

Since the 1960s, Americans have been in the midst of another great awakening, this time a spiritual reaction spawned by the rampant effects of materialism, the paranoia of worldwide totalitarianism, the threat of atomic annihilation, the destruction of the environment, and the assault on human rights. We remain in a difficult period of reorientation, seeking an understanding of who we are, how we relate to the rest of the universe, and what the meaning is of the manifold crises that threaten our sense of order.

According to the American religious scholar William McLoughlin, however, great awakenings and the revivals that are part of them are the results, not of depressions, wars, or epidemics, but of critical disjunctions in our self-understanding. They are not brief outbursts of mass emotionalism by one group or another, but profound cultural transformations affecting all Americans and extending over a generation or more. Neither are great awakenings periods of social neurosis, McLoughlin maintains, though they may begin in times of cultural confusion.

They are, rather, times of revitalization. They are therapeutic and cathartic, not pathological. They restore our cultural verve and our self-confidence, helping us to maintain faith in ourselves, our ideals, and our covenant with God even while they compel us to reinterpret that covenant in the light of new experience. Through awakenings, a nation grows in wisdom, in respect for itself, and into more harmonious relations with other peoples and the physical universe. Without them, our social order would cease to be dynamic; our culture would whither, fragment, and dissolve in confusion, as many civilizations have done before.[18]

The message of the American visionary tradition has a unique signature, however, in that it is at once optimistic, eclectic, and pragmatic in character. This is to say that, more than just generalizations that can be applied to any culture, there is a kind of filtering mechanism at work that has re-shaped all ideas from somewhere else, whether those ideas are as basic as science, government, and religion, or whether they take the form of more specific movements within these realms. Their continual Americanization suggests, as Theodore Rozak once said, that regardless of where we have come from and what tradition we represent, the stamp that is put on all new ideas is that once they are here they get reshaped, if only because of our belief that we are still unfinished animals with astonishing possibilities.

Whereas there is much more that could be said about this visionary tradition, there are two main points I want to emphasize. First, I believe that over the course of the late twentieth century, this tradition has come to define the heart of American popular consciousness. It is the essential filtering mechanism through which all foreign influences must now pass in order to have an impact on American culture, regardless of their source or content. Thus, by psychologizing them, by imbuing them with a teleology, by reifying them into a worldview, and by retailing them into a mass-market commodity, we have Americanized such diverse influences as Darwinian evolutionary theory, logical positivism, Freudian psychoanalysis, and Zen Buddhism.

Second, though the archetypal goal of mystical Christianity in the West is based on the turning of the soul inward toward God, the separation of spirit from matter, and the ascent of the soul to heaven, the main thrust of the American visionary tradition has been a more pragmatic blending of science and religion, spirit and matter, mind and body. Reason and revelation together make a whole person; consciousness can be transformed to see the arising of spirit in matter; mind and body are not radically distinct but, rather, co-arise.

We need to understand this tradition. Although its impact on individual lives and on social institutions in American history has been immense, its influence as a shadow culture remains largely unrecorded. Yet its definitive reconstruction would be a major undertaking. One can only hope here, in the compass of so short a space, to hint at its deep historical roots, the enormity of its scope, and its power as a force for constructive social change. To do this, I would like to develop a single point; namely, that there are important underlying continuities among divergent periods in American cultural and religious history, which, when taken collectively, help to define this visionary tradition.[19]

Notes

1. Similar examples are chronicled in popular works such as Ruth Norman, *Touched by the Light: Eyewitness Accounts of Personal Healing* (New York: Unarius, 1997). See also the Web page for the Society for Near-Death Experiences.

2. Recounted in a special series of articles in *Newsweek,* November 27, 1994, which the *Newsweek* editors based on extensive interviews with me.

3. Jack Huber, "Through an Eastern Window," in Gardner Murphy and Lois Murphy, *Asian Psychology* (New York: Basic Books, 1968).

4. Patricia Hopkins and Sherry Ruth Anderson, *The Feminine Face of God: The Unfolding of the Sacred in Women* (New York: Bantam Doubleday Dell, 1992); Robert Bly, *Iron John* (Reading, MA: Addison-Wesley, 1990); James Hillman, *The Soul's Code: In Search of Character and Calling* (New York: Random House, 1996); Robert Coles, *The Spiritual Life of Children* (Boston: Houghton Mifflin, 1990); M. Scott Peck, *The Road Less Traveled: A New Psychology of Love, Traditional Values, and Spiritual Growth,* 2nd ed. (New York: Simon & Schuster, 1998); and Pope John Paul II, *Varcare la Soglia della Speranza* (Crossing the threshold of hope), ed. Vittorio Messori, trans. Jenny McPhee and Martha McPhee (New York: Knopf, 1994).

5. Harvey Cox, *Fire from Heaven: The Rise of Pentecostal Spirituality and the Reshaping of Religion in the Twenty-first Century* (Reading, MA: Addison-Wesley, 1995); Martin E. Marty and R. Scott Appleby, eds., *Fundamentalisms Observed: A Study Conducted by the American Academy of Arts and Sciences* (Chicago: University of Chicago Press, 1991); and Timothy Miller, ed., *America's Alternative Religions* (Albany: State University of New York Press, 1995).

6. Charles Laughlin Jr., John McManus, and Eugene G. d'Aquili, *Brain, Symbol, and Experience: Toward a Neurophenomenology of Human Consciousness* (New York: Columbia University Press, 1992), take up a similar theme to Francis O. Schmitt, *The Never-Ceasing Search* (Philadelphia: American Philosophical Society, 1990).

7. David Lukoff, "From Spiritual Emergency to Spiritual Problem: The Transpersonal Roots of the new DSM-IV Category," *Journal of Humanistic Psychology,* 38:2 (1998): 21–50.

8. William James, *The Varieties of Religious Experience* (New York: Longmans, 1902); Abraham Maslow, *Motivation and Personality* (New York: Harper's, 1954); C. G. Jung, *Psychological Types: Or, the Psychology of Individuation,* trans. H. Godwin Baynes (London: Kegan Paul, Trench, Trubner & Co.; and New York: Harcourt, Brace & Co., 1923).

9. Harold Bloom has recently attempted to grasp this state of affairs when he concluded that American religious life was profoundly Gnostic in character; see *The American Religion: The Emergence of the Post-Christian Nation* (New York: Simon & Schuster, 1992). But he failed to differentiate among the rational, scientific lineage of Judeo-Christian high culture (which is more denominational and theological in character), popular culture (which is more secular), and the shadow culture (which is at once spiritual and psychotherapeutic). The Dutch religious scholar Wouter J. Hanegraaff has recently fielded probably the most comprehensive attempt to define this alternative reality tradition: *New Age Religion and Western Culture: Esotericism in the Mirror of Secular Thought* (Albany: State University of New York Press, 1998). He identifies the Gnostic, Neoplatonist, alchemical, hermetic, and occult lineage that he believes underlies modern New Age movements. But, I would maintain, the very reference to this cultural force as New Age religion suggests that this is more a survey of its European counterparts without a focus on its unique character in American religious consciousness beyond the stereotypes that the mainstream interpreters have placed on it. Hence, he falls into such gross overgeneralizations as "the primary characteristic that everyone can agree on is that New Agers all believe in reincarnation." My contention is that, quite to the contrary, no such generalization of this kind is possible.

This is also to say, however, that I am by no means the first to take up this topic. In a brilliant series of books published more than a decade ago, Robert Charles Fuller wrote *Mesmerism and the American Cure of Souls* (Philadelphia: University of Pennsylvania Press, 1982), as well as such works as *Americans and the Unconscious*

(New York: Oxford University Press, 1986) and *Alternative Medicine and American Religious Life* (New York: Oxford University Press, 1989), all of which contain enormous amounts of historical material and analyze the popular healing tradition but from the more generalized standpoint of American studies. However, his knowledge of the history of psychology seems weak; of depth psychology, unsystematic; and of the Asian traditions, nonexistent.

10. Mystery religions have flourished for thousands of years. A popular look at Egyptian conceptions is E. A. Wallace Budge's *The Book of the Dead* (New York: Dover; and London: Arkana, 1989). For a perspective on Greek culture, see Gordon Wasson, Carl Ruck, and Albert Hoffmann, *The Road to Eleusis: Unveiling the Secret of the Mysteries* (New York: Harcourt Brace Jovanovich, 1978). For background on Gnosticism, see Daniel Merkur, *Gnosis: An Esoteric Tradition of Mystical Visions and Unions* (Albany: State University of New York Press, 1993); or Stephen Heler, *Jung and the Lost Gospels: Insights into the Dead Sea Scrolls and the Nag Hammadhi Library* (Wheaton, IL: Theosophical Publishing House, 1989). For a readable introduction to alchemy, see Johannes Fabricus, *Alchemy: The Medieval Alchemists and Their Royal Arts* (London: Aquarian Press, 1976); and Jonalde Jacobi, *Paracelsus: Selected Writings* (Princeton, NJ: Princeton University Press, 1971). A work on thirteenth-century Jewish mysticism is J. Dan, ed., *The Early Kabbalah* (New York: Paulist Press, 1986). For some occult works on the Rosicrucians, see Manly P. Hall, ed., *Codex Rosae Crucis: A Rare and Curious Manuscript of Rosicrucian Interest* (Los Angeles: Philosophical Research Library, 1971 (originally published in 1938); and Arthur Edward Waite, *The Brotherhood of the Rosy Cross* (London: W. Rider & Son, 1924). An introduction to the Arthurian cycle is Emma Jung and Marie Louise Von Franz, *The Grail Legend* (Boston: Sigo Press, 1986); and for an overview of the same subject, see Oliver Davies, *God Within: The Mystical Tradition of Northern Europe* (New York: Paulist Press, 1988).

11. Robert Ellwood, *Religious and Spiritual Groups in Modern America* (Englewood Cliffs, NJ: Prentice Hall, 1973).

12. A potent example can be found in the work of John Gray, who has chronicled the transplantation of African spiritual traditions such as Umbanda, Candomble, Palo Monte, voodoo, and Santeria. See John Gray, ed., *Ashe, Traditional Religion, and Healing in Sub-Saharan Africa and the Diaspora: A Classified International Bibliography* (Westport, CT: Greenwood, 1989). See also M. V. Kamath, *The United States and India, 1776–1976* (Washington, DC: Embassy of India, 1976), for examples of American-Hindu syncretism. A similar work, based on common visions and prophesies, in the Native American tradition is William Willoya and Vinson Brown, *Warriors of the Rainbow* (Healdsburg, CA: Naturegraph, 1968).

13. Wilhelm Wundt, *Elements of Folk Psychology: Outlines of a Psychological History of the Development of Mankind,* trans. Edward Leroy Schaub (New York: Macmillan, 1916).

14. According to the historian of psychology Ryan Tweny, Wundt published the larger work first, starting with the two big volumes on language in 1900. The 1916 *Elements of Folk Psychology* (an authorized translation by Schaub [see previous note] of the 1914 German original) is actually an outline on a very different plan. Whereas the larger work treated language, religion, myth, law, etc., as separate domains, this smaller book treats the development of mind in "synchronous" fashion: first, primitive language, art, myth, etc., then the "Totemic Age," then the "Heroic Age," and finally the "Modern Age." In the large work, Wundt used a "comparative" method across cultures and history to illuminate each domain separately; in the smaller work, he used each domain to illuminate the history of humanity (personal communication with the author, 1998).

15. There are actually advocates of folk psychology in the neuroscience community. See the essay by Joseph Margolis, for instance, in John D. Greenwood, ed., *The Future of Folk Psychology: Intentionality and Cognitive Science* (New York: Cambridge University Press, 1991), pp. 242–262.

16. William G. McLoughlin, *Revivals, Awakenings, and Reform: An Essay on Religion and Social Change in America, 1607–1977* (Chicago: University of Chicago Press, 1978).

17. Robert V. Bruce, *The Launching of American Science, 1846–1876* (Ithaca, NY: Cornell University Press, 1988). See also Gerald Holton, *Science and Anti-Science* (Cambridge, MA: Harvard University Press, 1993); and D. N. Livingstone, *Darwin's Forgotten Defenders: The Encounter Between Evangelical Theology and Evolutionary Thought* (Grand Rapids, MI: W. B. Eerdmans, 1987).

18. Ibid., pp. 1–2, closely paraphrasing McLoughlin's own words.

19. Some general surveys of religious life in America are useful to place specific examples of this visionary tradition. A good study of colonial religious life is Cedric B. Cowing, *The Great Awakening and the American Revolution: Colonial Thought in the Eighteenth Century* (Chicago: Rand McNally, 1971). One handy reference guide to the big picture remains Elmer Clark, *The Small Sects in America* (New York: Abingdon, 1949), an authentic study of almost 300 little-known religious groups in the United States. A classic work on the development of mainstream religious thought in America is Israel Daniel Rupp, *Religious Denominations in the United States: Their History, Present Condition, and Doctrines* (Philadelphia: Charles Desilver, 1861). Meanwhile, two interesting books that give the contrasting picture of an alternative reality tradition to the mainstream are J. Stilson Judah, *The History and Philosophy of Metaphysical Movements in America* (Philadelphia: Westminster Press, 1967), and R. Ellwood, *Religious and Spiritual Groups*. A more recent compilation is Timothy Miller, ed., *America's Alternative Religions* (Albany: State University of New York Press, 1994), and a revealing study of the widespread acceptance of astrology and numerology is Herbert Leventhal, *In the Shadow of the Enlightenment: Occultism and Renaissance Science in Eighteenth Century America* (New York: New York University Press, 1976).

Chapter Two

Puritans and Mystics of the First Great Awakening

ACCORDING TO THE LATE PERRY MILLER, HARVARD HISTORIAN and Puritan scholar, from its very inception, America has been a psychologically oriented culture.[1] From the intellectual life of the mind to the care and salvation of the soul, the inward domain of consciousness was always the great battlefield upon which the armies of bondage and liberation conducted their various campaigns. Light skirmishes between mere opinion versus fact, and superstition versus reason, alternated with great pitched battles waged between good and evil. The inward condition of human experience was the primary focus of Puritan theology.

But the other story that still needs telling is the inner spiritual biography of the American visionary tradition, the religious experience of alternative realities lived by men and women who did not represent

Puritan high culture, who did not attend Harvard or Yale, who were not the denominational movers and shakers normally recounted in the history books. These were men and women who took full advantage of the freedom the New World afforded to pursue religious life unfettered, in any way they saw fit.

These visionaries almost always lived near the frontiers, where they were more likely to find the frontier of social consciousness. They lived solitary lives, away from the civilized world and material goods, because they had loosened the psychological bonds to material attachment. They tended to be self-sufficient, relying less on the new and making do with the old. They were more apt to live near nature than in established settlements. They resided by Native American Indian communities and often knew how to speak their languages, inhabiting a kind of no-man's-land between the red and white civilizations. These were some of the early pioneers of the American visionary tradition.

In order to help define this visionary tradition as it first emerged in the colonial period, one must keep in mind a few benchmark dates that help to define the religious atmosphere of the day. Virginia, the earliest organized colony, was chartered by the king of England in 1606 as a joint stock company. The religious persuasion of its early settlers was almost homogeneously Anglican. The Pilgrims, literalists in biblical interpretation who had little interest in formal theology and who felt themselves separate from the Church of England, landed at Plymouth Rock in 1620 and settled on the Maine coast, in the Connecticut River valley, and around eastern Connecticut. The Huguenots, members of the Reformed Church who were sponsored by the Dutch West Indies Company, began to arrive in the late 1620s, settling New Amsterdam, which later came to be known as New York. The Massachusetts Bay Colony was chartered by the English in 1629 and was soon flooded with Puritans, religious refugees who had sought to reform or purify the Church of England. The first true democratic colony was Rhode Island, founded in 1635 by Roger Williams, who had been hounded out of Massachusetts for his liberal ideas. Rhode Island became the only colony at the time to separate church and state and to grant complete religious freedom to all sects. It also later became the site of the first Jewish synagogue in America.

In general, the dominant religious trend in the colonies during the 1600s, with the exception of the work of a few Catholic missionaries, was derived from the teachings of the theologian John Calvin. Calvinism held strictly to such doctrines as the sinfulness of the flesh, the idea that souls were predestined to heaven or damned to hell, and a belief that only the elect could be saved. Calvinists also held to the necessity of public disclosure: One had to confess to God's grace before official church membership, and therefore social respectability, could be conferred. Although the ruling governments tended to be secular, the Calvinist ministers nevertheless maintained deep ties to the local magistrates, who legislated church tithes, Sunday blue laws, and clerically determined codes of public conduct.

After 100 years of this kind of religion, the Calvinist tide took a serious dip and was revived only through an evangelical wave that swept through the Northeast. This resurgence of religious sensibilities was initially led by a charismatic young preacher from Connecticut, Jonathan Edwards, who blended his rational arguments with the passionate fire of pulpit rhetoric thus stirring up a fervent emotionalism in the ranks of the congregation. Other ministers followed suit, until the movement had spread up and down New England like a spiritual epidemic. By one estimate, 250,000 converts were made and 250 new churches established in the early years, causing religious scholars to call these years between 1720 and 1750 the "First Great Awakening."

Jonathan Edwards at Northampton

WHEREAS EDWARDS REPRESENTED THE EPITOME of the orthodox Calvinist church in the colonies, himself being a New World product of European and English high culture, he was nevertheless an unwitting contributor to the emergence of a visionary folk psychology because of the impact he had on the future of experiential evangelism. He was born in 1703 in East Windsor, Connecticut, the only son of eleven children.[2] His father was a Congregationalist minister and his mother a Congregationalist minister's daughter. A child prodigy, he entered Yale in 1716 at the age of thirteen. There, his Christian faith was both challenged and tempered by his encounters with the ideas of Locke and Newton. From Locke, he derived the understanding that nothing is in the mind that is not first in the senses. This made of him a thoroughgoing empiricist, and he thus came to believe that God could be known only by what we experience through sensations. Accordingly, he would later encourage his parishioners in their pews to feel the fires of hell, rather than just think abstractly about being damned. From Newtonian physics, he derived a naturalistic conception of the universe, which he promptly saw was at odds with traditional Christian belief but had somehow to be tempered to it. His response was to develop a theology based on a rational explanation of sensory experience.[3]

Edwards graduated with a master's degree in 1720 and soon underwent an intense religious experience. He called it "a calm, sweet Abstraction of the Soul from all Concerns of this World; and a kind of Vision, or fix'd Ideas and Imaginations, of being alone in the Mountains, or some solitary Wilderness, far from all mankind; sweetly conversing with Christ, and wrapt and swallowed up in God. The sense I had of divine Things would often of a sudden as it were, kindle up a sweet burning in my Heart; an ardour of my Soul, that I know not how to express."[4] His main lesson was that religion is an affair of the heart—an experience that comes through the emotions. Thus, a full hundred years before an overemphasis on reason and the senses became the vogue, the youthful Edwards began to wrestle with an answer to the conflict between the highly subjective, lived experience of spiritual awakening and the objective description of reality presented by rational theology and empirical science. The result was America's first articulation of a science of religious consciousness, although scholars instead count Edwards as the originator of the first uniquely American theology.

At the age of twenty, Edwards was called to a parish in New York City, followed by one in Connecticut. In 1724, however, he returned to Yale as a tutor, where he remained for two years until called to his grandfather's parish in Northampton, Massachusetts, as assistant pastor. About the same time, he married Sarah Pierrepont, whom he had known at Yale and who subsequently bore him twelve children.

When his grandfather died in 1729, Edwards inherited a congregation that numbered nearly 600 members. This pastorate lasted for the next twenty-three years, and it would eventually cast him as the single most important spiritual and political influence in western Massachusetts. He was little known in the beginning but gradually developed a reputation as a faithful Puritan minister. In 1731, he was invited to deliver his first sermon to the elite society of ministers in downtown Boston, with favorable results. He presented them with the new learning, a rational God who could be known through the senses but was still clothed in the strictest Calvinistic terms. The Boston listeners divined he had something important to say, but they were not sure at first what it actually was. They were soon to discover it.

Based on Edwards's new scientific idea of divinity, a spirit of exhortation had entered his preaching by 1735 that pitched the fear of a wrathful God into his congregation in vivid new terms. He encouraged them with stark realism: "To help your conception, imagine yourself to be cast into a fiery oven, all of a glowing heat, or into the midst of a glowing brick-kiln, or of a great furnace, where your pain would be as much greater than that occasioned by accidentally touching a coal of fire, as the heat is greater." He then exhorted each person to imagine having to lie there and suffer for a half hour, full of fire; how long that half hour would feel. And if it seemed unbearable after just the first minute, how much worse would be the other twenty-nine. Next he instructed them to think about having to lie there for a full twenty-four hours, and if they could imagine that, then how about an entire year, or a thousand years, or, for that matter, for all eternity? "That after millions of millions of ages, your torment would be no nearer to an end than it ever was; and that you never, never should be delivered."[5]

Shamed and frightened into righteousness by such preaching and overwhelmed by these convincing reasons to be good, numerous young people in his congregation began to have spontaneous conversion experiences. Similar but more transient episodes of religious enthusiasm had been known in the church under his late grandfather. The present effect was a renewed wave of moral and ethical enthusiasm for Christian doctrines at a time when "lascivious and lewd behavior" and the frequenting of taverns seemed to have become the order of the day. The young now, however, fervently admitted their sins, prayed for forgiveness, and professed to experience an opening into a new spiritual life.

First one and then another listener became infused with a heightened experience of religion, although the episodes were different for each person. Then people from across town began to recount similar episodes. Church attendance began to rise, civility returned to public discourse, bickering and petty quarrels ceased, and a pleasant countenance and humane agreeableness were everywhere. It started with the young people and then spread to the older ones. Parishioners would gesticulate and fall into a trance. They would make unusual noises and appear giddy, then undergo a conversion experience.

Edwards preached on Sunday and gave a separate lecture during the week, and the attendance at both events quickly swelled to overflowing. Soon, throughout the week, four to five parishioners a day would come by Edwards's office seeking personal guidance. He would counsel them much like a modern-day psychotherapist. To accommodate the increasing numbers, he arranged for groups of people to meet and talk together about their religious experiences. Instead of abating, spiritual inflammation spread to other neighborhoods. This went on for six or eight months, until finally the ever-mounting excitement ended when two of the townspeople got into such a frenzy that they committed suicide. The conversions abruptly ceased, people again returned to their senses, and the religious hysteria died down. Edwards noted, however, that the effects on most people's personal lives were not transient, but enduring.

Edwards published his observations of these phenomena in 1737, in a tract titled *A Faithful Narrative of the Surprising Work of God*. Therein, he wrote about certain steps in the experience of conversion that he had witnessed. First, an individual is overcome, suddenly or gradually, with a sense of misery and guilt. Life looks as black as midnight, and it seems there is no help. At this point, the person touches bottom. He recognizes that he has no claim on God—indeed, he would like to kill him. He gives up. Then, in the next stage, comes a calm, a composure, a recovery of power, as the self-confessed sinner realizes that, although he deserves nothing, God does after all have something for him. Although he cannot help himself, if he will put his trust in God or Christ, he need no longer be fearful and distressed. Life will straighten itself out for him. Looking back upon his past, it will seem to him as though his former self, with its old interests, standards, and practices, had died. Now he is a new individual, facing a new world with a clear eye for its novelties. Edwards wrote that "the light and comfort which some of these converts enjoyed gave a new light to their common blessings and caused all things about them to appear beautiful, sweet, and pleasant. All things abroad, the sun, moon and stars, the clouds and sky appeared with a cast of divine glory."[6]

These episodes were but a prelude, however, to events of the Great Awakening that were to unfold throughout the colonies beginning in 1740 with the arrival on the American scene of George Whitefield. Whitefield, an ordained English Methodist, had been an innkeeper's son, a boyhood truant, and an aspiring actor. He converted to Methodism in 1735, was ordained by the Wesleys, and became a specialist in extemporaneous dramatic preaching. He traveled as an itinerant preacher in America and Britain and so excited congregations that he was soon excluded from entering the local English churches. Undaunted, he led a crowd of 20,000 out into the fields. After being denounced by the bishop of London in 1739, he went again to America, where he preached to tens of thousands of people at a time along the eastern seaboard, in Philadelphia, in Maryland, and as far south as Georgia. On Boston Common, he held a crowd of 50,000 completely enraptured while he gave evidence for the impending millennium. For this, he was censured by the Anglicans in Boston, the conservatives in Philadelphia, and, in 1744, denounced by the faculty at Harvard as an "enthusiast," meaning pejoratively one who mistakes some mechanical or psychological disturbance for the Word of God.

Whitefield preached at Edwards's church four times in 1740. Edwards then accompanied him to other churches and afterward himself set out to preach throughout the region. The uproar he caused led to entire crowds weeping and shrieking. In the midst of wailing voices, convulsions were common, as was speaking in tongues. The fervor in large audiences was enormous. Edwards later wrote an extensive analysis of these episodes in order to assure the Puritans of New England that this was still respectable religion. In 1741, he published *The Distinguishing Marks of a Work of the Spirit of God,* in which he outlined the various signs, both negative and positive, that confirmed whether such an experience was genuine or counterfeit.[7]

He listed a series of questionable signs that would at first seem to discount the experience, but he expressed these in the double negative—that is, these signs were not to be used to reject such an experience. An experience, he said, cannot be considered inauthentic just because it is different from what is considered normal or just because the person manifests exaggerated bodily movements or evinces tears, trembling, groans, loud outcries, agonies, or the failing of bodily strength. It should not be discounted just because it has worked a great influence on people's imagination, or because one person appears to be imitating the experience of another in the manner of social contagion. Great imprudence and irregularities of conduct are no reason to discredit such awakenings, and neither are they to be rejected even if satanic delusions are intermingled with divine revelations. If people fall into error or scandalous practices, this does not discount the larger movement. Further, it is not to be discounted if it seems to promote voices that invoke the terror of the devil or other results that seem to come about by such practices.

On the other hand, Edwards affirmed at least five positive signs by which conversion, awakening, or rapture could be immediately judged as good. These he gave to assuage the misgivings of even conservative Christians. The experiences are to be deemed genuine, he said, when they raise the esteem of Jesus, born of the Virgin and crucified outside of Jerusalem. They are genuine if they impel people away from sin and lust. They are genuine if people are led back to the teachings of the Bible; if people are led to truth instead of error; and, above all, if they promote love among people. Under these circumstances, awakenings of the kind he reported were to be promoted and not hindered.

In 1746, Edwards composed a more extensive tract titled *A Treatise on Religious Affections,* in which he more fully elaborated the development of the spiritual side of personality and enumerated a series of signs by which one knows that spiritual experiences are genuine because of their enduring fruits. He was led by these insights to review the standards by which the elect were designated as full members in his congregation, an issue that earlier had been significantly liberalized by his grandfather, who permitted people only halfway on the spiritual journey to also become members of the church. Edwards, however, believed the standard had to be tightened again, which raised the ire of those who did not fully support him within his own congregation. The political reaction to his new dictum became strong enough that, in 1750, after a bitter struggle, he was summarily dismissed from his pastorate, after holding the same pulpit for twenty-three years.

He retired with his family to Stockbridge, then a primitive village in the wilderness, where he was charged with bringing Christianity to Native Americans. Under these conditions, he wrote and thought as a solitary scholar for seven years. His most enduring work during this period was *The Freedom of the Will,* a tract that subsumed human willpower under the faculty of reason.

In 1757, due to the unexpected death of his son-in-law, Edwards was called to replace him as president of the College of New Jersey (this college was later renamed Princeton). But the following year, Edwards, ever the believer in the new science, submitted to the new treatment of being inoculated against smallpox; due to complications that immediately set in, he died from the procedure, having held his new office for only two months.

Conrad Beissel and the Ephrata Mystics

EDWARDS, ALTHOUGH A REVIVALIST, was actually an errant conservative within the then-burgeoning circles of American high culture—a man who set the tone of New England theology for the next hundred years. He has yet to be compared to one of the most important examples of the American visionary tradition—one that can be found in the community of German mystical Pietists who first settled in Pennsylvania. Among them sprang up the Ephrata Cloister, composed of radical separatists from mainstream Protestantism who lived as celibate monks and nuns on the American frontier beginning in the early 1730s.[8]

The first of its kind in the New World, Ephrata has been characterized as a missing link between the monastic communities of Europe and the great American experiments in utopian communalism. Its success for almost half a century was due largely to the spiritual inspiration of its leader, Johann Conrad Beissel, an uneducated German peasant who adhered to a mystical vision of early Christianity that he made come alive on the harsh and unforgiving terrain of the Pennsylvania wilderness.

Beissel was born in 1690 in what is now Bavaria and raised in a poverty-stricken and fatherless household until he was orphaned at age seven.[9] He was endowed with a robust intellect and an introspective temperament, but during subsequent wanderings alone in the world, his talents were dissipated. This all changed when as a young man he joined the Pietists, a spiritual community founded by the seventeenth-century mystic P. J. Spener (1635–1705), who rejected the materialism of the new science that was developing and simultaneously spoke out against the uninspired pretensions of the Lutheran Church. Spearhead to a powerful religious awakening in Germany, the Pietists rejected formal church order and cultivated instead an ascetic inward transformation of consciousness as the true basis for Christianity. Entering their order, Beissel took up a life of intense inward contemplation and renunciation of the material world.

Through the Pietists, Beissel was soon initiated into the mystical, occult, and millennialist underground of European Christianity. He began to have contact with numerous secret societies, among them the Society of Philadelphia, a mystical fraternity owing its inspiration to Jakob Böhme (1575–1624). He also encountered the Inspirationists, a Pan-European movement that advocated the rejection of dogma and mere reason in favor of spiritual renewal by religious fervor, exaltation, and prophesy. In such groups, possession by the Holy Spirit, ecstatic religious visions, speaking in tongues, and the report of miracles were common. From there, Beissel was led to the teachings of the Kabbalah and to the esoteric rites of the Rosicrucians. He began to worship the mystical virgin Sophia, a symbol of the Gnostic tradition. He and many others believed they were participating in a historic renewal of Christianity.

Meanwhile, Europe at the time was a continuous theater of political wars, bloodshed, and religious persecution. As a result, entire sects migrated to places such as Pennsylvania, where William Penn, the English Quaker, had launched a "Holy Experiment" and opened large tracts of land to fleeing religious groups. The Amish, Mennonites, Dunkers, Inspirationists, Schwenkenfelders, and Moravians responded en masse, settling around what is now Germantown and the surrounding area north and west of Philadelphia.

In this region, German religious communities arose everywhere based on a welter of beliefs. Many practiced Christian pacifism. Some rejected all oaths of fealty to government. Others restricted baptism only to adults who could comprehend its meaning. Many, like members of the numerous utopian experiments in Europe that had preceded them, advocated a radical return to apostolic Christianity and a withdrawal from the material world. Such communities lived according to the ideal of mutual aid within a close-knit society and showed a pastoralism reinforced by a deep sense of stewardship for the land.[10]

Along with these hordes came Conrad Beissel, who wanted nothing more than to live by himself as a mystic in one of the many isolated caves along the Wissahickon River. But the power and force of his spiritual personality immediately drew others to him, and he was forced several times to move farther into the wilderness, until he finally stopped in a swampy area where he believed no one would venture. Within a short time, however, a significant settlement had again gathered around him, which came to be known as the Ephrata Cloister. Ephrata soon developed into a monastic community of men and women who would leave their mark on the American landscape long past the actual existence of the community.

Existing evidence gives us only a glimpse of the internal nature of the spiritual life of these people. When they first joined, members dropped their family names and took on new given names to eliminate blood ties and to promote spiritual cohesion. Most adopted celibacy and communal ownership. The women came from many walks of life. Some brought their entire family to join. Some had fled abusive husbands and harsh frontier life. Others came young and single. All of the women who came by themselves were "rebaptized into virginity." They constituted the Spiritual Virgins and cloistered together in their own monastic community. Single men banded together into a Brotherhood of the Angels, while married householders were permitted to live in an area of their own and to keep their own material goods. In addition to these social arrangements, the Ephrata community also included "The Solitary," a collection of ascetic men and women who voluntarily lived in isolation from each other and the rest of the cloister.

One of the main characteristics of their spirituality was that of visionary awakening to God. Here is one account of a visionary experience, taken from the *Chronicon Ephratense,* the main record of the Ephrata community. The experience was recounted by Catherine Hummer, a young Pennsylvania German associated with Beissel's community, who lived as a householder with her own family.

Hummer wrote that in October 1762, while sitting by her kitchen fire after everyone had gone to bed, she heard a knock at the door and found upon answering it that no one was there. A second time the knock came and Hummer answered, but still no one. Then, when she opened the door a third time, an angel appeared to her and began to speak about the cooling of love in her community. Hummer asked three times to be allowed to call the others from sleep, but each time the angel kept her, inducing her to sing songs about the vision of God and to fervently pray for the salvation of believers. During this discourse, she later recounted, she was absolved of her sins and remonstrated against worldly pleasures. After more singing and praying with the angel, the vision ascended to heaven, and Hummer went to bed:

After this I lay in a trance for the greater part of seven days and nights, so that my spirit was separated from the body. In this state I was led through strange conditions and dwelling places of spirits, and I saw such wonderful things that I greatly hesitate to reveal them. After this it became quite customary for me to talk with good spirits and angels, and also to be transferred in spirit out of my visible body into heavenly principalities, just as if it had happened bodily. The Almighty God in his mercy also allowed me to translate myself in spirit into eternity as often as I wished, either by day or night, and there to see, hear, and touch the divine wonders. My body was always as if asleep until my spirit returned. I wandered through indescribable habitations of the blessed, and saw innumerable hosts; and once I was told their number, I could not remember it. Oh, what joy and happiness did I there behold! There you feel a bliss that is inexpressible and cannot be described.[11]

Such accounts, in all likelihood, served several purposes. First, the individual is confirmed as a channel to the divine. We have the solitary, nighttime visitations of the angel, after which there are repeated trances, facilitating return to a blessed state that confirms repeated access into the higher and more interior domain. Second, personal experience then becomes an inspiration for the community. The woman tells her story and sings the songs of God, which serve to bring the community back to its original loving presence.

Whereas deep inward contemplation was the focus of religious life for each individual, the community also had collective experiences, such as fasting and penance. Agape, their love feast, included the humility of foot washing. Other ascetic rituals for physical and mental regeneration included ingestion of elixirs and forty days of solitary meditation in a forest hut in the wilderness. They held to the scriptural Sabbath on Saturday and were therefore relentlessly persecuted and periodically jailed in small groups by colonial authorities for working on Sunday. They held midnight prayer meetings, at which, after a ghostly procession and elaborate symbolic rituals accompanied by polyphonic hymns, they would openly espouse forgiveness of the sins of others and publicly unburden themselves of their own transgressions. They slept on wooden boards rather than mattresses, ate one meal per day, engaged in hard physical work, practiced vegetarianism, and for a time shaved their heads. They were also well known for the beauty of their singing and for their stirringly elaborate and original chorale.

Their communalism focused on defeating the calls of the flesh and heightening the claims of the spirit, yet their strict regimentation allowed for the erection of corporate enterprises otherwise impossible to attain. As a result, Ephrata became both prosperous and widely influential. At one point, it controlled the production of flaxseed, from which most of the printing ink in the colonies was made. The community was a major supplier of paper as well as farm produce. From its mills, members ground the highest quality wheat, which was in constant demand. It ran its own printing presses and produced the finest examples then known of illuminated manuscripts, called *Fraktur*.

The Ephratites also engaged in extensive missionary activity. The community distributed pumpernickel bread, ran schools, and raised cabins for the benefit of newcomers without charge. Having a deep respect for Native American culture, some members of the group were conversant with Indian languages and customs and would often mediate disputes between the colonial government and the various tribes. In addition, they would periodically visit neighboring Pietistic communities in search of converts. Their arrival always caused a great commotion, as all would stop and stare or step aside for the Ephrata pilgrims, who, barefooted, draped in cloaks and hoods, and carrying staffs, would proceed by in single file, completely silent, heads bowed in meditation. By all these means, Beissel and his followers promoted a powerful religious revival among Germans all over Pennsylvania. At one point, at the height of the Great Awakening, a contingent also traveled as far north as Connecticut, where they drew enthusiastic crowds to their message of renunciation and God-consciousness.

But the Ephratites were distinct from other religious groups in that they raised adversity and poverty to the status of a religion. Their intense morality, their penchant for mystical exhilaration through singing, their emphasis on what they called the "Way of Peace," their rejection of unclean foods, and their belief in the spiritual necessity of shunning private wealth set them far apart from other German religious groups and from the prevailing Calvinist Evangelicalism of the day. Today, we do not even remember them. The only vestiges left in our collective memory come from the continued existence of their distant neighbors, the Amish and the Mennonites.

The question we must now ask ourselves is, why, if the Great Awakening was actually a widespread movement in the West, is it referred to by historians of American religious life as somehow unique to New England? And why, if it was inspired so significantly by the Pietists in Germany and if in Ephrata we have such a vibrant New World example, do we never hear about the monastic, inward communities that existed on the American frontier, except perhaps as a footnote to the greater glory of mainstream Protestant theology?

At first, it would seem that the answer is that we document what we know best. Mainstream historians, in other words, do not write the history of the shadow culture because its worldview is so different and they have been so well schooled in the mainstream view. They know not only the most intimate details of the mainstream, but also its context, whereas they are not at all familiar with the context of the shadow culture, if the idea even occurred to them. For them, there is only one history, the history of their own civilized world.

To the mainstream historian, Beissel was a German mystic, while Edwards was a Puritan theologian. Beissel advocated a return to apostolic Christianity in which higher consciousness deepened the spiritual life of the individual, and the religious affections that resulted bound his little spiritual community together. Edwards's concerns were denominational, congregational, and oriented toward the elevation of mainstream Protestantism. Beissel turned to monasticism in the Pietistic tradition of the visionary shadow culture. He and his followers were loyal only to God. Edwards had, in addition to God, the English Crown to consider. To be religious in Edwards's parish was defined by how well one obeyed the laws of the church and conformed to English colonial law. Beissel's group recognized no union between church and state; they remained profoundly indifferent to town and county registrations, refused to swear oaths of any kind, and resisted paying taxes with supremely successful strategies of passive nonviolence.

Mainstream historians might struggle to account for these differences through economic, political, or social analyses. But what was so radically different between Beissel and Edwards was the psychology of their respective worlds. Although they both cleaved to experience, their very definition of the term could not have been more opposite. Beissel was certainly a man who tended to his community, which takes observation, clear thinking, and pragmatic response; but inwardly, his orientation was primarily intuitive and emotive. He was not interested in doctrinal disputes or adherence to creeds. Edwards was primarily oriented toward the sensory and the rational. Beissel advocated the direct experience of ecstatic rapture, while Edwards condoned it but made it sanitary enough for the rationalists by objectively describing it. Beissel advocated sensory withdrawal from the material world, while Edwards's focus was a theological and moral justification of the material world. Beissel cultivated the experience of visions, while Edwards cultivated the exercise of the will in service of reason. Beissel's goal was self-realization, while Edwards's was adjustment to the norms of Puritan society. No more important elements demonstrate this than Beissel's espousal of complete sexual abstinence, while Edwards proved himself procreative in the extreme. Moreover, Beissel's complete rejection of outward authority only served to highlight the fact that Edwards, during his political and religious reign over New England, for all intents and purposes, represented the very kind of outward authority that had driven Beissel into the wilderness.

Both, however, had a tremendous impact on the American scene. Edwards rescued a declining Calvinism but at the same time participated in a liberalization of Protestantism up and down the eastern seaboard, which sounded the death knell of Anglican Puritanism in the colonies and helped set the stage for the American Revolution. In addition, Edwards defined the direction that white evangelical Protestantism continues to take to this day. Beissel, on the other hand, created a community that lasted up to the Revolutionary War, the elements of which were to be repeated many times over in the numerous utopian social experiments that were to come.

Notes

1. Perry Miller, *Errand into the Wilderness* (Cambridge, MA: Belknap Press, 1956); Perry Miller, *The Life of the Mind in America, from the Revolution to the Civil War* (New York: Harcourt, Brace & World, 1956); Perry Miller, *The New England Mind* (Boston: Beacon Press, 1953–1954); and Perry Miller, *Consciousness in Concord: The Text of Thoreau's Hitherto "Lost Journal," 1840–1841* (Boston: Houghton Mifflin, 1958).

2. Adapted from E. I. Taylor, "Jonathan Edwards," in *Encyclopedia of Psychology* (Washington, DC: American Psychological Association and Oxford University Press, 1999).

3. This discussion is best developed in Perry Miller, *Jonathan Edwards* (New York: William Sloan Associates, 1949), which essentially presents the Harvard view. For the Yale view, see W. E. Anderson, ed., *The Works of Jonathan Edwards: Scientific and Philosophical Writings,* vol. 6 (New Haven, CT: Yale University Press, 1980).

4. Adapted from Ola Elizabeth Winslow, ed., *Jonathan Edwards: Basic Writings* (New York: New American Library, 1978), pp. xiii–xiv.

5. Miller, *Jonathan Edwards,* pp. 160–161.

6. Adapted from Arthur Cushman McGiffert, *Jonathan Edwards* (New York: Harper & Bros., 1932), pp. 56–57. Showing that he, too, was affected by inspirational movements, Edwards followed with an apocryphal statement on the spiritual destiny of America, *An History of the Work of Redemption,* in which he put forth the idea that American civilization exists for the salvation of the world, and if there was to be a world transformation, then it was meant to begin right then and there.

7. Jonathan Edwards, *The Distinguishing Marks of a Work of the Spirit of God* (1741), in *The Select Works of Jonathan Edwards* (London: Banner of Truth Trust, 1965), pp. 75–147.

8. E. G. Alderfer, *The Ephrata Commune: An Early American Counter-Culture* (Pittsburgh: University of Pittsburgh Press, 1985). The primary source for information on the Ephrata community is the *Chronicon Ephratense,* the first edition of which, in German, appeared in 1786. For an English translation recently reprinted, see *Chronicon Ephratense: A History of the Community of the Seventh Day Baptists at Ephrata,* trans. J. Max Hark (New York: Burt Franklin, 1976). For a survey of monastic life along the Wissahickon, also known as the "Ganges of the New World," see E. G. Alderfer, ed., *Johannes Kelpius: A Method of Prayer* (New York: Harper, 1951).

9. Walter Conrad Klien, *Johann Conrad Beissel: Mystic and Martinet, 1690–1768* (Philadelphia: University of Pennsylvania Press, 1942).

10. Alderfer, *The Ephrata Commune,* p. 9.

11. Jon Alexander, *American Personal Religious Accounts, 1600–1980: Toward an Inner History of American Faiths* (New York: Edwin Mellen Press, 1983), p. 93.

Chapter Three

Early Visionary Communities: The Quakers and Shakers

WITHIN THE VISIONARY TRADITION, AS IN ANY SOCIAL GROUPING, we encounter the paradox of the relation of the one to the many: What is the relation of the individual to the group, if the inward journey is so solitary? And what, then, is the nature and fate of the visionary community that follows the solitary prophet? The idea that a life quest toward self-realization must be launched alone would at first sound odd as a source of spiritual community. Yet once seekers experience an opening of the inward doors of perception and commit themselves to a new life path, it seems that, soon, unknown friends always appear. These may be guardians to the inner door who turn out to be guides and allies, those who, like angels, arrive spontaneously and unbidden at various points to help the spiritual pilgrim through his hour of difficulty. Or they may appear as other human souls similarly predisposed to interior exploration who cross their path at various stages on the way, perhaps at some prescient moment. Sometimes by accident and sometimes by design, seekers often gravitate together into spiritual families that concretize themselves into living communities. The psychology of such spiritual communities is complex and deserves to be more thoroughly interpreted.

The Society of Friends

CONSIDER, FOR INSTANCE, THE QUAKERS, who were responsible for the founding of Pennsylvania and therefore gave harbor to Conrad Beissel and the Ephrata Cloister. More formally known as the Society of Friends, the Quakers were so named by outsiders because of their occasional involuntary movements during ecstatic trance. Their founder, the Englishman George Fox (1624–1691), believed that God comes directly into each person through the Inner Light. This light lay within; it could be appealed to at any time; and Quakers held firm to their contention that it was the ultimate vehicle of religious truth.

Fox's own life was one of repeated trances, which he believed brought him into the presence of divinity. While in these states, Fox recounted numerous direct calls from the Lord. In one instance, God told him to rush barefoot in the snow through the streets of a small English town, cursing the inhabitants; he meanwhile recounted that he saw rivulets of blood running to a great red pool in the marketplace. Later, upon coming out of this state, he learned that a thousand Christians had once been martyred there. Thus he said: "So I was to go, without my shoes, through the channel of their blood in the market-place, that I might rise up the memorial of the blood of those martyrs, which had been shed above a thousand years before, and lay cold in their streets. So the sense of this blood was upon me, and I obeyed the word of the Lord."[1]

Elsewhere, Fox described his ascent to a purity of spirit commanded by God, but a purity that put him at odds with the world:

When the Lord sent me into the world, he forbade me to put off my hat to any, high or low: and I was required to "Thee" and "thou" all men and women, without any respect to rich or poor, great or small. And as I traveled up and down, I was not to bid people Good morning, or Good evening, neither might I bow or scrape my leg to any one. This made the sects and professions rage. Oh! the rage that was in the priests, magistrates, professors, and people of all sorts; and especially in the priests and professors: for though "thou" to a single person was according to their accidence and grammar rules, and according to the Bible, yet they could not bear to hear it; and because I could not put off my hat to them, it set them all into a rage. Oh! the blows, punchings, beatings, and imprisonment that we underwent for not putting our hats off to men!"[2]

Similarly, the prominent American Quaker John Woolman (1720–1772), ardent abolitionist and pacifist who was born in New Jersey, has left an extensive account of his increasing awareness of the Inner Light. He recounted a wanton and pleasure-filled life up to the time of a serious illness, when, in the midst of great suffering, he had an intimation of Christ's presence. He later said that in the face of shame and humility, he believed he was healed. Afterward, he alternately slipped back into his old life and would then feel remorse when the Inner Light would again come to him, until:

One evening I had spent some time in reading a pious author, and walking out alone I humbly prayed to the Lord for his help, that I might be delivered from all those vanities which so ensnared me. Thus being brought low, he helped me; and as I learned to bear the cross I felt refreshment to come from his presence; but not keeping in that strength which gave victory, I lost ground again, the sense of which greatly affected me; and I sought deserts and lonely places and there with tears did confess my sins to God and humbly crave help from him. And I may say with reverence he was near to me in my troubles, and those times of humiliation opened my ear to discipline.[3]

Because the actual experience of the Inner Light was the central focus and transcended all outward forms, Quaker prayer meetings were simple, usually conducted in silence in a plain hall with no adornment. Occasionally, individuals rose and spoke as the spirit moved them. Men and women were considered equal, and both sexes spoke freely. There was no liturgy, no priesthood, no vestments of holy office. The Quaker garb was distinctively simple, and, after the teachings of their leader, their speech was punctuated by "thee" and "thou" in the old biblical style. Historically, they have been known for their pacifism and have always been conscientious objectors to war.

As a sect of deviants from both Puritan and Anglican theology, the Quakers were mercilessly persecuted in England in the middle of the seventeenth century because they posed a major threat to the alliance between the state church and the English throne. To be a Quaker in England or the colonies in the early 1660s was at one point punishable by death. Early Quaker missionaries to America, mostly women, arrived beginning in 1656 and were promptly arrested, tortured, and deported. Four such followers, all of them women, were hanged on Boston Common before the death penalty was rescinded in 1664.

Whereas various forms of persecution continued until 1725, the most notable success of the Quaker movement, as mentioned, was the founding of Pennsylvania in 1682 under William Penn. Born in 1644, the son of a knighted British admiral, Penn was raised under strict Puritan influences. Despite this, or perhaps as a direct reaction to it, he recounted later that at the age of twelve, he had an ecstatic experience. He was "suddenly surprised with an inward comfort" and, as he thought, with "an external glory in the room, which gave rise to religious emotions, during which he had the strongest conviction of the being of a God, and that the soul of man was capable of enjoying communication with Him."[4] He joined the resistance against the rigor of Anglican statutes while a student at Oxford and endured the first of many punishments for his religious beliefs. Severe recriminations also followed from his family. He became a Quaker at the age of twenty-three, and, on the basis of public statements he made regarding his belief in the freedom of religious conscience, he was sent to prison. Through his father's high influence, he was able to obtain release, but he immediately became the equivalent of a minister in the Quaker denomination and began to enter public debates. His writing career in the name of religious freedom commenced from his first imprisonment.

Not long after, he was again sent to prison for his scathing attack on the loose and unchristian lives of the clergy and for refusing to recant his views. Again his family connections and powers of written persuasion secured his release. He continued to preach and write on the ideals of the Society of Friends and eventually became close friends with its founder, George Fox.

Upon his father's death in 1670, Penn inherited a small fortune and a financial claim upon the Crown, which he later parlayed into a tract of land in the New World. This land in 1681 officially became the colony of Pennsylvania. The first Quaker enclave, Pennsylvania also became noted for the extreme diversity of its population, for its liberality in religious matters, and for being the largest and most successful of the proprietary provinces. Penn himself envisioned his colony as a refuge not only for Quakers, but for all religious groups seeking protection from persecution. He eventually died in England in 1718, and the proprietary rights to Pennsylvania, held by his descendants, ended in 1790. The Quaker experiment in civil government had already ended by the 1760s, however, when the political reins of state government passed to the Scotch-Irish Presbyterians.

The Quakers, meanwhile, because of their intense religiosity, fairness in financial dealings, and peaceful ways, were mostly spared by warring Native American tribes. They continued to play a major part in the government of other nearby states, and eventually they became quite prosperous and politically active in what we would today identify as liberal causes. Exerting an enormous influence that far exceeded their small numbers, they controlled the whaling trade in New England in the nineteenth century; they were among the foremost groups to outspokenly oppose slavery; and since then, they have long been involved in international humanitarian aid.

Over their history, Quakers in the United States have split into several divergent groups. In 1827, the followers of Elias Hicks (a cousin of Emily

Post) withdrew from the main body of the Society of Friends because they believed that formalism among the elders had obliterated the freedom of individuals to act according to the dictates of their own Inner Light. A second separation occurred in 1847, when the followers of John Wilber reacted against the attempted establishment of biblical Scripture as a form of ultimate authority. Thus, to this day, the Quakers maintain several actively recognized religious conventions, each one spawned by the urge to preserve the sanctity of individual spiritual experience.

The United Society of Believers

WE MAY COMPARE THE INDIVIDUALITY of the Society of Friends to the communal impulse of the Shakers. Accounted as the oldest and most successful of the utopian experiments, the Shakers, more formally known as the United Society of Believers in Christ's Second Appearing, represent a central example of the American visionary tradition. The first Shaker colony was launched in the United States in 1775, just before the advent of the American Revolution. Its founder, Mother Ann Lee, was born in 1736 in Manchester, England, one of eight children, the daughter of a blacksmith. Throughout her life, she could neither read nor write. Thus, instead of tracts and ideas, her ministry was intuitive, ascetic, and devotional. In 1758, her parents first affiliated with a sect of the Society of Friends called "the Shaking Quakers," so named because when they would go into trance their bodies would shake.

As a young woman, Lee followed in this religious path, enduring social ostracism and imprisonment. On one such occasion, while in jail in 1770, she received the experience of Divine Light, at which time she said the testimony of salvation and eternal life was revealed to her. She saw Jesus in all his glory, who satisfied all the longings of her soul. All of spiritual reality unfolded before her. She saw into the mystery of iniquity, understood the source of human depravity, and witnessed the first act of transgression by man and woman, the sexual union of Adam and Eve in the Garden of Eden. The lustful gratifications of the flesh were revealed to her as the source of all corruption and all sin. As a result of this vision, she was reborn into celibacy. All those who would follow her on this path, she proclaimed, were assured of redemption and resurrection. Thereafter, she was acknowledged by other believers as a Mother in Christ and hence was called Mother Ann.

By the time of this vision, she had already been married and produced four children, all of whom had died in infancy. But after her vision, she returned to the home of her parents. Gathering an increasing number of followers around her, Lee had another vision in 1773 that she was to lead her people to America, where she would establish the Second Christian Church.

With a party of nine, she landed in New York City in the summer of 1774, and there the group struggled for a year. Finally, in 1775, they moved up the Hudson River and settled just north of Albany at Watervliet. Their commune, inspired by Mother Ann's preaching, was established on the basis of strict self-discipline, complete celibacy, and suppression of the passions.

After five years of toiling by themselves, they were joined by a band of new converts who had recently come from a major religious revival then going on nearby among the Baptists. Soon, Mother Ann's doctrines had spread beyond upstate New York into Connecticut and Massachusetts. Wherever she traveled, she purportedly preached, healed the sick, and performed miracles.

Although Mother Ann died in 1784 at the age of forty-eight, her communities continued to thrive. By 1785, more than 5,000 people had joined her society, and eighteen communities existed throughout New York, Kentucky, New Hampshire, Vermont, and Massachusetts, occupying a total of more than 40,000 acres of land. They developed an extensive herbal pharmacopoeia, based largely on Native American lore, which they parlayed into a lucrative cottage industry. They sold and distributed seeds throughout New England. They developed techniques for the mass production of crafts, and they pioneered in progressive forms of agriculture and animal husbandry.

The Shakers held to a unique blend of religious beliefs. To join, all one had to do was settle one's accounts with the material world, confess all earthly sins to God before an elder as witness, and earnestly seek forgiveness. The Shakers did, however, maintain their own internal theology. Although they saw themselves as Christian and followed the teachings of the Bible, their main tenets were based on direct revelation. They believed, for instance, that the beginning of Christ's Kingdom on Earth commenced with the founding of the first Shaker society. They also believed that Christ was a spirit that may have appeared first in the body of Jesus but later in the form of Mother Ann. For this reason, they held that God was a dual entity, both male and female. This meant that men and women were accounted as absolutely different to eternity yet were equal before God. Women might do the cooking and sewing while men worked the fields, but in all forms of religious worship and in political activity regulating the affairs of the community, women had a status equal to men.

The Shakers lived by the principles of the Pentecostal Church, which they believed the orthodox denominations had abandoned. These principles included common property, celibacy, nonresistance, separation of church and state, and power over physical disease. They rejected the doctrine of the Trinity, believed in communication on the after-death plane, and thought that spiritual perfection was attainable in this life. They also recognized that there was an important intrinsic relation between the inwardly oriented Shaker experience and the way people lived in the outer world. The Shaker life was not for everyone, and they understood that they were supported by and a complement to the outer world. They did not oppose the outer world but only believed it was a lower order of existence.

Though their way of life appeared on the surface to be rigid and ascetic, it was actually designed to promote inward beauty through attention to the spiritual world. They lived communally in families of thirty to a hundred people. Their houses and barns were large but absolutely plain in appearance. Most of their floors were without rugs but clean and highly polished. Their dress was simple, not ostentatious, and changed with their needs. Men wore shirts and long coats without ties. Women wore floor-length dresses and almost always had their heads covered by bonnets with long lappets, so one could not at first tell old from young. They had no pictures hanging on the walls, as these harbored dust and dirt. They had contact with the outer world but kept it to a minimum, preferring instead to make their own cloth, grow their own wheat, bake their own bread, and can their own foods. In everything they made, they found great beauty in simplicity and perfect order.

In their dealings with others, they were scrupulously honest and fair. They soon developed a reputation for efficient farming, and their efforts yielded only the highest quality produce. Whatever they made beyond their basic sustenance they reinvested in land; thus they eventually accrued extensive holdings. They also used the banking system at the time and had savings accounts that were always earning interest. Their penchant was to save and not spend. They never borrowed and never, under any circumstances, contracted any debt.

Their ceremonies of courtesy and forms of religious worship also reflected their inwardly oriented lifestyle. With the exception of personal needs, for instance, there was no privacy. Individuals in the community always knew where everyone else was at every minute. Men and women had occasional meetings, but these always took place under tightly controlled conditions. They ate in the same room but at separate tables. They slept in rooms on different sides of the hallway and passed down stairs at different times. No passing of the sexes through transit doors was permitted except in the presence of a third party. Nor was spontaneous physical contact ever allowed.

Interaction of the sexes was permitted, however. On Saturday nights, groups of six to eight women would visit an equal number of men for an hour to sing hymns and exchange pleasantries. When infatuations developed, these were quickly reported or confessed to the elders. Immediate recognition of worldly desires and instant public atonement were important corrective devices. At the same time, confession of sins was constant, and the primary means by which the inner emotional life of the community was made known and kept were evenly regulated.

Shaker religious services were spartan in the extreme. They would take place in either the expansive meeting house or the large assembly hall of each family house. There was no altar and no images of any kind. Benches lined the walls, and all else was a vast open space. Members of the family, as they entered, would take their accustomed places, standing up in ranks formed specially for worship. The men and women faced each other. The elders of each sex stood up front, with a long empty corridor separating the two groups. After a hymn, one of the male elders would typically give a brief address on the holiness of living and consecration to God, after which a woman of equal rank would also speak.

The ranks would then be broken, and a smaller group of men and women would begin singing a lively hymn, which all would take up as they marched around the room becoming entranced in unison.

These activities often varied. Sometimes a single person particularly moved would bow to an elder and then begin a solitary whirling, which would continue for some time. Occasionally, a brother or sister would receive inspiration from the spirit land and, entranced, deliver a message of warning or comfort out loud. Sometimes the entire group would be asked to kneel in prayer by one of the elders. In their marching and dancing, the entire group would sometimes use hand gestures to alternately gather blessings up from the invisible or distribute them to particular individuals in need.

Shaker Visions

Trance consciousness was the primary source of inspiration in Shaker spirituality. Without understanding this, nonbelievers could have no comprehension of their way of life. The standard was established in the biographical details of the group's founder. Mother Ann left to her followers an account of her own spiritual awakening, which she described in the metaphor of birth:

> Thus I laboured, in strong cries and groans to God, day and night, till my flesh wasted away, and I became like a skeleton, and a kind of down came upon my skin, until my soul broke forth to God; which I felt as sensibly as ever a woman did a child, when she was delivered of it. Then I felt unspeakable joy in God, and my flesh came upon me, like the flesh of an infant.[5]

That mortifications could be endured in this condition is suggested by Mother Ann's account of a severe beating she received at the hands of one of her brothers, in which a staff was used on her body until one end splintered: "But I sensibly felt and saw the bright rays of the Glory of God, pass between my face and his staff, which shielded off the blows. . . . I felt my breath, like healing balsam, streaming from my mouth and nose, which healed me, so that I felt no harm from his strokes."[6]

Dreams, visions, and clairvoyant events were also a part of the lore of the United Society of Believers. One Shaker eldress, Eunice Bennett, remembered one of Mother Ann's dream visions in which "she saw the glories of God round about her head and pillow like the colours of the rainbow. . . . Twelve angels come into the room, placed in the form of a heart, six males on one side and six females on the other."[7]

Mother Ann, it was reported, also saw the coming of certain converts in visions before they appeared. One such man dreamed he was to come to her, and when he arrived, she herself reported having seen him coming in a dream. She gave accounts of clairvoyant journeys she would often take into the underworld:

> I felt the power of God come upon me, which moved my hands up and down like the motion of wings; and soon I felt as if I had wings on both hands; and I saw them, and they appeared as bright as gold. And I let my hands go as the power directed, and these wings parted the darkness to where souls lay, in the ditch of hell; & I saw their lost state.[8]

While she was alive, Lee enjoyed the reputation of a charismatic and powerful personality, and this perception only grew after she died. People who were weak and sick would report instant rejuvenation upon touching her. They also believed that she could communicate with the dead. When one Shaker brother visited Lee, he felt himself to be in the presence of God and "under great weight of body and spirit," but he did not know the cause. Lee purportedly said to him at the time, "You know not what you feel. I see the dead around you, whose visages are ghastly and very awful. Their faces almost touch thine. . . . Be of good comfort and be not cast down; for the dead gather to thee for the gospel, which thou hast received."[9]

It was also believed that Mother Ann could see into the spiritual purity of her followers. One elder reported:

> When she felt a gift of God to reprove . . . wickedness, the power of the spirit seemed like flames of fire, and the words of her mouth more dreadful than peals of thunder; so that the most stubborn and stout-

hearted would shake and tremble in her presence, like a leaf shaken with a mighty wind.[10]

Indeed, Mother Ann was thought to have power over events. The story is told of a band of attackers that she turned away at her door. They boldly rode up to seize her, and she commanded them to draw back. When they failed to do so, she beckoned menacingly toward them. The men seemed as if they had collectively lost their will, and their horses ran backward from the house, turned, and galloped down the road.[11]

Mother Ann was not the only one to leave a record of such experiences. In the late 1830s, Shakerism underwent a significant revival due to the collective phenomena of trance consciousness. The new phase began in the Watervliet community, when a group of young Shaker girls playing by themselves began to shake and whirl as if "driven by the wind." They kept this up for so long that they attracted the attention of the entire community. After they collapsed, they were put to bed, whereupon they began to report communication with angels. As they spoke, they made graceful motions with their hands and talked audibly so everyone in the room could clearly understand the nature of the spirit realm they had entered. Finally, when they recovered their senses, they were able to report everything they had seen.[12]

Shortly thereafter, a group of young boys had a similar experience. Soon, adults, too, were reporting such incidents, until the influence finally spread to all eighteen communities. People would become entranced and dance in circles for hours. Others would bow, jerk, whirl, or fall down upon the floor. Conversations in an unknown language were held for weeks with the spirits. Hymns were composed in a spiritual language and set to music.

Several members, acting as instruments for communication with spirits beyond the grave, reported visions from Mother Ann herself, who instructed them to entertain large bands of Native Americans. Visions of Indians appeared at the windows of the Shaker religious services, and these spirits were invited in to take part in the dancing. As before, similar visions swept through all eighteen Shaker communities in the United States. Subsequently, members of various Native American tribes, followed by blacks and a rising number of spiritualists, showed up in the flesh and became new converts.

Group visions then became quite common. On one occasion, nine Shakers testified that they had all heard the sound of a mighty trumpet and seen an angel standing on the roof of the meeting house, horn in one hand, roll book in the other. On another occasion, others reported that angels brought them rich garments, food, and gifts of jewelry, which they passed around at meetings. Others reported receiving eyeglasses to see into the invisible world. Still others received messages from Hebrew prophets, such as Ezekiel, Micah, and Noah. Several books of spirit communication were also published by the Shaker communities during this time, including *The Sacred Roll and Book,* which contained messages from the prophets and Shaker testimonials as to the divine influx, and *Holy and Eternal Wisdom,* a denunciation of sin and a description of God's impending wrath.

Beginning in 1841, the Shakers collectively experienced a succession of visits from Holy Mother Wisdom, or Christ in his feminine aspect. Villages set their affairs in order and practiced ascetic rituals in preparation for the appointed hour of arrival. At the Mount Lebanon community, on the designated day, Holy Mother Wisdom began to speak through her chosen instrument, Miranda Barber. Gifts were bestowed on every member, and then each family in their turn went through an inventory to determine which was a true vessel of God and which was unworthy of redemption. The purpose of the ceremony was to set a mark on each believer so that when the hour of the destroying angels came, the Shakers would be passed over and thus saved. Afterward, between 1841 and 1842, Holy Mother Wisdom came to Mount Lebanon again on several occasions and visited other communities as well.[13]

In 1842, another revelation, this time involving an elaborate ritual for the healing of nations, came from Mount Lebanon. The revelation soon spread to all the other communities. Each group was to build a holy place of worship on a nearby hill, the exact location of which would be designated through the local mediums. The site was to contain a specially enclosed area with a stone slab, which only to the eyes of believers appeared as a spiritual fountain spewing forth abundant water. Semiannual all-day religious services were held at these locations in which the worship was especially intricate and ecstatic. Men, women, and children would whirl around the fountain, sway in unison, and march and sing for many hours while "instruments," or chosen people, would converse with departed spirits. At the Harvard Shaker village, at a place called the Holy Hill of Zion, it was reported that 40,000 such spirits at one meeting were seen encircling the hilltop in a mighty host.[14]

One commentator claimed that all of these collective phenomena of trance consciousness then ended in 1844, as abruptly as they had begun six years earlier. Others, however, have made a point that Shakers were always known for their trance worship and alleged psychic abilities. Still on display at the Harvard Society is a spirit cabinet, in front of which believers would sit, waiting for a communication from the beyond. Adult-size cradles were used to transport the aged and the sick between buildings or to rock those who were too ill to attend meetings, so that their sins, too, could be shaken from them.[15]

By these means, the Shakers have left a twofold legacy. First, they were major contributors to the American handicraft tradition. We have only to think of the circular saw, wooden clothespins, the disc harrow, cut nails, flat brooms, and wooden matches to remember their influence. A revolving oven, the first metal pen, and the lazy Susan were also products of their inventiveness. They are best known, however, for their finely crafted but simple furniture, vintage pieces of which still bring outrageously exorbitant prices on the modern antique market. Second, the Shakers taught spiritual values that still appeal to American counter-culture. They believed in the equality of men and women; they preached vegetarianism and the abolition of slavery; and they practiced Christian pacifism in the face of anger and violence. The Shakers thus remain a living legend by combining the ideals of efficiency, neatness, and functional utility with an intense inward spirituality.

The Social Psychology of the Visionary Community

What can be said, then, about these examples of a uniquely American visionary psychology? First, with regard to visionary spiritual communities, there seem to be important analogies between the visions of the individual and those experienced by the group. If consciousness is a field with focus and margins, in the case of the visionary, we would expect one to spend the most time in the twilight region of contemplative meditation, on the margin or periphery of the waking state, in the exaltation of the transcendent, or struggling to overcome control by some lower-order condition. Waking consciousness thus becomes less the norm than a domain of necessity to which one must periodically, if not reluctantly, return, if only for the benefit of preserving the biological vehicle that allows for the experience of those other states. The other question is, can one even return to waking reality after a vision of the divine? The mystical literature is as replete with cases of ecstatic trance in which the person has to be constantly cared for by others as it is with accounts of people who have learned to successfully and simultaneously navigate both the domain of waking consciousness and that of the interior life during spiritual practice.

If, in the case of Mother Ann Lee, the leader is prone to witness visions, then the collective will likewise reflect this capacity. If mediumistic powers or clairvoyant events are common to the individual, they will also likely be so to the group, the experiences of which will likewise be filled with fortuitous events and simultaneous occurrences. If individuals go into trance consciousness, there will also likely be similar socially sanctioned events incorporated into the ritual of the community, such as those seen in Shaker dancing and singing.

Indeed, the psychology of the visionary seems to be written in larger letters only regarding the identity of the group. If the leader lives in a mythic, visionary, and numinous world that communicates higher spiritual ideals, then others will necessarily be inspired toward similar ideals. Such communities, in addition to their normal outward and observable behavior, and along with the capacity to live rationally in a state of waking consciousness, often also live by the belief that insight and intuition are the links to higher and more illuminated states of consciousness. Spontaneous motor automatisms such as involuntary dancing or speaking are then alternative ways to release the energy of the unconscious, but in socially sanctioned ways. Because of a certain hypersuggestibility of mass consciousness, spontaneous psychic events may travel through a group or even among distant communities in the same way that the germ theory of disease predicts the spread of physical contagion.

Visionary communities are also defined by the nature of the guru-disciple relationship—that is, by the unique bond that each individual has to the inspired personality. This bond may or may not be as totalitarian and complete as the experts in cults would have us believe. Indeed, in some Tibetan schools, the student of meditation always has two teachers: the one whose sole function is to inspire the student to higher attainment, and the other whose job is to instruct, to discipline, and to maintain the standards of practice. With regard to the guru-disciple relationship, there can be mentors as well as direct teachers, although the entire concept is little understood in the West.

Moreover, the form that teaching takes can be surprising. Teaching may come from a homeless man spouting philosophy in the subway, or it may come inadvertently out of the mouths of young children. It may not always come in the form of an advanced spiritual practitioner of some esoteric tradition or a bishop or rabbi or other person of high order. A spiritual teacher might be a complete failure in the material world yet exert a life-changing force on the person simply through his state of consciousness. Similarly, a teacher may be thoroughly immersed in materialism and yet be able to directly guide the inward journey.

In such apparently conflicting cases, we in the West may be suffering from an insufficient appreciation of the Hindu conception of devotion, or *bhakti*. To revere spiritual teachings wherever we hear them; to know when we are in the presence of a divine state of consciousness; to be prepared to receive spiritual instruction, even from the most unexpected quarter; to know complete loving surrender to some higher purpose—these are qualities that have only recently emerged into our collective consciousness in the West and must always seem foreign to traditional, mainstream ways of thinking, at least for the time being.

Finally, visionary communities often recognize a direct relationship between consciousness and healing. Herbs, the sweat lodge, the absorbing and conquering of pain, the miraculous recovery from illness that then gives one the power over that illness, the discovery of energy in the hands, the healing powers of the trance, the capacity to participate in the dance, the recuperative power of the voice, the shamanic journey within—all these suggest that there is some intrinsic relationship between one's ability to heal and the attainment of some specific state of interior consciousness. In these ways, visionary communities come to be centers of healing for those individual visionaries who participate in them.

Notes

1. In William James, *The Varieties of Religious Experience* (New York: Longmans, 1902), p. 8.

2. Ibid., p. 292.

3. Jon Alexander, *American Personal Religious Accounts, 1600–1980: Toward an Inner History of American Faiths* (New York: Edwin Mellen Press, 1983), p. 78.

4. From *Encyclopedia Britannica,* 11th ed. (London, 1911), p. 99.

5. Jean Humez, "'Ye Are My Epistles': The Construction of Ann Lee Imagery in Early Shaker Sacred Literature," *Journal of Feminist Studies in Religion,* 8:1 (Spring 1992): 100.

6. Ibid., p. 101.

7. Ibid., p. 92.

8. Ibid., p. 93.

9. Ibid., pp. 81–103.

10. Ibid., p. 94.

11. Ibid., p. 97.

12. Slater Brown, *The Heyday of Spiritualism* (New York: Hawthorne, 1970), pp. 68–72.

13. Stephen J. Stein, *The Shaker Experience in America* (New Haven, CT: Yale University Press, 1992), pp. 174–175.

14. Clara Endicott Sears, *Gleanings from Old Shaker Journals* (Boston: Houghton Mifflin, 1916), pp. 209–211.

15. Harriet E. O'Brian, *Lost Utopias,* 3rd ed. (Harvard, MA: Fruitlands Museum, 1947).

Chapter Four

The Swedenborgian and Transcendentalist Milieu

ON COMMENCEMENT DAY AT HARVARD, IN JUNE 1821, THE same year Ralph Waldo Emerson graduated and spoke as Class Day Poet, a young aspirant to the Swedenborgian ministry named Sampson Reed rose to the same podium to receive his master of arts degree and deliver a little homily he had written, titled "An Oration on Genius." In its form and delivery, those who were there remembered it as charismatic and oracular: "There is something in the inmost principles of the individual, when he begins to exist, which urges him onward; there is something in the centre of the character of a nation, to which people aspire; there is something which gives activity to the mind in all ages, countries, and worlds. This principle of activity is love."[1]

It was not the usual Harvard speech exalting reason and the senses over other forms of knowing. Rather, it was an affirmation of the spiritual nature of the mind—understanding enlivened by the affections—and of the manner in which true genius is formed, not by the light of ideas alone, but by the added warmth of the highest spiritual feeling, purified of every selfish and worldly passion. Whether geniuses are individuals of strong understanding, exquisite taste, or deep learning, their powers of divine truth are always derived from the hidden, spiritual source of all thought. Thus we have our Luthers, our Shakespeares, our Miltons, and our Newtons.

It was Reed's position, echoing the eighteenth-century scientist and mystic Emanuel Swedenborg, that all culture and all society, all art and all science, are expressed through the soul of individuals. This soul, however, does not simply generate truth out of itself. It is rather a conduit for the divine, expressed through the intelligence of the understanding, graced by the affections of the heart. All true geniuses see that the truth to which they aspire flows through them but is meanwhile not of their own making. Each person may become a genius in his own right by the perfection of this inward capacity. Moreover, Reed predicted, the knowledge of this process will constitute a transformed science of the mind in the future.

The eighteen-year-old Emerson sat in the audience, and when he heard Reed's homily, he declared it "native gold." He managed through his brother to get a copy of the text, which he "kept as a treasure" and which lived on in his mind for years. Later, Reed would develop the speech into a little book, *The Growth of the Mind* (1826), which Emerson used as a model for his own first book, *Nature* (1836). Eventually, historians would recount Reed's work as the first admonitory indictment of formalism in the liberal church, an altogether fresh approach to nature, and, indeed, the first salvo of the transcendentalist movement.

The main theme that Emerson derived from Reed's work was the Swedenborgian idea of correspondences—that God speaks to man through nature. The reason for this, Swedenborg maintained, was that every facet of the natural world is somewhere reflected in the life of the soul. In the hands of the transcendentalists, this meant one had to place oneself in natural surroundings in order for divinity to become visible to consciousness. Nature had to be preserved in order to remain an effective transmitting medium, and character had to be perfected so the light could shine through. Hence we have Christopher Cranch's caricature of Emerson as a fantastic eye, dressed in tuxedo and top hat, contemplating the sky from a country hill, to which Cranch appended the caption, quoted from *Nature:*

> *Standing on the bare ground—*
> *my head bathed in the blithe air,*
> *and uplifted into infinite space,—*
> *all mean egotism vanishes.*
> *I become a transparent eyeball.*[2]

The main psychological influence of the Swedenborgian idea of correspondences was to reinforce the powers and mechanism of symbolism. Nature in its many facets needed to be interpreted. Each perception told a story as both a bare fact of the natural world and a spiritual truth about the domain of inward consciousness. Each leaf was rich in poetic meaning; each twig a light toward self-knowledge; each breeze the breath of God. All of nature was an open book, laid before us as a set of glyphs, waiting to be translated by the powers of the mind into its divine message.

Transcendentalism, according to one Harvard historian, was the first uniquely American literary aesthetic to develop independent of European roots.[3] Certainly the ideas of German transcendentalism were in the air, as German romanticism was being retailed by Thomas Carlyle in England and Victor Cousin in France. But by the time the term "transcendental" became widely known, it had become uniquely American. Emerson's essays "American Scholar" and "Self-Reliance" outlined a new era of the New England intellectual class; Henry David Thoreau created the first literature of place by consecrating the American wilderness; Nathaniel Hawthorne depicted an American literary psychology closest to modern psychosomatic medicine when he showed the mental and physical consequences of defying Puritan standards of public conduct; Margaret Fuller wrote one of the first works celebrating American women, delving into the psyche of individual personalities. The letters, essays, and speeches of the transcendentalists were collected together to become landmark books of an American renaissance, and their articles became the new literary journals, such as the *Dial,* the *Boston Quarterly Review*, and later the *Atlantic Monthly.*

First stirring in the 1820s, transcendentalism was an intuitive movement that grew out of controversies surrounding the Calvinists, whose Puritan religion dominated the colonies, and the Unitarians, perhaps the most liberal wing of the New England churches to spring up after the American Revolution that could still call itself Christianity. Supernaturalism, the doctrine of the elect, and the concept of the depravity of man were supplanted by the validity of sense perceptions, the laws of reason and technological progress, and the idea that Jesus was, after all, just a man. Congregationalist churches converted their pulpits to Unitarianism in droves.[4]

But transcendentalism, representing an exaltation of the individual spirit, went a step further. Divinity, the transcendentalists said, could be known to each person not through the clouded lens of the historical churches, but directly through the inward contemplation of nature. The approach was through insight, not theology. Transcendentalists proclaimed the inextricable relation between God and man through human personalities and maintained that mere reason alone could not suffice to explain the whole.

Here the transcendentalists made a radical distinction between reason and understanding. The function of reason, they claimed, was not the discovery of truth, but that of arranging, methodizing, and harmonizing verbal propositions in regard to it. Understanding, however, was much larger. It was the cultivation of reason, emotion, and intuition in the same person; it was the perfection of the higher self, the discovery of divinity within.

With such an aesthetic, transcendentalism eventually became the popular but unchurched voice of an era. Its influence was pervasive, and its tenets would soon be taken for granted by subsequent generations. It appealed because it was not merely a critique of rationalism and materialism, as if a few minor corrections would fix the perceived drift into mediocrity and decadence. On the contrary, it exuded what Frederick Henry Hedge called a fierce disquiet and a dissatisfaction with the whole mechanism of society. More than that, transcendentalism pointed the way to a new alternative that was uniquely American, suiting the American temperament.

The official beginning of the Transcendentalist Club dates from the Harvard commencement of 1836, fifteen years after Reed and Emerson had graduated. Feeling that Harvard as an institution was out of touch with their thinking, a group of individuals who had been invited to the commencement decided to meet instead at the home of George Ripley. Besides Ripley, in attendance were Emerson, Orestes Brownson, Convers Francis, and Bronson Alcott. Breaking convention, they admitted women at subsequent meetings—Margaret Fuller, Sophia Ripley, and Elizabeth Peabody all took part. Others, such as Christopher Cranch and Caleb Stetson, also became regulars. Even the great Unitarian divine William Ellery Channing came once.

When the group began to import members from elsewhere, such as Henry James Sr. (1811–1882), who lived in New York City, the members changed their name to the Town and Country Club. But eventually, it became quite clear that Boston, the "Athens of America," had become a mere suburb of Concord, Massachusetts, as far as the transcendentalist movement was concerned: Concord was its intellectual epicenter. Soon, the now-famous Saturday Club was formed, which brought all the important local thinkers into Emerson's orbit. Much later, by the 1870s, when even these meetings became too big and too fashionable, the aging transcendentalists convened the Chestnut Street Radical Club. Emerson was still there, as were Henry James Sr., Benjamin Peirce, Oliver Wendell Holmes, and others. Despite the fact that the club met behind closed doors at a private residence, and by invitation only, the detailed contents of its proceedings always appeared in local newspapers the next morning.

That first month in 1836, Emerson had already showed signs of leading the way. *Nature* had appeared a few weeks earlier, and though it was slow to receive wider recognition, the little band that met at Ripley's understood that the work captured prevailing sentiment. The *Dial*, cofounded by Emerson and Fuller, began publication in 1840; communal experiments from Brook Farm to Walden were launched; experimental schools appeared, first under Alcott and then Franklin Sanborn. Establishments such as the Old Corner Bookstore became local havens;

publishers such as Ticknor & Fields sprang up to meet the public demand for transcendentalist writings. Essays, novels, and poetry appeared in a flood. Allying itself with progressive causes such as women's suffrage and the antislavery campaign, spiritualism and mental healing, and utopian socialism, transcendentalism soon became a political and spiritual, as well as a literary and philosophical, movement.

In all this, the transcendentalists also became deeply involved in the prevailing popular psychology. Emerson's second wife, Lidian, practiced a form of naturopathic medicine. Thoreau avidly studied Native American culture. Fuller had her books printed and distributed through Fowler & Wells, the phrenological publishers in New York. Hawthorne depicted the still-prevailing sentiments regarding witchcraft. A diet fad called Grahamism, among other food crazes, was practiced for its influence on promoting a purified state of spiritual consciousness at Alcott's utopian community, Fruitlands, in Harvard, Massachusetts. Such food trends were repeated at Brook Farm in West Roxbury. Alcott and others also practiced hydrotherapy—the naturopathic regime of taking cold-water baths and vigorous exercise upon awakening—even in midwinter.

At the same time, the transcendentalists showed themselves to be avid enthusiasts of orientalism. Emerson had read Persian and Sanskrit literary sources from the library of Henry Wadsworth Longfellow. Members of the editorial staff of the *Dial,* mainly Emerson and Fuller, had access to recent Sanskrit translations of the Hindu Upanishads, the Bhagavad Gita, the Laws of Manu, and the Vishnu Puranas. Appearing also in the *Dial* were French translations of Chinese sources on Confucianism and Taoism. Thoreau was most interested in yoga. Both James Freeman Clarke and Lydia Maria Child wrote influential textbooks on world religions. Then, with the passing of transcendentalism after the Civil War and its absorption into the philosophy of mental healing, the stage was set for the next generation, when Asian techniques in breath control, yoga, and meditation were enthusiastically taken up by Theosophists and New Thought practitioners.

An Intuitive Psychology of Character Formation

At the heart of transcendentalist philosophy lay an intuitive, dynamic psychology of inner experience. Based on immediate access to the subconscious, it appealed to a large number of unchurched spiritual seekers by emphasizing the highest moral and aesthetic capacities of personality. It was a philosophy for self-starters. It fostered the development of willpower, and it proclaimed that destiny was in one's own hands. And there stood Emerson at its center, preaching from the public lectern on the gospel of what he called the "Over-Soul." His message was that beyond the bounds of the individual ego lies something more vast and infinite, the source of all religion, the basis for ethical behavior, the foundation of individual belief. So the Concord Sage had said:

> The Supreme Critic on the errors of the past and the present, and the only prophet of that which must be, is that great nature in which we rest . . . , that Over-Soul, within which every man's particular being is contained and made one with all other; that common heart of which all sincere conversation is the worship, to which all right action is submission; that over-powering reality which confutes our tricks and talents, and constrains everyone to pass for what he is, and to speak from his character and not from his tongue, and which evermore tends to pass into our thought and hand and become wisdom and virtue and power and beauty.[5]

Emerson's view was all inward and, therefore, psychological. In his lectures on the Philosophy of History in 1836, he delineated what he called a "science of the mind," the center of which was that portion of ourselves that "lies within the limits of the unconscious," the "unfathomed sea of thought and virtue," the "universal soul within or behind . . . individual life." He understood the nature of the dynamic unconscious, when, in his lecture series titled "Demonology," delivered in 1839, he spoke on "the witchcraft of sleep," which "divides with truth the empire of our lives." And in this sleep,

> *Night-dreams trace on memory's wall*
> *Shadows of the thoughts of day,*
> *And thy fortunes as they fall*
> *The bias of thy will betray*

Of the stream of consciousness, he wrote: "As with events, so with thoughts. As I watch that flowing river, which out of regions I see not, pours for a season its streams into me, I see that I am a pensioner; not a cause but a spectator of this ethereal water; that I desire and look up and put myself in the attitude of reception, but from some alien energy the visions come."[6]

He also conceptualized personality in terms of double consciousness. Reason, by which he meant the higher intuitive faculties of the idealist, and understanding, the cognitive and sensory faculties of the materialist, "diverge every moment and stand in wild contrast." We are self and not-self, head and heart, animal and spirit.[7] So he said in 1833,

Man begins to hear a voice that fills the heavens and earth saying that God is within him. . . . I recognize the distinction of the outer and the inner self; the double consciousness that within this passionate erring, mortal self sits a supreme, calm, immortal mind, whose powers I do not know; but it is stronger than I; it is wiser than I; it never approved me in any wrong; I seek counsel of it in my doubt; I repair to it in my dangers; I pray to it in my undertakings. It seems to me the face which the Creator uncovers to his child.[8]

And insofar as the transcendentalists sought for a unification of these dichotomies, Emerson articulated a spiritual transformation of personality, in terms of both its process and its content:

Man is the dwarf of himself. Once he was permeated and dissolved by spirit. He filled nature with his overflowing currents. Out from him sprang the sun and the moon; from man, the sun, from woman, the moon. The laws of his mind, the periods of his actions externalized themselves into day and night, into the year and the seasons. But, having made for himself this huge shell, his waters retired; he no longer fills the veins and the veinlets; he is shrunk to a drop.[9]

Verily, he said in *Prospects,* "man is a God in ruins." The regeneration of consciousness stands before us, in other words, as but an aspiration.

Only when the lessons of the unconscious are assimilated to consciousness through the revitalization of myth will the actual transformation take place. Only in this way can our highest ideals be made real, as he made clear in "The American Scholar": "The preamble of thought, the transition through which it passes from the unconscious to the conscious, is action." The transformation is initiated by an "act of reflection" that places life "in perspective." We gain access to the hidden power of the unconscious by separating truth "from unconscious reason" and making it "an object of consciousness." In this way, "any sentiment or principle" can be "disentangled from the web of our unconsciousness." We acquire self-knowledge by "detaching from the general instinct of life and moral principles which we feel to be the ascendant stars in our inner firmament." Then we act on them to make them real in the world.

Such ideas were revolutionary for the times because they raised a daring question: What good are religious dogma and the priestly caste if divinity truly lies within? The transcendentalists answered that self-realization—based on an inward-looking, contemplative witness of God in nature—is far superior to the parochial ecclesiasticism of the denominations and the barren ritual of the church. Popular consciousness, already attuned to the most unfettered experiments in spiritual expression through the rising tide of mental healing, could run wild with the possibilities of inward freedom. Meanwhile, however, Emersonianism was castigated by the pundits of high culture. After the students at Harvard Divinity School invited Emerson to lecture in 1838, the faculty rose in condemnation, and he was banished from the halls of his alma mater for more than a quarter of a century.

Shrugging off the denunciation, members of the Concord circle proceeded on their own course, articulating to an eager public the outlines of a generic psychological theology based on their own inward experience. Emerson began in the Unitarian Church pulpit and ended up on the public lecture platform after discovering that people would listen attentively to the same subjects on Wednesday evening that they appeared anesthetized to on Sunday morning. Thoreau preached from the woods and the riverbank, enshrining nature as the mother church. Alcott launched the Concord School of Philosophy to discuss topics that were denied a hearing at Harvard and Yale; and, believing, as Emerson had said, that transformed individuals will create a transformed society, Alcott spurned the traditional convention of the isolated nuclear family, took up utopian socialism, and founded his experimental Fruitlands in Harvard. By all these means, transcendentalism emerged. But there is more to the story.

Margaret Fuller:
The New Psychology of the Feminine

IN NO OTHER PERSONALITY among the transcendentalists do we find such close analogies to the contemporary scene of American folk psychology than that of Margaret Fuller, a major contributor to the transcendentalists' understanding of the feminine side of personality. A child prodigy, she was probably more intelligent than most of the men around her, yet she was also a catalyst for their own genius. A groundbreaker of the American women's movement, a writer, editor, journalist, translator, and historian, she remains, nevertheless, largely unsung today. There have been a few recent studies of her, but the most compelling among them is a series of books and dramatic performances by the New York author and actress Laurie James, who has shown the various ways in which Fuller was a leader in the uniquely American visionary tradition.[10]

Sarah Margaret Fuller was born on May 23, 1810, in Cambridgeport, Massachusetts. She was the eldest child of Margaret (née Crane) and Timothy Fuller, a lawyer, politician at the state and national level, Jeffersonian Democrat, and abolitionist long before the word was coined. From an early age, she was diligently schooled by her well-educated father. She studied English grammar and could read Latin by the age of six, after which she began memorizing Virgil. She was opinionated enough at the age of seven to insist on changing her name, dropping "Sarah," so that for the rest of her life, she was known simply as Margaret.

In her younger years, she read widely in European literature, both classical and modern. (But according to Laurie James, Fuller's diaries show that, as a result of the stress from overlearning at an early age, Fuller was the little genius by day but wracked by spectral illusions, nightmares, and somnambulism by night.) Her imagination was filled with the Greek and Roman gods and goddesses of whom she had read. She learned to sing and play the piano, and she studied penmanship and music with tutors. She also developed the habit of gazing into a carbuncle and other gems, where she saw "neverending depths" and was transported "into never-ending spheres." Her friend Frederick Henry Hedge described her when she was twelve as "so precocious in her mental and physical developments that she passed for eighteen or twenty . . . as a lady full grown . . . a blooming girl of a florid complexion and vigorous health, with a tendency to robustness of which she was painfully conscious."[11]

She grew up in the company of Oliver Wendell Holmes, anatomist and professor at the Harvard Medical School; Henry Ware, the Harvard Divinity professor; Richard Henry Dana, later the author of *Two Years Before the Mast;* James Russell Lowell, the poet; the luminary William Ellery Channing; and a host of other Harvard lights, including Charles Eliot Norton and Thomas Wentworth Higginson. By the time she entered boarding school at the age of twelve, she found her teachers rather pedestrian. She later wrote, "I was . . . in the hands of teachers who had not, since they came on earth, put to themselves one intelligent question as to their business there."[12] They required mere memorization from a young girl who had known "great living minds."

She completed her formal education at age fifteen. Since colleges were not open to women, she set up a rigorous routine of study for herself, while her male peers went on to Harvard, preparing for professional careers. (Later, she would help her brothers through Harvard.) Her goal was to travel to Germany, where she could research and write a life of Goethe, whom she felt had been ignored and misunderstood by the American intelligentsia. Some of her own translations soon appeared through the efforts of George Ripley, whose published series introduced Americans to the work of Continental authors.

Fuller made numerous friends, but men were often simultaneously fascinated and threatened by her intellect and wit. She knew the highly gifted Lydia Maria Child, well-known writer of children's books and later biographer of Madame de Staël; she became close to Caroline Sturgis; she brushed shoulders with the fugitive antislavery campaigner

William Lloyd Garrison; and she developed a friendship with the English writer and abolitionist Harriet Martineau.

Fuller also developed intellectual relationships with young men who advocated women's rights, such as Hedge, Clarke, and Samuel Ward. She inspired confidences in them, and close friendships followed. But they did not reciprocate emotionally. When it came to romance, they would choose the stereotypical girl of the day—a young attractive woman who had been groomed to keep a home and raise children. Fuller's recurrent headaches, it is surmised, were connected with these heartbreaks and the inability to find love. To alleviate the headaches, her physicians sometimes prescribed leeches, a commonly used treatment. Other times Fuller took to the woods to walk for many hours.

On one of these excursions, trying to find rejuvenation, she recounted a mystical awakening:

> Suddenly the sun shone out with that transparent sweetness, like the last smile of a dying lover, which it will use when it has been unkind all a cold autumn day. . . . I remember how, a little child, I had stopped myself one day on the stairs, and asked, how came I here? How is it that I seem to be this Margaret Fuller? What does it mean? What shall I do about it? I remember all the times and ways in which the same thought had returned. I saw how long it must be before the soul can learn to act under these limitations of time and space, and human nature; but I saw also that I MUST do it—that it must make all this false true,—and sow new and immortal plants in the garden of God, before it can return again. I saw there was no self; that selfishness was all folly, and the result of circumstance; that it was only because I thought self real that I suffered; that I had only to live in the idea of the All, and all was mine. This truth came to me, and I received it unhesitatingly; so that I was for an hour taken up into God.[13]

Fuller later recounted that her earthly pain at not being recognized "never went deep after this hour," having "passed the extreme of passionate sorrow." From then on, she felt that "all check, all failure, all ignorance, were only temporary" and could not affect her as before. She felt that she had "touched the secret of the universe" and had become "invested with talismanic power." Her life had become a church, her thoughts devout and full of solemn music. Whatever hardships she would face thereafter would only help her grow; she now welcomed adversity instead of shunning it.

Issues such as abolition, peace, temperance, Grahamism, free public schools, communitarianism, and prison and asylum reform were in the air. In the early days of the antislavery movement, abolitionists were thought to be so radical that, in Boston, they couldn't even be asked to dinner. They were considered "coarse, unworthy of respect, of no influence . . . and of disreputable deportment," and words such as "illiterate," "ill-mannered," "crazy," and "long haired" were used to describe them.[14] As Anne Braude has shown in her work *Radical Spirits,* it was no accident that social movements such as abolition and spiritualism were made up of many of the same people who championed women's rights.[15] Such radical ideas as the right of women to hold property and to vote were promoted, and Fuller participated intellectually and socially in this atmosphere in the circles that linked Boston, Cambridge, and Concord.

Fuller was admitted into the august company of the Transcendentalist Club with full honors. She attended Emerson's Phi Beta Kappa address at the Harvard commencement on August 31, 1837, and a day later met at Emerson's house with the club. Her two greatest contributions to this most impressive body were the opportunities she opened for women to be heard and her editorship of the *Dial.* In the first instance, in order to make money, she conceived that she would launch a discussion series for women. Since men were constantly being called upon to recite what they knew and give their opinion, why not women? For this opportunity, the participants would pay her a fee—$20 for ten sessions. The first series of "conversations," held on the subject of Greek mythology, was convened at Elizabeth Peabody's bookstore.

On November 6, 1839, at eleven o'clock in the morning, some twenty-five women gathered together. Fuller's intense personality dominated the discussion with illustration, wit, and imagination. Once the conversation was opened, Fuller encouraged the women to speak up, listened appreciatively to all that was said, and steered the conversation toward coherent themes. At the end, she offered a summary and finished by presenting her own views. She found that some of the women shied away from principles while others cleaved to details, but a small handful among them had real talent, and all in all the experiment was judged a success.

The conversations became "singularly prosperous." They attracted the cultivated, the well connected, and the politically active. Such eminent women joined as Lydia Maria Child, Mrs. Josiah Quincy, Mary Greeley (Mrs. Horace Greeley), Maria White (the fiancée of James Russell Lowell), Lidian Emerson, Marianne Jackson (Oliver Wendell Holmes's sister-in-law), and Julia Ward Howe, author of "The Battle Hymn of the Republic." The network grew to more than forty and for one season even included some men—Emerson, Ripley, Alcott, and a few others.

Then, about that same time, after the men in the Transcendentalist Club had also voted their approval, and largely because Emerson really did not want the job himself, Emerson offered Fuller a position as editor of the new transcendentalist magazine, the *Dial*. There would be nothing like it yet on the market, he proclaimed. Established periodicals such as the *North American Review* put readers to sleep, and the pulp magazines appealed only to the more prurient aspects of public taste. Here would be a vehicle of self-knowledge and high thoughts—the main avenue for expression of the new higher philosophy.

Fuller accepted the offer because she believed in the cause; as well, she hoped she might earn a salary from the work. Emerson even offered to be her assistant. But what she found was meager funding from a low subscription base and a cast of male characters who had promised a steady flow of manuscripts but whose commitments suddenly vanished as soon as each deadline neared. The first issue came out later than announced and received mixed reviews. Subsequent issues were more well received, although Fuller had to keep filling up space with her own material.

The issues contained prose, poetry, essays, and reviews. Leavening the text, the editors also included liberal quotes from the Upanishads, the Laws of Manu, the Bhagavad Gita, and the Confucian Analects. Fuller continued the job for two years before turning it over to Emerson. All in all, her editorship was a historic feat, not only because she was a woman, but because she helped initiate a new and unique genre of national literature that Emerson had called for in "The American Scholar."

Thoreau and Other Naturalists

It is supposed today that ecological psychology is something new, or at least that it dates from the time of Thoreau; but reverence for the land has always been a part of American folk consciousness. One of the foremost examples from folklore is the legend of John Chapman, better known as Johnny Appleseed, "the picturesque sower of a two-fold seed." Chapman was an itinerant nurseryman who planted apple trees throughout the United States. Born in Leominster, Massachusetts, in 1774, he was attracted to the wilderness at an early age, which led him to spend forty years roaming thousands of miles between the Ohio River and the Great Lakes and west from the Alleghenies to Indiana. He obtained seeds from cider presses in western Pennsylvania, planted primitive nurseries, protected them with fences, and then sold or gave away the young trees to any farmers who wanted them.

One of his other ventures was to rescue broken-down horses that had been abandoned by settlers in their desperate rush westward. These animals he would leave in corrals near the poorest settlements, paying nearby residents to care for them while he was away on his long journeys.

While Chapman distributed trees and tended animals, at each settlement he also left Swedenborgian pamphlets describing the New Jerusalem. These he had made by cutting up sections of Swedenborg's works by chapter, which he then disseminated like a lending library. He would leave a section at each house and then return to get it, leaving a new section on each visit. He also preached and read Swedenborg's doctrine around roaring campfires to all who would listen.

His philosophy of life was totally nonviolent and guided solely by spiritual principles. A vegetarian, he went about the wilderness unarmed, a friend to wasps, snakes, and people alike. In dress he was eccentric in the extreme, wearing no shoes, an old coffee sack for clothing, and an old pot for a hat. Whereas the more educated settlers thought him half-witted, he was dearly loved by children and venerated by Native Americans as a powerful medicine man.

As settlers pushed into Ohio, he kept ahead of them by moving farther west into Indiana. It is said that he died alone outside a frontier cabin near Fort Wayne at the age of seventy-two. A monument now stands nearby for the edification of future generations.

Vachel Lindsey placed him in his context:

> He was the New England kind of saint, much like a Hindu saint, akin to Thoreau and Emerson who came after him. . . . He preached Swedenborg to the Indian witch doctors in his youth, and in his old age to the Disciple preachers and other stubborn souls on the frontier. . . . And he kept moving for a lifetime toward the sunset . . . , leaving in his wake orchards bursting and foaming with rich fruit, gifts for mankind to find long after.[16]

Chapman, we now see, was a transcendentalist before anyone had heard the name.

The best-remembered naturalist of the Concord movement, however, was Henry David Thoreau, a man who elevated simple living to the level of a spiritual discipline. Two years after Thoreau's death, Emerson acknowledged this when he said that "Henry pitched his tone very low in his love of nature,—not on stars and suns . . . but tortoises, crickets, muskrats, suckers, toads, and frogs. It was impossible to go lower."[17] At different times a woodsman, surveyor, essayist, philosopher, and pencil-maker, Thoreau was born and raised in the vicinity of Concord and graduated from Harvard in 1837. After college, he taught at a small private school for a few years until it closed. In 1841, he made an arrangement to live with the Emersons in exchange for odd jobs and gardening. He left after a short time, saying that he found their prosperity "dangerous" to the life of the spirit.

He now wished to be as self-sufficient as possible and to live with only the essentials, free from regimentation and constraint. The communities at Fruitlands and Brook Farm were options, but it was not society he sought. To immerse himself in nature seemed the most desirable course.

With this end in mind, he went into the town of Lincoln, which neighbored Concord, and petitioned the Board of Selectmen to grant him a permit to build a small hut on the shores of Flint's Pond, an idyllic body of water that served as the town's chief drinking supply. His request was denied. It seems that a few weeks earlier, while fishing on the Sudbury River, Thoreau had been cooking some fish for his lunch and had accidentally started a forest fire. Lincoln did not want the same thing to happen at Flint's Pond. Thoreau went back, hat in hand, to Emerson, who suggested Thoreau stay at Walden Pond, where Emerson had just purchased some property. Thoreau arranged to clear brush in exchange for the right to squat on the land.

At Walden, he built a small cabin with a chimney and lived there for a year. Although it was a utopian experiment of one, so to speak, he went there not to become a hermit, but to see if he could transact the business of living with the fewest obstacles possible: "I went to the woods because I wished to live deliberately, to front only the essential facts of life, and see if I could not learn what it had to teach, and not, when I came to die, discover that I had not lived."[18] He documented life around the pond through the cycle of the seasons; he communed with the animals and wrote *A Week on the Concord and Merrimack Rivers*. He was also not far from town and went in frequently to wash his clothes and obtain provisions. People came to visit him and he them.

The ecopsychology Thoreau evolved (to borrow a contemporary term) was based on the conservation of consciousness. His outward analogies all conspired to train the spotlight on character, suggesting that environmental conservation has everything to do with the light of self-knowledge. So he said: "The surface of the earth is soft and impressible by the feet of men; and so with the paths which the mind travels."[19] And elsewhere:

I saw a striped snake run into the water, and he lay on the bottom, apparently without inconvenience, as long as I stayed there, or more than a quarter of an hour; perhaps because he had not yet fairly come out of the torpid state. It appeared to me that for a like reason men remain in their present low and primitive condition; but if they should feel the influence of the spring of springs arousing them, they would of necessity rise to a higher and more ethereal life.[20]

Thoreau learned from his experiment that plain living did not necessarily lead to high thinking and that simplicity is a quality in the mind, not a lowered level of one's standard of living. He also discovered that

if one advances confidently in the direction of his dreams, and endeavors to live the life which he has imagined, he will meet with a success unexpected in common hours. He will put some things behind, will pass an invisible boundary; new, universal, and more liberal laws will begin to establish themselves around and within him; or the old laws will be expanded, and interpreted in his favor in a more liberal sense, and he will live with the license of a higher order of beings.[21]

We may well wonder about the source of these ideas, and, of course, Thoreau's answer was that they came from within. The interior spiritual domain was his ever-constant quest. All during his youth, Thoreau used to regularly experience heightened states of consciousness and glimmerings from the beyond. But as he got older, these faded. He spent his mature years as a transcendentalist trying to bring back these experiences by somewhat artificial means. He would put his ear to the telegraph wires in an effort to induce an altered state from the vibrations. He would sit at the shores of Walden Pond and look for two suns; that is, he placed himself strategically so that the sun in the sky and its reflection in the water could both be seen at once. Contemplating the reflection in the water would induce a slight dissociated state, inviting all of nature to then open up to the inward eye.

Thoreau's civil disobedience, in the context of a heightened environmental consciousness, represents a protoexistentialist response to the pretensions of modern culture. It takes a special set of circumstances to get a glimpse, even if just for a moment, of pureness. Turning to the inward contemplation of nature allows us to step outside the bubble of a strictly man-made world.

In such a vision, there is both hope and inspiration of historic proportions. Just as Thoreau, Emerson, and Fuller informed their philosophy with insights from the Hindu Gita, so, too, did Gandhi a century later borrow a page from the transcendentalists for his campaign of *satyagraha*—nonviolent noncooperation. Martin Luther King Jr. then followed by borrowing back this cup of sugar as a key ingredient in the American civil rights movement of the 1960s.

Beyond these developments, Thoreau has come to stand for the right, even the duty, of the individual in a free society to protest against the status quo. Civil dissent is not a form of psychopathology; it is a necessary corrective to the ossification and corruption of authority as a fixed and immovable entity that would quell the spirit of the individual for the sake of an ideology. Thoreau himself refused to pay taxes, and he protested against slavery and the waging of war, considering dissent to be the responsibility of a free man. Walden, moreover, has become a touchstone for generations of spiritual seekers, inspiring the counterculture even today.[22]

Another nineteenth-century naturalist of the transcendentalist bent was John Muir, a pioneer conservationist, mystic, and wilderness wanderer. A shining example of the American visionary tradition, Muir's life itself represented the transcendental ideal in practice.

Muir (the name, appropriately, means "moor" or wild stretch of wasteland) was born on April 28, 1838, in Dunbar, Scotland. On February 19, 1849, at the age of eleven, he arrived in the United States from Glasgow, motherless, accompanied by his brothers and sisters and their father, who was a religious zealot and former shopkeeper. The family made their way through the Erie Canal to Wisconsin, where they settled down and began a farm. Muir remembered only working very hard as a youth under the eye of his stern father. He also remembered as a teenager being unmercifully beaten each day by this man, who proclaimed that a thrashing was warranted even without provocation, lest there was something hidden that had not yet been discovered.

One benefit of farm life, however, was that Muir became quite handy with tools. At this point in his career, he also showed the exceptional skills of a budding inventor. Muir left home in 1860 and made his way to the University of Wisconsin at Madison. He showed himself to be largely self-directed. He lived frugally, studied only what he wanted, and left without a degree. Years later, however, he received honorary doctorates not only from Wisconsin, but also from Harvard, Yale, and the University of California.

After he left Madison, a period of indecision set in. To remedy it, Muir took a thousand-mile walk from the Midwest down into the South and across to Florida. He slept in cemeteries for protection, talked with people from all walks of life, and kept a journal. During this time, the naturalist in him also emerged.

From Florida, he went to Cuba in 1868, trying unsuccessfully to press on southward to the Amazon. Instead, he came back by way of New York and, a short time later, traveled across the country to California. When he arrived in San Francisco, he wasted no time getting from the city out into the country. The westward rim of the Yosemite valley filled him with awe, and around that valley he spent the rest of his life.

Like Thoreau, Muir chose to live simply. He worked only enough to get by. The rest of the time he spent on wilderness expeditions. Believing that civilization "drives its victims in flocks," he preferred the solitary life of a tramp in the mountains.[23] When he traveled, it was often without blanket or cloak and with nothing more than a sack of dried bread and some water. Like John Chapman before him, he never carried a weapon and was never attacked by a wild animal. He walked all over Yosemite and beyond and would stay away for long periods. In fact, he seemed to be completely oblivious to the passage of time, not in any hurry to get to the next brook or hill, using only nature as his watch. Through all this, he declared once to his sister, "I have not yet in all my wanderings found a single person so free as myself."[24]

In 1869, Muir spent the summer in the high sierras tending a flock of 2,500 sheep. Another sheepherder did most of the work while he supervised, so he had plenty of time for his beloved treks. Comparable to Thoreau's youthful experience at Walden Pond, an account of that summer appeared much later from Muir's pen, *A Record of My First Summer in the Sierras*.

In all his travels, he also made numerous contributions to natural science. He discovered many species of plants and animals. Mountain peaks he charted were named after him. Moreover, he became involved in a national controversy when he put forth the theory that Yosemite had been formed by the movement of glaciers. His ideas were opposed by the professors of geology, who claimed that truth could not possibly come from a mere shepherd. He spent three painstaking years tracing all the streams in Yosemite to prove his point and presented his results in a series of *Sierra Studies* in 1873, which confirmed his theory and brought him wide acclaim.

Muir married and started a family in 1880. During his most active domestic period, he leased land from his father-in-law and grew extensive crops, focusing on the Tokay grape. He became the first to ship grapes to Hawaii. Financially, he did quite well over a ten-year period, but he then abandoned his commercial interests. Money did not concern him. His attitude was that a rich man who could never get enough was actually poor when compared to the man with a little who thought he had plenty. Much of Muir's own extra funds went toward trying to procure tracts of land to protect them against the ravaging effects of logging and ranching.

Thus, instead of Mammon, nature became both his laboratory and his temple of worship. To him, everything was the handiwork of God, and his belief in the healing power of nature verged on spiritual exaltation. He led the preservation of Yosemite as a national park; he deserves major credit for saving the Grand Canyon and the Petrified Forest; and he was the co-founder and first president of the Sierra Club. When he died in 1914, he was still trying to keep part of the Yosemite valley from being flooded to produce an unnecessary source of drinking water for San Francisco. His legacy lives on today in the environmental movement he helped to create.

But Muir was also a transcendentalist. Although he never actually called himself one, his spiritual roots lay with his Concord colleagues. He had first read Emerson in college, and he carried with him *The Prose Works of Ralph Waldo Emerson* (1870), which he read and reread during his travels in the high sierras. Later in his life, he kept photographs of Emerson and Thoreau in his study on a mantelpiece that served as a hallowed, dust-covered altar that no one was ever permitted to touch.

Muir and Emerson even met in 1871, when Emerson and eight others, including the younger James brothers, Wilkinson and Robertson, traveled across the United States starting out on the Appalachian Trail to visit the Yosemite valley. Muir was thirty-three and Emerson sixty-eight. Muir was working in a sawmill at the time and tramping up into the mountains on botanic expeditions whenever he could. They talked heartily, the old sage drawing out the young naturalist wherever possible. Muir was so delighted to meet Emerson that he proposed to accompany him into the mountains for a camping trip, luring him with the idea that up there was the new heaven and the new Earth.

Emerson was in the autumn of his life, however, and his hosts, thinking of his welfare, steered him toward the hotels and rest houses. Muir was considerably warmed by his presence but disappointed. He wished to spend a wild Emersonian night under the stars with a huge bonfire. "But the house habit was not to be overcome," Muir later wrote, "nor the strange dread of pure night air. . . . So the carpet dust and unknowable reeks were preferred. And to think of this being a Boston choice! Sad commentary on culture and the glorious transcendentalism!" [25]

But they did ride up to see the sequoias together. When they got there, Muir declared to Emerson, "You are yourself a sequoia; stop and get acquainted with your big brethren." Emerson, for his part, wandered among the giants as if in a trance, sensing their great age. When the group mounted to continue on, leaving Muir to walk back later on his own, of all the party, Emerson was the last to pass over the hill. Turning, he looked back to wave with his hat.

Later, the two wrote letters and Emerson sent books, but they never saw each other again. Emerson counted Muir in his list of "My Men." After seventeen years had passed, Muir at last stood in Concord, under the pine trees on a hill in Sleepy Hollow Cemetery. There, he later said, he fancied he saw Emerson, but this time from the higher sierras, again waving his hat in farewell and friendly recognition.

Hawthorne and Melville: The Dark Side

Another important facet of the transcendentalists' intuitive psychology of character formation, largely overlooked, is exploration of the dark side of the unconscious as a vehicle of spiritual transformation. Nowhere is this better revealed than in the relationship between Nathaniel Hawthorne and Herman Melville. Hawthorne was an acquaintance of Emerson's: They walked together and visited on occasion. Hawthorne was actually on more friendly terms with Fuller and Thoreau and not a permanent member of the transcendentalists' circle per se, because he lived in Concord on only two occasions.[26] His novels, dark and brooding, hardly partook of the bright side of the transcendentalists' doctrine. Hawthorne believed that mesmerism, one of the transcendentalist pastimes, was the nineteenth-century equivalent of witchcraft, and although he knew about the existence of occult practices, he generally disdained them. Nevertheless, his writings showed a sophisticated understanding of dynamic unconscious processes.

Melville, for his part, never evolved through the Unitarian phase of his Congregationalism, and so he never passed beyond into the sunlit view of the transcendentalists.[27] He seemed to be cut from a different cloth. He was from New York rather than Massachusetts. He never went to college; instead, the sea became his Harvard and his Yale. Consequently, his metaphors differed from those of his contemporaries. Where others looked up into the clouds for inspiration, he looked into the deeps. And because of certain events that befell him, he was an atheist from the standpoint of orthodox Christianity. He nevertheless had a remarkable spirituality that unflinchingly regarded the abject horror of things. His character Ahab could be judged a transcendentalist, though a mad one.

Hawthorne was born on July 4, 1804, in Salem, Massachusetts. His ancestors were seamen and magistrates, one of whom, a jurist, witnessed the hanging of alleged witches of the infamous Salem trials. This forebear punished female adulterers in the 1630s by fixing signs on them in the public marketplace announcing their sins and even by having them flogged in the streets half naked. When Hawthorne was four, his father, a sea captain, died from fever. His mother became a permanent recluse, dependent on the aid of others. Consequently, the family eked out an existence in impoverished circumstances.

In 1821, through the efforts of his uncle, Hawthorne entered Bowdoin College in Brunswick, Maine. There, for the first time in his life, he began to thoroughly enjoy himself. He became an idle student, paid huge fines for skipping class and church, and learned how to drink and play cards. He also developed close friendships with fellow classmates such as Henry Wadsworth Longfellow, the future poet, and Franklin Pierce, the future president.

Upon graduation, instead of pursuing business or adventure, Hawthorne retreated to a small room under the eaves of his uncle's house. There, domiciled in the same building with his mother and sisters, he lived for twelve years. In this "dismal and squalid chamber," as one biographer called it, he began to write, and in that place, he made his literary reputation. He later wrote about the room:

> [It] deserves to be called a haunted chamber, for thousands upon thousands of visions have appeared to me in it; and some few of them have become visible to the world. If ever I should have a biographer, he ought to make great mention of this chamber in my memoirs, because so much of my lonely youth was wasted here, and here my mind and character were formed.[28]

During this period, he read more than a thousand books, mostly novels and local history. He began to write fiction and to publish in obscure places. At one point, strictly for money, he fell to editing such works as the *American Magazine of Useful and Entertaining Knowledge*. One of his early pieces, "The Haunted Mind," is interesting for the descriptions of wraithlike visions the author describes in "a sort of conscious sleep."

Twice-Told Tales, which appeared in 1837, marked the end of Hawthorne's seclusion. Longfellow praised it, and Hawthorne became known throughout New England. One result was that the reclusive writer soon received an invitation to visit the home of his neighbors, the Peabody sisters in Salem. It proved to be a fortuitous event, for one of them, Sophia, would later become his wife.

At this point, Hawthorne moved from his native Salem and began working for the Boston Customs House. He also became involved with Ripley's utopian community, Brook Farm, in West Roxbury. He hoped that he could shovel manure in the morning in order to buy time to write in the afternoon. This bold experiment was not a success, although he did later write about his Brook Farm experiences in *The Blithedale Romance*.

At the age of thirty-eight, Hawthorne married the thirty-two-year-old Sophia, and the newlyweds moved to Concord. Their home was the Old Manse, which had been built by Emerson's grandfather. Now residing in that sanctified hall, Hawthorne became a full-fledged transcendentalist. During his idyllic and secluded time there, he produced more stories, such as *Mosses from an Old Manse* (1846), which again increased his reputation and cemented the public view that he was on intimate terms with Emerson and Thoreau.

After four years in Concord, Hawthorne's next move was back to Salem to work in its customs house. The job, apparently a patronage position, lasted until 1849, when, because of a change in the political scene, he was fired. Fate appeared to conspire against him in other ways, as well; at just that time, his mother died. It was his darkest hour, he later said, but there is every reason to believe that the event emancipated the grown man from his morbid childhood dependence on the grand old recluse.

His reaction to losing his job was, "God bless my enemies," for it gave him time to write his greatest and best-known romance, *The Scarlet Letter* (1850). In this work, we have Hawthorne the psychologist at his peak. Its main theme is the moral wound that cuts deeper than any mere physical incision, a wound that has severe ramifications for both body and mind. Hawthorne reveals a modern, dynamic understanding of unconscious processes. In one passage, he presciently describes the extraordinary relationship established between patient and therapist:

A man burdened with a secret should especially avoid the intimacy of his physician. If the latter possesses negative sagacity, and a nameless something more,—let us call it intuition; if he show no intrusive egotism, nor disagreeably prominent characteristics of his own; if he have the power, which must be born with him, to bring his mind into such affinity with his patient's, that this last shall unawares have spoken what he imagines himself only to have thought; if such revelations be received without tumult, and acknowledged not so often by an uttered sympathy as by silence, an inarticulate breath, and here and there a word, to indicate that all is understood; if to these qualifications of a confidant be joined the advantages afforded by his recognized character as a physician,—then, at some inevitable moment, will the soul of the sufferer be dissolved, and flow forth in a dark, but transparent stream, bringing all its mysteries into the daylight.[29]

And elsewhere in the book, Hawthorne notes that "a bodily disease, which we look upon as whole and entire within itself, may, after all, be but a symptom of some ailment in the spiritual part."[30] So he advises that, in order for the physical part to be healed, patients had to confess first the wounded troubles of the soul.[31]

Hawthorne's primary insight in *The Scarlet Letter* is into the reality of the buried idea. By exploring the effects of keeping a secret, he stumbles on what dynamic psychology today calls the "psychogenic hypothesis." Here, traumatic events and mental conflicts are actively put out of the mind or are completely forgotten by consciousness, only to return later, disguised in the form of a symptom.

Thus we see Reverend Dimmesdale under the weight of an untold secret—that he has fathered the child of a married woman, Hester Prynne. As a result, Dimmesdale becomes melancholy and emaciated, driven at times to near lunacy. He moves about as if in a dream. He has visions that pass in front of him. He dreams in his waking moments and walks in his sleep. And the secret, far from diminishing his spiritual powers over the years, seems to strengthen them. Even as his physical constitution slowly deteriorates, Dimmesdale becomes a charismatic and powerful figure, a commanding presence over the very flock that has cast the woman out. But in the end, the hidden idea causes him to waste away and die.

As for Hester, one can imagine the pressure weighing on her when the penalty for adultery is death. The court shows mercy on her, however. She is required only to submit to a public shaming for three hours and to wear an embroidered red "A" on her clothes for the rest of her life.

The alchemy that this works serves to cast her outside of culture, consigning her in many ways to a fate worse than death. Her public vilification is unending. Ministers pass her on the street and, pointing to her, begin extemporaneously preaching on sin. Under her mother's sign, Hester's illegitimate daughter grows up isolated from other children ("In many ways," Hawthorne notes, "running along by her mother's side she was the likeness of the scarlet letter"). Each newcomer to the village ogles anew upon learning the story and thus reopens the original wound. Hester Prynne wanders without rule or guidance in a moral wilderness.

But although heaven has indeed frowned upon her, Hester has not died. As it was for Hawthorne and his lost customs house job, her fate has set her free. She does not flee but settles at the edge of town, on the fringe of public consciousness, to eke out a living doing embroidery. But then, by degrees, her handiwork unconsciously becomes the fashion. She is continually repulsed by the sanctimonious matrons of the town, yet she also enters into an occult sympathy with certain women whom she intuitively knows have escaped detection for the same act. She becomes almost like a mendicant, helping the sick and the poor. She can go where others dare not, and she sees things that they do not see, because she is forced to always walk in the shadows. Moreover, as an otherwise righteous woman consigned to the dark side, she becomes disciplined to truth, so that she cannot lie.

These charged and astute readings of psychological dynamics formed the basis for the huge success of Hawthorne's novel. While the other transcendentalists philosophized on the new psychology, Hawthorne sharpened many of its elements and made them more widely accessible to the reading public in the form of a romance.

He now continued to build on this literary psychology. From Salem, he moved to Lenox, Massachusetts, where he produced his chilling tale *The House of the Seven Gables*. He then moved back to Concord, when he bought the Alcott House in 1853. But his life quickly took a dramatic turn away from writing.

No sooner had Hawthorne settled his family in their new surroundings than he was offered the consulship at Liverpool. He had written a biography of Franklin Pierce as part of Pierce's campaign for the U.S. presidency, and once elected, his old classmate did not forget the favor. Hawthorne needed the money and accepted. He held the post with distinction for five years and stayed abroad with his family another two before returning to Concord and to his literary friendships with Longfellow, Holmes, Lowell, and especially Thoreau. He published a few more volumes, but by then his fires were burning low. He died in 1864 at the age of sixty.

Herman Melville, fifteen years Hawthorne's junior, was born August 1, 1819, in New York City. His mother, Maria, was a Gansevoort, descended from well-to-do Dutch traders from Albany. His father, Allen, came from more humble beginnings, although the paternal line could boast that Major Thomas Melvill, Allen's father, had been a dressed-up Indian in the Boston Tea Party. Because his father had an uncertain business career, Herman's educational experience was somewhat uneven. He spent time at the prestigious Albany Academy under the tutelage of the famous Joseph Henry, only to find himself shortly thereafter attending New York public schools, where he became just another cog in the wheels of the Lancaster System of Instruction, an almost leaderless self-help regime in which the more advanced students taught the slower ones.

Driven by bad debts and poor health, Allen died when Herman was only thirteen. The father appeared to have gone insane at the end, although subsequent medical analysis suggests that he may have contracted lobar pneumonia, which has a characteristic maniacal phase. In any event, it was a blow of unequaled proportions from which, some commentators believe, Herman never recovered.

To make matters worse for the young boy, there is some speculation among older Melville scholars that the very moral and upright Allen may have sired an illegitimate daughter and that, after the father's death, Herman may have been informed of this by his uncle. This apparently caused a psychic wound that never quite healed. According to one version, after he had gotten over the initial shock, Melville became fixated on finding out the identity of this girl in order to bring her back into the family. He had an unsuccessful time of it, and, partly the result of an argument over the matter that he may have had with his mother, the situation escalated unbearably. Twenty-one at the time, he tried to escape from his personal torment by going to sea.

Melville's experiences over the next four years changed him dramatically. He sailed to the South Pacific and jumped ship to live among the cannibals. Then he worked from rig to rig and island to island as a beachcomber and roustabout. He finally returned to Boston on the frigate *United States* in October, 1844.

What he saw in the unfathomable depths of the ocean and in the hearts of men made him give up a belief in the Christian God of his youth, yet he became even more attracted to the spiritual realm. He identified so strongly with the Polynesian worldview that he never again had respect for Christian missionaries, whose real message, he thought, was sickness and death, or for the commercial businessmen who plundered nontechnological cultures in the name of progress. Somewhere out there, where there is only the mind and the sea, he had become a searing and skeptical critic of the entire Western edifice.

When Melville returned from seafaring, he began to write. Thus he said, "From my twenty-fifth year, I date my life."[32] Sea yarns like *Typee, Omoo,* and *Mardi* flowed from his pen. He started to develop a reputation. Having given up his quest to unite with his mythical half sister, he married the daughter of Massachusetts Chief Justice Lemuel Shaw. They moved to the Berkshires in western Massachusetts, near Lenox, and there Melville began working on what some have called the greatest American novel of the nineteenth century, *Moby-Dick.*

In the middle of this task, Melville met Hawthorne. They were to know each other intensely for almost a year and a half. After that, with the exception of some letters, they were never to connect again. But that one window of opportunity was decisive.

Melville had already formed an impression of the transcendentalists. When he went to an Emerson lecture in February 1849, he thought he would hear oracular gibberish but instead found a man "elevated above mediocrity." Afterward, he wrote to his publisher about the event, declaring, "I love all men who *dive*."[33]

He soon encountered Hawthorne, who, like Emerson, he found, was weighty enough to plummet to the very bottom of things. They first met on August 5, 1850, at a literary picnic. The company included, besides Hawthorne and Melville, Oliver Wendell Holmes Sr., known as the "poet at the breakfast table"; James T. Fields, Hawthorne's publisher; Evart Duyckinck, Melville's publisher; Cornelius Mathews, a literary critic; David Dudley Field, a lawyer; and a gaggle of their women.

The party climbed Monument Mountain, near Stockbridge, drank iced champagne in a sudden downpour, spouted poetry, and teetered on the edge of a cliff before returning to Fields's house for a sumptuous meal and more wine. As tongues loosened, a lively discussion ensued about the superiority of American over European authors. Afterward, journal entries were abuzz with details, letters and gifts flew back and forth, and a series of articles about the event, written by Mathews, appeared in print. Hawthorne wrote to a friend, "I met Melville the other day, and liked him so much that I have asked him to spend a few days with me before leaving these parts."[34]

Melville went back to his own house and penned a two-part review for *Literary World* titled "Hawthorne and His Mosses." Posing as a Southern writer and signing the review anonymously, he leapt overboard with exaggerated flattery. As a finale, to the embarrassment of many admirers but to the great pleasure of Sophia, Melville favorably compared Hawthorne to Shakespeare.

Melville had numerous visits with the Hawthornes. He and Nathaniel would go for walks or shut themselves up behind closed doors to talk, smoke cigars, and drink port. Melville seems to have done most of the talking, while Hawthorne absorbed it all into his own great silence. On one occasion, while Melville was lounging around waiting for Hawthorne to finish his regime of daily writing in another room, Melville confessed to Sophia, to her complete amazement, that he, in fact, was the author of the anonymous review.

The most significant impact of these exchanges, however, was that Melville became more expansive. Something was unlocked in him at a spiritual depth that made him completely change his mind about what he was writing. In the alchemy of their relationship, Melville's new style suddenly showed that he could be allegorical, metaphoric, and mythic. He abandoned the draft of *Moby-Dick* that he had been working on and started again. This time, the text was suffused with dynamic undercurrents. It was no longer merely a sea adventure, but a resonating symbol of the present. Each line became a projective stimulus for the reader to plunge into the here and now. The great unconscious forces at work in the world suddenly became visible in a text that was at once literature, psychology, and metaphysics. In gratitude, he dedicated the work to Hawthorne, and in a double boon to the literary world, it appeared a year after publication of *The Scarlet Letter*.

Melville was never again to reach the literary fame that followed from his story about the whale. He published a number of other volumes, works such as *Pierre or the Ambiguities,* an autobiographical novel; *The Confidence Man,* in all likelihood a disguised tale about his father; and *Clarel,* a poetic narrative of his trip to the Holy Land. But he soon faded from public memory, remembered only as an author at midcentury. A few short stories appeared over the years. The last was the novel *Billy Budd,* which, like *Moby-Dick* and *Bartleby the Scrivener*, was made into a Hollywood movie more than a century later.

Meanwhile, Melville had become an obscure customs house inspector in New York. By the time he died in 1891, no one knew who he was. When the *New York Times* finally published a tardy obituary, it apologized to the American public for its oversight. A first biography by the Columbia scholar Raymond Weaver would not appear for more than a quarter of a century. But Melville would rise again when a renaissance of interest in his work began in the 1930s. In the context of a widespread fervor for psychoanalysis, the older dynamic literary psychology again breached the surface of American cultural consciousness.

James Freeman Clarke on Spiritual Self-Realization

Finally, perhaps the clearest summary of the transcendentalists' intuitive psychology of character formation can be found in the work of Reverend James Freeman Clarke. Born into a famous Unitarian family in 1810, Clarke graduated from Harvard in 1829 and from its Divinity School in 1833. He tried his luck in the Midwest for a few years, editing the *Western Messenger,* but he returned to Boston to establish his own church in 1841. He had become a devotee of Carlyle at an early age and, in 1832, had accompanied Johann Gaspar Spurzheim on his grand tour of Boston when phrenology was first introduced into the United States. But Clarke's primary role, and the one for which he is best known, was that of militant transcendentalist.

The work of Clarke's that most clearly expresses the literary psychology of the transcendentalists is *Self-Culture.* Originally delivered as a series of public lectures in downtown Boston and first published in 1880 near the end of Clarke's life, the book immediately proved its popularity by going into eight editions in two years.[35] In it, Clarke outlined a system of personality grounded in phrenology but interpreted in the context of a transcendentalist Christianity. Transcendentalism suggested what was generic to the inner transformative experience, while the Bible provided specific scriptural examples of what God intended us to become. Phrenology (discussed in more detail in the next chapter) described the faculties of personality minutely and allowed for each trait to become its own projective stimulus, giving the common man a systematic, secular language of inner experience with which to analytically approach the problem of character formation.

Clarke's main thesis rested on a redefinition of what we mean by "education." Instruction, or knowledge communicated to the intellect, was the most commonly held definition of the term. Traditional educators believed that the primary job of the student was to learn facts and apply them. But for Clarke, education also meant the exercise of the faculties of intelligence. In the classical sense, this meant primarily refining the capacities for sensory experience and logical analysis. Intuition and insight were completely neglected. Yet because the transcendentalists believed that intuition was the ground of all logical and clear thinking, as well as the conduit through which we come to experience the divine, it constituted the core of the intelligent person. Education in the transcendentalist sense, therefore, also meant not simply learning, but development—the unfolding of the entire personality.

In this larger view, schools and colleges played a significant but small part, for as Clarke put it, "Nature educates, life educates, society educates." Outward circumstances, inward experiences, and social influences make up the larger part of human culture. It is therefore absolutely essential, he felt, to see that the activities of our schools work in harmony and not in conflict with the largest goals of education: namely, the development of character.

Self-Culture opens with a discussion of how instruction in culture begins in childhood. Why, Clarke asks, if we keep children in school for fourteen years, do they leave knowing so little? His rule was to patiently and reverently study the methods of nature and copy her principles instead of working in direct opposition to them. Children will put ten times the amount of effort into play than into work; why not, then, use the principles involved in play to acquire knowledge? Since the child's first language is learned by constant usage in social settings, why not teach a second and a third by the same means? Nature is always holistic, teaching all the faculties at once, while we are too analytic, teaching largely by memory alone. We educate only part of the person.

Our faculties, Clarke believed, like anything else in nature, are God-given, and it is our duty to use them for growth. Hence it is a basic law of the mind to "Use and improve, or lose." For our lifework, we must have the earnest desire and purpose in our soul to grow, to become larger, deeper, higher, nobler, year by year. This is the theme struck in all of Clarke's succeeding chapters. His practical framework is to show, using the vocabulary of phrenology without directly identifying it as such, those individual faculties our educational system needs to develop.

Clarke's command was to nurture a consciousness of the physical body.[36] We need also to train ourselves in the most efficient use of time. We need to consciously attain self-knowledge. We need to develop our powers of observation, perception, and intuition. To the intuitional, we must add the imaginal. We must also educate the conscience, the ability to distinguish between right and wrong. We must develop our emotions and our social affections, nurture our capacity for reverence, and cultivate an even temperament. We should develop the habits of wide reading and recreation as a means of culture. We should systematically develop courage. We should also cultivate the capacity to see a task through to the end, as well as the expectation of hope. Most important, however, is education of the will. Clarke envisioned two kinds of will. One is natural, organic, instinctive, belonging to the brain and blood. The other is spiritual, linking us to the higher spheres.

In his conclusion, Clarke summarized the transcendentalist psychology of the entire era: Namely, each one of us has a particular gift to develop as our contribution to the whole. Its cultivation allows us to appreciate differences in opinions, tastes, and temperaments among people. Although ultimate perfection may not be possible, the task facing every educated person is to use the skills for self-knowledge that we have available as an advanced society. With these tools, he implored the reader, each one of us must do the best that we can.

And out of the cultivation of this unique self comes our solitary men and women of genius, those movers and shakers who define the cutting edge of culture by being the first to lay down new paths for the rest of us to follow. Emerson was such a person, as were Thoreau and Fuller. They all believed, as Sampson Reed had earlier proclaimed, that the depth of one's self-knowledge was the yardstick against which the character of a nation could be measured.

Notes

1. Sampson Reed, "An Oration on Genius," in Perry Miller, ed., *The Transcendentalists* (Cambridge, MA: Harvard University Press, 1971), pp. 49–52.

2. Ralph Waldo Emerson, *Nature* (Boston: J. Munroe & Co., 1836), p. 13.

3. This was Professor Donald Fleming, expounding an idea indelibly impressed in the minds of all Harvard freshmen who took his first-semester course in American history.

4. This was, of course, the expedient thing to do. According to Conrad Wright, American church historian, however, these churches became Unitarian in name but remained Congregational in polity.

5. Ralph Waldo Emerson, "Over-Soul," in *Essays: First Series* (Philadelphia: David MacKay, 1888), p. 287.

6. Ibid., p. 262.

7. Likewise, Thoreau says, "Our very life is our disgrace ... the divine allied to beasts." He continued to believe, however, that we can elevate ourselves and learn "to eat, drink, cohabit, void excrement and urine" in a spiritual fashion; see Joel Porte, "Emerson, Thoreau, and the Double Consciousness," *New England Quarterly,* 41 (1968): 40–50.

8. Quoted in M. Bickman, *American Romantic Psychology* (Dallas: Spring Publications, 1988), p. 81. Bickman has made extensive comparisons between the analytic psychology of C. G. Jung and such nineteenth-century literary psychologists as Emerson, Poe, Hawthorne, and Melville.

9. Quoted by Jeffrey Steele, "Interpreting the Self: Emerson and the Unconscious," in Joel Porte, ed., *Emerson: Prospect and Retrospect* (Cambridge, MA: Har-

vard University Press, 1982), pp. 94–95, in a most perceptive essay on Emerson's psychology of inner experience.

10. I am referring here to Laurie James, *Men, Women, and Margaret Fuller* (New York: Golden Heritage Press, 1990). Other works by James include: *The Wit and Wisdom of Margaret Fuller* (New York: Golden Heritage Press, 1988); *Why Margaret Fuller Is Forgotten* (New York: Golden Heritage Press, 1988); and *Outrageous Questions: The Legacy of Bronson Alcott and America's One Room Schools* (New York: Golden Heritage Press, 1994). Additional works on Fuller include Joan von Mehren, *Minerva and the Muse: A Life of Margaret Fuller* (Amherst: University of Massachusetts Press, 1994); and Robert N. Hudspeth, *The Letters of Margaret Fuller,* 6 vols. (Ithaca, NY: Cornell University Press, 1994).

11. James, *Men, Women, and Margaret Fuller,* p. 35.

12. Ibid., p. 37.

13. Ibid., p. 55.

14. Ibid., p. 65.

15. Anne Braude, *Radical Spirits: Spiritualism and Women's Rights in Nineteenth-Century America* (Boston: Beacon Press, 1989).

16. From Marguerite Block, *The New Church in the New World* (New York: Holt, Rinehart & Winston, 1984), pp. 115–117.

17. Porte, "Emerson, Thoreau, and the Double Consciousness," p. 50.

18. These words are carved into the sign by Thoreau's cabin at Walden Pond.

19. Quoted in David Shi, *In Search of the Simple Life* (Salt Lake City, UT: Peregrine Smith Press, 1986), p. 171.

20. Ibid., p. 168.

21. Ibid., p. 171.

22. In 1983, with the impending dissolution of the Soviet Union, Nikita Pokrovsky, a professor of philosophy at Moscow University, published the first Russian biography of Thoreau: *Henry Thoreau* (Moscow: Progress Publishers, 1989; originally published in Russian in 1983). In this work, Pokrovsky details the influence of Thoreau and the transcendentalists on, for instance, Leo Tolstoy, a man who also read the works of Henry James Sr. Pokrovsky has also written the first biography of Emerson in Russian. These little volumes are significant because they are emblematic of a burgeoning interest in the New England transcendentalists among the emerging countries of the former Soviet bloc. Ethnic minorities, whose inward spiritual life sustained them during decades of occupation, according to Pokrovsky, view their survival as the result of passive resistance and nonviolent noncooperation. This took the form of preserving their older culture through folk dances, traditional music, and religious ritual, despite the attempt by the outward order to completely remake their society.

Moreover, there has been a recent groundswell of public opinion rising in American popular culture to save Walden Pond from developers. Plans were launched in the mid-1990s to build a giant office park near the pond, as well as a high-density multifamily housing complex. Although there has always been a strong vocal minority of people in Lincoln and Concord to preserve Walden as a national historic site, they were no match for the money and political influence that was about to take over the area in the name of private enterprise. It took the interference of celebrities—including entertainers such as Don Henley, Kirstie Alley, Paula Abdul, Arlo Guthrie, and Carrie Fisher; social activists such as the late Cesar Chávez and Jessie Jackson; and politicians such as Ted Kennedy and Chester Atkins—to gain national attention for the Walden cause. Concerts, social benefits, and nature walks to raise money eventually netted millions of dollars, so that the area surrounding Walden Pond could be purchased from private owners and turned over to a public trust. Here is a modern-day example of the American visionary tradition at work: Artists, environmentalists, and visionaries, with the weight of history behind them, acted successfully to preserve what many believe is a national treasure. See, for instance, Don Henley and Dave Marsh, *Heaven Is Under Our Feet: A Book for Walden Woods* (New York: Berkely Books, 1991).

23. Edwin W. Teale, *The Wilderness World of John Muir* (Boston: Houghton Mifflin, 1954), p. xvii.

24. Ibid., p. xvi.

25. Ibid., p. 162.

26. Material on Hawthorne is developed from James R. Mellow, *Nathaniel Hawthorne and His Times* (Boston: Houghton Mifflin, 1980).

27. All the ideas stated here about Melville are those of the late Henry A. Murray, whose unpublished Melville biography cast a long shadow over Melville scholarship in the mid-twentieth century. Contemporary Melville biographers, such as Laurie Robertson Laurant, doubt the accuracy of Murray's interpretation of Melville and maintain that it was more a reflection of Murray's own archetypal struggles.

28. Philip Young, *Hawthorne's Secret* (Boston: Godine, 1984), p. 18.

29. Nathaniel Hawthorne, *The Scarlet Letter* (New York: Washington Square Press, 1948), pp. 127–128.

30. Ibid., p. 140.

31. Ibid., p. 141.

32. Henry A. Murray, "Young Melville," unpublished ms., Murray Papers, Pusey Library, Harvard University Archives, quoted by permission.

33. Ibid.

34. Mellow, *Nathaniel Hawthorne,* p. 333.

35. James Freeman Clarke, *Self-Culture: Physical, Intellectual, Moral, and Spiritual* (Boston: James R. Osgood, 1882).

36. Likewise, ideas can improve physical health: "One day we shall have a mind-cure hospital, where bodily disease will be relieved by applications to the mind. Meantime, how much can be done for invalids by visits from cheerful, bright, entertaining visitors,—by religious influences which inspire faith and hope, not doubt and fear" (ibid., p. 68).

Chapter Five

Homeopathy, Phrenology, and Mesmerism

SPIRITUALISM AND MENTAL HEALING REPRESENTED THE EMER-
gence of a distinct folk psychology devoted to the development of personality and consciousness in American culture during the nineteenth
century. But they did not just appear out of thin air. On the contrary, esoteric practices that were the accepted legacy of European Renaissance
culture existed from the beginning in the early American colonies.[1] The
Ptolemaic theory of the universe—that the heavens rotated around the
Earth—was still taught at Yale as late as 1717. Astrology, the prediction
of events by reading the progression of the stars across the sky, was
taught as part of the curriculum at Harvard at least to 1731. During the
same period, physicians who did medical bleeding would often prescribe
their treatments at designated astrological moments. Belief in witchcraft,

an offshoot of the European mental epidemics, still persisted, and women in Salem, Massachusetts, were hanged as a result. Alchemical studies, which included astrological medicine, formed part of Rosicrucian teachings at the Ephrata settlement near Lancaster, Pennsylvania. Indeed, the almanacs, which were widely used and second only to the Bible in popularity, were full of astrological references, folk remedies, herbal prescriptions, and homespun psychology.

Although it is true that ideas from the European Enlightenment eventually supplanted these influences in medicine and higher learning, the earlier tradition continued to exist as an integral part of American folk culture. As the medical doctors went off in droves to study in Europe, physical and mental health for the everyday American remained largely a personal affair. Left to themselves, individual families chose the remedies they thought best. Many who were healed by various methods sometimes became healers and practitioners of those same methods themselves. Self-drugging, home remedies, and a host of popular therapies abounded, and a wide variety of regimes were constantly in use by practitioners mostly outside the medical profession.[2]

We have no better example of this self-care than the books on popular medicine that appeared at the time. William Buchan's *Domestic Medicine* was first published in Edinburgh in 1769 and enjoyed wide circulation in America. In 1816, it was republished in New Haven under the title *Every Man His Own Doctor*. In 1826, Anthony Benezet, a medical graduate of the University of Pennsylvania, produced *The Family Physician,* "calculated particularly for the inhabitants of the western country." Already available were texts such as *The American Medical Guide for the Use of Families* (1810) and *The American Family Physician* (1824), and Benezet's works were soon followed by J. C. Gunn's *Domestic Medicine: Or Poor Man's Friend* (1830), which went into 100 editions by 1870. Even as late as 1869, *Our Home Physician* by George Miller Beard presented the latest scientific advances, packaged as a new encyclopedia of family medicine. Beard wrote "in plain language with copious illustrations for those beyond the ready call of a physician."[3] The work covered basic anatomy and physiology, minor surgery, common illnesses, and herbal preparations; and though it debunked clairvoyants, astrologers, and chiromancers, it gave an extensive home physician's manual of homeopathic medicines.

As a result of these trends toward self-help, numerous alternative therapeutic systems of both a medical and a psychological nature flourished in the first half of nineteenth-century America. Alternative medicine was readily accepted for a number of reasons, not the least of which was the disorganized state of allopathic or Western European medicine at the time. Blistering, bleeding, purging, and heroic drugging were the accepted medical interventions of the day. Mental illness, in contrast, was more often than not treated by incarceration, restraint, and a limited number of medicinal preparations, many of which, like mercury and belladonna, were either poisonous or addictive. In addition, shifting tides of religious liberalism, the rapid expansion of the American frontier, extreme fluctuations in the economy caused by the gold rush, large-scale immigration, and the meteoric rise of industrialization in the midst of what formerly had been an agrarian society all contributed to an exciting but highly unstable atmosphere. Into this milieu poured a number of streams that converged by midcentury into a torrent that has been collectively referred to as the "Mental Healing" or "Mind-Cure" movement.

Homeopathy

Thompsonianism and Grahamism were two of the most popular medicinal regimes that Americans practiced in the first part of the nineteenth century. The first of these was a naturopathic system based almost exclusively on herb lore that rejected the use of common poisonous compounds used by European-trained physicians and American doctors of the mainstream medical establishment. Grahamism, on the other hand, relied on fresh air, exercise, pure foods, and coarse grains, rejecting for philosophical reasons any kind of medicinal preparations altogether. But the first major organized effort within the American alternative reality tradition to firmly establish itself as a tested therapeutic regime was homeopathy. Wildly popular, homeopathic physicians also successfully criticized the state of orthodox (or what homeopaths still call "allopathic") mainstream medicine at the time.

Homeopathy originated in Germany in the late 1790s with the work of Samuel Hahnemann (1755–1843), a physician and chemist. Hahnemann, in a significant departure from prevailing theory, believed in two ideas new to medical practice: the "law of similars" and the "doctrine of infinitesimals." The law of similars, Hahnemann said, means that like cures like—*similia similibus curentur.* He believed that giving sick patients small doses of medicinal preparations that mimic the symptoms of a particular illness would produce a natural healing reaction that would allow the patients to get well. In order to substantiate this principle empirically, Hahnemann instituted what he called a system of "provings," or clinical trials, whereby a given substance was administered to groups of healthy men and women in gradually increasing doses. The results of these administrations, known as "drug diseases," were carefully recorded. After repetition on many "provers," the particular substance was duly entered into the homeopathic materia medica with the corresponding symptom it produced. In this way, a large body of data was amassed relating specific drugs to specific illnesses, which in no way conformed to established allopathic medical pharmacopoeias of the time.

Although the homeopathic pharmacopoeia is the feature most emphasized by modern historians of medicine who try to fathom what homeopathy was, the equally important but most frequently misrepresented principle in Hahnemann's system was his theory of dosage, which he based on the doctrine of infinitesimals. Whereas drug dosage was increased in healthy subjects during proving trials, Hahnemann maintained that with sick patients, the dosage should be significantly *decreased.* The homeopathic physician achieved this by a succession of dilutions, until a "mother tincture" was finally reached. Contrary to all known medical reason, Hahnemann claimed that the dynamizing function of a drug was achieved when it had been subdivided to its fullest extent. The more subtle the drug's action, the higher its curative, spiritual potency, for he believed that "it is only by means of the spiritual influence of a morbid agent that our spiritual, vital power can be diseased, and in like manner, only by the spiritual operation of medicine can health be restored." [4]

There can be little doubt that this law of cure was held as a belief by doctor and patient alike, and it must therefore have played an important role in harnessing the patient's own resources for self-healing. Hahnemann himself understood the importance of psychological factors in illness, no doubt the result of his running a private asylum for the insane at one point in his career in Germany.

Homeopathy as a medical movement produced a number of important changes in its day. It successfully challenged prevailing allopathic remedies of heroic drugging. It influenced the development of the medical procedure for inoculation, which significantly altered the epidemiological course of the most dangerous diseases to public health, such as diphtheria, lockjaw, typhoid fever, tuberculosis, and bubonic plague. It also anticipated the concept of self-limiting disease—*vis medicatrix natura,* that left to its own, nature will cure itself. More important, homeopathy became an integral part of the psychological fabric of different folk cultures when it spread throughout Europe and England between 1810 and 1831. But it was in the United States that homeopathic medicine gained its widest acceptance.

Hans Birch Gram (1786–1840), a student of Hahnemann, first brought homeopathy to America in 1825. He is also credited with publishing the first treatise on the subject in English, "The Characteristics of Homeopathia," a nearly unreadable translation of an essay by Hahnemann. Gram first practiced in New York with a small circle of acquaintances. Most of these were Swedenborgian students.

Emanuel Swedenborg, an eighteenth-century scientist and interpreter of religious experience, had been a member of the Swedish nobility and the Royal Assessor of Mines for the first part of his career. Having mastered most of the known sciences of his day, he was a craftsman and inventor as well. He introduced the calculus into Sweden, wrote the first Swedish algebra, and edited the first scientific periodical in his country. In addition, he made various contributions to astronomy, mineralogy, and cosmology, which led to a European reputation and membership in the Swedish Academy of Sciences.

His main interest, however, was to use science in search of the soul. In this quest, he moved through mathematics, geology, and astronomy to anatomy and physiology and then on to sensory psychology. Finally confronted with his own consciousness as an object of scientific investigation, he developed a primitive but workable method of dream interpretation that gave him access to his own interior states.

This precipitated a religious crisis, however, and he later recounted that, in 1774, God came to him and told him to begin writing a new interpretation of the books of the Bible, based on the internal spiritual meaning of the Word. While undertaking this task over the next ten years, Swedenborg had numerous visions and developed apparent psychic abilities. His five-volume spiritual diary gives an account of the domains of the heavens and hells as shown to him by God's angels. He also had a vision of the Final Judgment, which he interpreted to mean the transformation of worldwide spiritual consciousness. He wrote more than thirty volumes on the subject of what this New Jerusalem looked like.

Swedenborg died in 1772, having been driven from Sweden for contravening the teachings of the state Lutheran Church. What sprang up in his wake instead of a globally transformed Christianity was an entirely new Christian denomination called the Church of the New Jerusalem. Its main centers were England, France, and the United States. The denominational membership has always been quite small, while an even greater number of nonmembers read Swedenborg's writings for the affirmation they gave to the process of spiritual self-actualization. In fact, the Swedish seer became one of the most widely read authors of the nineteenth century in American popular culture.

The association between homeopathy and Swedenborgianism was to have important consequences. The two ideologies spread throughout America hand in hand, and it was in no small measure that homeopathy became indigenized through this connection with the Swedenborgians. Homeopathic medical colleges developed in Philadelphia, Cincinnati, Boston, and elsewhere, in many cases involving members of the local Swedenborgian societies. The major homeopathic apothecaries in the East—namely, Boericke & Tafel in Philadelphia and Otis Clapp in Boston—were also the major distribution houses for Swedenborg's writings in America.

The Hahnemann Medical College of Philadelphia, too, had numerous Swedenborgians associated with it, most notably Constantine Hering and Charles Raue, both of whom lectured on the psychological principles underlying homeopathic treatment. In New England, the present Boston University School of Medicine was originally founded as a homeopathic medical college for women. Samuel Worcester, an ordained Swedenborgian minister as well as a graduate of Harvard Medical School, taught courses at Boston University on the homeopathic treatment of insanity. In addition, the Boston University School of Medicine was closely associated with the Westboro State Hospital, a local asylum that used homeopathic methods to treat the insane, which was supported by the taxpayers of Massachusetts, a state wherein numerous Swedenborgian churches flourished.[5]

Homeopathy was a popular medical regime for several reasons. Mothers were assured that the effects would be mild but effective on their babies, while the religiously inclined were attracted to its spiritual principles of healing. It was also a psychophysical approach that was compatible with other systems of healing and self-development then in vogue, such as phrenology and magnetism.

Phrenology

A second major European import to sweep the American therapeutic scene in the 1830s was phrenology, an alleged science of personality based on reading the anatomical shape of the skull.[6] Probably as popular in the 1840s in America as psychoanalysis was in the 1930s, craniognomy, as it was originally called, was first formulated by Franz Joseph Gall (1758–1828), a German-born Roman Catholic who took his medical training in Vienna. Gall had noted while in medical school that those gifted with good verbal memory had very prominent eyes. Subsequently, more detailed observation led him to suppose that character and intellect were the combined function of what he called specific "organs" of the brain, which he believed were located in different parts and could be measured on the outside of the human skull.

Gall developed his theory into a new science by mapping out the different organs of the skull during the time he practiced medicine at an insane asylum in Vienna. He also made numerous visits to prisons and schools during this formative period. Soon, he attracted students, and in

1800, he was joined by a man who would become his emissary abroad, Johann Gaspar Spurzheim (1776–1832), who had also studied medicine in Vienna.

By 1802, Gall was forbidden to practice by the Austrian government on the grounds that phrenology was an enemy of the church, an official act that had the effect of drawing only more public attention to his work. Spurzheim and Gall began traveling, and the two collaborated on researches into the anatomy and physiology of the nervous system. Only partially successful in Paris, phrenology finally took hold in England, and from there, mostly as a result of Spurzheim, it spread to America, where it grew to proportions beyond anyone's wildest expectations.[7]

As it traveled, phrenology developed through several distinct stages. Under Gall, it was a theory of cerebral localization, which significantly influenced French and English clinical medicine. Under Spurzheim, it became a theory of character reading, an early form of personality psychology that later influenced the social sciences. Spurzheim and two other recent converts, the Scotsman George Combe (1788–1858) and the American physician and controversialist Charles Caldwell (1772–1853), became proselytizers of the new science among the upper classes, appealing to clergymen, doctors, and philosophers in Europe, England, and America.

But it was not until the doctrine fell into the hands of Orson Squire Fowler (1809–1887) and his brother in New England that phrenology took on mass appeal. It became a lucrative source of income as individual character readings were instituted for a small fee. In America, as nowhere else, not even in Britain, phrenology found its surest footing. Considered an applied science in the 1840s, phrenology was used in prison reform, the education and rearing of children, the selection of employees, and even in diagnosing the effects of poor diet and tight corsets. Publication of phrenological books went into the tens of thousands and was supported by the establishment of lecture bureaus and specialized publishing firms.

Despite its major flaw—that the size of different bumps on the surface of the head did not correspond to any underlying, fixed faculties of personality—phrenology was successfully put forward as an applied science because it was grounded in empirical measurement and could be understood in the context of a theory that was functional, developmental, and predictive. The detailed map of personality characteristics effectively put a working vocabulary for self-development in the hands of anyone who could read or write. However, it was left up to the early magnetizers, the name given to hypnotists, to provide the wider reading public with the means to alter their state of consciousness and gain access to the inward domains.

Mesmerism

Although phrenology found a ready foothold in American folk psychology, the foundation of the mental healing movement as it later developed throughout the nineteenth century was unquestionably based on the introduction of mesmerism, or, as it was also known, animal magnetism, beginning in the 1830s. Franz Anton Mesmer (1734–1815), physician and founder of the early science that bears his name, was denounced in his own day as a charlatan and mountebank. He was forced to leave his native Vienna for Paris, where he was also attacked by members of the medical and scientific profession. His method fared only a little better in England, where it underwent a series of transformations on being taken up by physicians such as James Braid, who renamed it "hypnosis." James Eisdale had even greater success in India performing painless surgery on mesmerized patients. But, like homeopathy and phrenology, mesmerism gained its widest following in America, not only as a science and a religion, but also as a new form of psychotherapy.

The American Swedenborgian literature of the late 1790s shows evidence of interest in mesmerism, yet it was not until the 1830s that a Frenchman, Charles Poyen, self-proclaimed professor of the new art, began a thorough dissemination of Mesmer's techniques by means of systematic lectures across New England.[8] Poyen believed that the single most important discovery of animal magnetism as a science was the somnambulistic or trance state. He sought to promote an interest in trance consciousness by holding flamboyant demonstrations that employed an assistant and volunteers from the audience who agreed beforehand to be hypnotized. Poyen was then able to demonstrate to all observers the typical characteristics of hypnosis, including complete oblivion to loud noises, foul smells, and the effects of pinpricks, as well as complete forgetfulness on the part of his subjects after awakening to all that had transpired during the demonstration. The effect of these public demonstrations, however, was to disenfranchise animal magnetism from any claim to scientific validity. Nevertheless, through its entertainment value alone, Poyen was able to heighten public interest in the subject.

In the wake of Poyen's travels throughout New England, many of his subjects reported obtaining medical cures from their trance experience. Others allegedly demonstrated spontaneous feats of extrasensory perception. Numerous people entranced by him went on to develop their own personal powers along mesmeric lines and thus became the early promulgators and prime movers of mesmerism as a new mental and spiritual science.

One among these was Thomas Lake Harris (1823–1906), trance poet, prophet, and utopian socialist. Originally a Unitarian minister, Harris renounced his pulpit to follow the spiritualist teachings of another trance healer, Andrew Jackson Davis. After an ill-fated attempt to run a utopian community at Mountain Cove, Virginia, Harris migrated to New York, where he gave numerous lectures that were successful from the standpoint of public attendance. But he failed in his efforts to have the local spiritualists accept him as their new prophet. It was at this stage of his career that he composed most of his epic trance poetry. In 1859, he went to England to spread the new spiritualist doctrine and drew the attention of Laurence Oliphant and his mother, both members of the British royalty. The Oliphants were swayed to commit both their persons and their purses to manual labor at a utopian experiment Harris launched in Brocton, New York, from which they were able to extract themselves only after some twenty years of entanglement.

Another among Poyen's converts was John Bovee Dods (1795–1872), Universalist minister and itinerant preacher from Maine, who propounded eclectic religion before turning his attention to mesmerism, spiritual development, and what he called the "new electrical psychology." Raising some of the major theological issues of the day through his writings—especially his *Thirty Short Sermons, Both Doctrinal and Practical*—Dods maintained that the traditional Calvinist religion only played upon people's fears and insecurities. He called for a revolution within the church, a new birth that would foster the development of a more exuberant and joyful potential of the spirit. Animal magnetism soon proved for him the ideal method for achieving spiritual regeneration, for the mesmeric state suggested the opening up of internal life to the full view of consciousness.[9]

Dods's theory, which was physiologically as well as metaphysically grounded, saw man as a single psychophysical entity. Drawing on the latest developments in electrical science and clinical physiology then coming into vogue, chiefly from France, Dods believed that there was only one primary cause of disease: namely, the electricity of the system thrown out of balance. His fame, generated by public demonstrations and numerous cures of his patients, was sufficient to elicit an invitation to lecture before the U.S. Congress in the 1830s. He also became an ardent foe of spiritualism, or communication with the dead. His explanation of such phenomena was based on his medical knowledge of the involuntary nervous system. The involuntary system, Dods maintained, could be made to carry a superabundant electrical charge that produced phenomena hidden to the waking self. He believed that mediums who had these experiences mistakenly attributed such manifestations to supernatural sources.[10]

Probably more than anyone else, another figure, the Reverend George Bush (1786–1859), was responsible for associating the religious teachings of Swedenborg with the philosophy and methods of mesmerism. A Presbyterian minister and professor of Hebrew languages and literature at New York University, Bush wrote *Mesmer and Swedenborg,* which led numerous people to convert to Swedenborg's teachings. In this work, Bush maintained that the facts of mesmerism had been scientifically established. His own review of the voluminous literature, along with experiments he himself had conducted, served to convince him that entranced subjects in fact gained entry into higher planes of consciousness. In Swedenborg's writings, Bush found detailed descriptions of inner dimensions of consciousness, which he believed mesmerism also revealed.

Bush was a severe critic of writers such as Ralph Waldo Emerson, who had called Swedenborg a mystic in *Representative Men.* Nevertheless, Bush was chiefly responsible for introducing Swedenborg's works to the grandfather of American spiritualism, Andrew Jackson Davis (1826–1910). Davis, an uneducated cobbler's apprentice from Poughkeepsie, New York, had, like so many others, developed his remarkable healing abilities as a result of exposure to Poyen's original demonstrations. Poyen had come through Poughkeepsie and mesmerized one Stanley Grimes. After Poyen left, Grimes in turn tried but failed to mesmerize the eighteen-year-old Davis. Later, others who tried again were able to entrance Davis. While in this condition, Davis, it was reported, exhibited remarkable powers of clairvoyance that allegedly were tested beyond dispute.

For a period of many months, Davis was put into a trance to assuage public curiosity and to continue tests on his powers of internal sight. As time passed, he discovered that he had the power to see people as transparent beings whose entire anatomy appeared visible to him in glowing colors, which he described as auras. He also found that he could heal people of their afflictions. Thereafter, he ceased to participate in public demonstrations and requested that he be entranced only for purposes of utility—namely, to cure disease, to prescribe remedies, and to receive communications from the spirit world.

Sometime in 1844, after more than a year of continuous entrancements, Davis reported that he had been visited by Galen, the Greek physician, in a vision, as well as by Swedenborg. Galen passed Davis a magic staff, by means of which he was able to learn about disease and its cure. Further, he gave Davis knowledge of a therapeutic system based on the premise that disease afflicted only the bodies of living beings but not their internal spiritual life. God within was the internal creative spirit, and one's contact with him was the essence of health and healing. To be disconnected from this source was to court disease. To be reconnected to him was to banish illness. In the same vision, Swedenborg allegedly told Davis that he would guide him on his life's journey and make of him a prophet of the great change that was to come by teaching him the details of the inward universe. The major thrust of Davis's career, however, was not as a healer, but as a philosopher of human nature. In this role, his ideas formed the basis for much later spiritualist philosophy.[11]

The significance of Davis's career for the development of occult psychotherapy rests in the transition that took place in him from induced mesmeric sleep to spontaneous trance mediumship. In the beginning, Davis required a magnetizer to place him in the trance condition. Gradually, as his experiences in the inner state became more frequent and as he felt his powers growing, he was able to dispense with the mesmerist and place himself in the trance state directly. Accounts of his personality suggest a remarkable transformation, for in his normal condition he was the young, plain man from Poughkeepsie, poorly educated, who had failed to master any trade. But in the trance state, he rose to the level of the scientist-philosopher, able to discuss illness and its cure by medical means and to speak in learned terms upon complex intellectual topics.

By that time, the only assistance Davis needed was someone to copy down his performances verbatim. His own writings were hugely popular, as indicated by his thirty-volume *Principles of Nature,* published between 1847 and 1885 and printed concurrently in London, which went into forty-five American editions, and by his autobiography, which went into ten American editions. By the end of his career, he had earned degrees in medicine and anthropology and was calling for similar training for other mental healers.

Another famous early pioneer in the American mental healing movement was Phineas Parkhurst Quimby (1802–1866). Quimby was a young clockmaker who had first heard Poyen lecture in 1838 in Belfast, Maine. Inquisitive in the extreme, Quimby had plied Poyen with questions and followed his lecture-demonstration tour around New England until 1840, when Quimby finally mastered the art himself. Quimby soon took on Lucius Burkmar, an easily entranced subject who helped him give public demonstrations. Like Davis, Burkmar showed remarkable clairvoyant abilities. During their demonstrations, Quimby would place Burkmar in the mesmeric state and then ask him to diagnose and prescribe treatments for patients selected randomly from the audience. According to the newspapers, these performances had outstanding beneficial results. Burkmar's herbal prescriptions often corresponded to standard medical classifications and therapeutics and then-current folk medicine. Occasionally, however, a remedy would be presented that was so outrageous as to have no connection to the described illness, yet patients continued to get well. Gradually, Quimby came to feel that Burkmar was not perceiving the patients' illnesses, but reading their minds. Perhaps what Burkmar clairvoyantly read was what the patients believed to be their illnesses. Quimby then concluded that disease must be a deranged state of mind. Treatment, he reasoned, consisted of (1) faith that the proposed cure would work, and (2) a change in the patient's belief system.

By 1865, Quimby had treated nearly 12,000 patients with ailments ranging from consumption, smallpox, cancer, lameness, and diphtheria to the largest class, nervous ills of a hysteric and neurasthenic nature. Soon, as his own clairvoyant powers began to develop, he abandoned the use of the mesmerized Burkmar. His method came to be direct contact with the patient. He diagnosed by visual imagery, sometimes using mesmeric passes, but mainly he talked with his patients, listening to what they said about their beliefs and working with them to overcome self-defeating attitudes.

Quimby's methods probably resembled shamanic practices more than modern-day psychotherapy. He would enter a state of extraordinary lucidity, a state that he conceived of as superior vision, where he could see "mental atmospheres" developing around the patient. In this state, he believed that he peered into inaccessible strata that contained forgotten memories and all the patient's ideas about right and wrong. His treatment involved reenergizing through a visual process he called "mental daguerreotyping." With his mind alone, Quimby would use his powers of trance visualization to suffuse the patient's mind with magnetic healing fluids. His own explanation was not sacrosanct, however. In fact, when once offered $1,000 for the secret of his cure, he was forced to reply that he himself did not know it.[12]

Thus, from the opening of the nineteenth century to about the time of the Civil War, Quimby, Davis, Dods, Harris, and others were the offspring of mesmeric influences originally imported from Europe but supported and sustained by an indigenous folk consciousness already well established within the newly emerging American scene. They were some of the key figures chiefly responsible for the Americanization of techniques such as mesmerism.

With the Civil War, the period of the 1860s became a turning point in American social history. The older folk psychology appeared to recede into the background as empirical science gained ascendancy. Professional education in medicine became more highly organized and experimentally sophisticated, while the trend toward specialization in the social and biological sciences proceeded in earnest. Scientifically informed culture and folk psychology began to diverge radically from each other as, more and more, the visionary tradition was forced underground. Psychology as an academic field of specialization attempted to pattern itself after the natural sciences, which severely restricted its content to only the measurable; and what could be measured was explained simply in the reductionistic and positivistic language of cause and effect.

At the same time, however, popular interest in mental healing grew rather than waned. Whereas the early part of the nineteenth century harbored the pioneers and fostered widespread local interest, the last three decades produced full-fledged organizations devoted to spiritual therapeutics that were national, even international, in scope, many of which have remained viable to the present day.

It should be noted in closing that one of the key reasons for this paradox—that the visionary tradition was gradually suppressed within American high culture because of the rising tide of positivistic science, while it not only flourished but expanded dramatically in the popular arena—was due in no small part to the growing feminist movement. The Civil War had left an entire generation of eligible young men dead on the battlefields and an extraordinary excess of single women in its wake. While women's needs became the new subject of commercial advertising and feminine ills became the new focus of medicine and psychiatry, feminine thinking, previously fueling the spiritualist movement at midcentury, now turned to more burning issues such as women's suffrage, fair employment, and equal opportunity.[13] In the domain of healing, men such as William Alexander Hammond, Silas Weir Mitchell, William Osler, and William Welch came to dominate the specialties of physical medicine, neurology, and psychiatry—the disciplines of mainstream science—while a new generation of strong, charismatic, and outspoken women, such as Mary Baker Eddy, Helena Blavatsky, and Katherine Tingley, representing the intuitive, the imaginal, and the transcendent, came to dominate the shadow culture.

Notes

1. See, for instance, Herbert Leventhal, *In the Shadow of the Enlightenment: Occultism and Renaissance Science in Eighteenth-Century America* (New York: New York University Press, 1976).

2. See, for instance, G. B. Risse, R. Numbers, and J. W. Leavitt, eds., *Medicine Without Doctors: Home Health Care in American History* (New York: Science/History Publications, 1977); and J. H. Young, *The Toadstool Millionaires: A Social History of Patent Medicines in America Before Federal Regulation* (Princeton, NJ: Princeton University Press, 1961).

3. George Miller Beard, *The New Cyclopedia of Family Medicine: The Good Samaritan* (Boston: Balch Bros., 1869).

4. Samuel Hahnemann, *The Organon of Homeopathic Medicine,* 3rd ed., with improvements and additions from the last German edition, and Dr. C. Hering's introductory remarks (New York: William Radde, 1848).

5. M. Block, *The New Church in the New World: A Study of Swedenborgianism in America,* with a new introduction and epilogue by Robert H. Kirven (New York: Swedenborg Publishing Association, 1984). For a picture of psychiatry as taught at a homeopathic medical school, see S. Worcester, *Insanity and Its Treatment: Lectures on the Treatment of Insanity and Kindred Nervous Diseases* (Philadelphia: Boericke & Tafel, 1882).

6. A good historical analysis is provided by John D. Davies, *Phrenology, Fad and Science: A Nineteenth Century American Crusade* (New Haven, CT: Yale University Press, 1955).

7. A. A. Walsh, "Phrenology and the Boston Medical Community in the 1830's," *Bulletin of the History of Medicine,* 50 (1976): 261–273; and David Bakan, "The Influence of Phrenology on American Psychology," *Journal of the History of the Behavioral Sciences,* 2 (1966): 200–220.

8. Charles Poyen, *Progress of Animal Magnetism in New England, Being a Collection of Experiments, Reports, and Certificates, from the Most Respectable Sources. Preceded by a Dissertation on the Proofs of Animal Magnetism* (Boston: Weeks, Jordan & Co., 1837).

9. Chauncey Townshend's *Facts in Mesmerism with Reasons for a Dispassionate Inquiry into It* (London: Baillerie Press, 1844), is the unofficial canon for American mesmerists, which jettisons Mesmer's clumsy theories about physical fluids in favor of a more sophisticated model of internal states of consciousness.

10. See J. B. Dods, *Six Lectures on the Philosophy of Animal Magnetism, Delivered in the Marlboro Chapel in Boston, Reported by a Hearer,* 12th ed. (New York: Fowler & Wells, 1854); J. B. Dods, *The Philosophy of Electrical Psychology in a Course of*

Twelve Lectures (New York: Fowler & Wells, 1850); and J. B. Dods, *Spirit Manifestations Examined and Explained, Judge Edmonds Refuted: Or, an Explanation of the Involuntary Powers and Instincts of the Human Soul* (New York: Dewitt & Davenport, 1854).

11. A. J. Davis, *Principles of Nature, Her Divine Revelations, and a Voice to Mankind* (New York: S. S. Lyon & W. Fisbough, 1847).

12. H. W. Dresser, *The Quimby Manuscripts* (Secaucus, NJ: Citadel Press, 1961; originally published, New York: Thomas Y. Crowell, 1921). I have also followed R. C. Fuller, *Mesmerism and the American Cure of Souls* (Philadelphia: University of Pennsylvania Press, 1982).

13. See Anne Braude, *Radical Spirits: Spiritualism and Women's Rights in Nineteenth-Century America* (Boston: Beacon Press, 1989).

Chapter Six

Utopian Socialism and the Second Great Awakening

BY THE MID-NINETEENTH CENTURY, THE SECOND GREAT Awakening was fully under way. It was a spiritual revolution of unprecedented proportions that swept across the Midwest and the American frontier, swelling the ranks of Protestant denominations such as the Baptists, Methodists, and Presbyterians. Revivalism, extended camp meetings, and ecstatic visionary experiences among normally staid individuals were common occurrences. The result was that new sects representing an expansion of liberal as well as conservative ideologies were founded at an amazing rate, their juxtaposition reaffirming American cultural consciousness as a spiritual democracy.[1]

Within this mix, an entirely new generation of utopian communities appeared in the United States, this time arising less from religious persecution than from Christian communalism and issues surrounding social justice and equality. Inspired by the French Revolution, more than forty phalanxes, or communal societies, following the writings of Charles Fourier had sprung up across the national map by midcentury. Meanwhile, the Perfectionist John Humphrey Noyes (1811–1886) established the Oneida Community, based on complex marriage relationships combined with male continence, mutual criticism, and the spirit of free inquiry. Etienne Cabet (1788–1856), author of the utopian novel *Un Voyage en Icarie* (1840), provided the blueprint that brought a colony of French peasants to Texas, where they established the first of several Icarian societies. The Amana colony, a German settlement founded in 1842, maintained strict discipline, a system of confession, ancient German customs, and a high standard of craftsmanship—all of which were combined with the excellent business abilities of its members. And, of course, the New England transcendentalists tried their hand at utopian socialism for a time, which caused their leading light, Ralph Waldo Emerson, to proclaim to his friend Thomas Carlyle, "The fever has gripped us so that not a man passes by who does not have some blueprint for a new community in his waistcoat pocket."

The Mormons

ONE OF THE MORE IMPORTANT EXAMPLES of communities inspired by visionary experience during the first half of the nineteenth century has been the Mormons, more formally known as the Church of Jesus Christ of Latter-day Saints.[2] Their founder, Joseph Smith, was born in Sharon, Vermont, on December 23, 1805. His parents were staunch New Englanders, descended from Lathrops and Smiths of English ancestry. (Others in the family tree included Henry Wadsworth Longfellow, Eli Whitney, Ulysses S. Grant [sixth cousin], John Foster Dulles, Franklin Delano Roosevelt, and Benjamin Spock, although none of these were Mormons.) Within a few years of Smith's birth, the family moved to New Hampshire, then back to Vermont, trying to survive financially.

His biographers recount that when Smith was seven, he developed a bone growth on his leg. The doctors prescribed immediate amputation, but his parents objected. As a result, the young boy underwent a long and bloody operation where the growth was surgically removed without anesthesia. He survived the ordeal but for the rest of his life limped slightly.

In 1816, the family moved to Palmyra in upstate New York, a rural area still sparsely settled today that was once the preserve of the Iroquois Confederacy. The first white settlers in the area had come in 1776. They had been followers of Jemima Wilkinson, the first native-born American to organize a religious society in the New World. Later, it became an area dominated by Baptists, Methodists, and Presbyterians, although the Quakers had also established a presence. The Smith family appears to have been unchurched, but both mother and father were prone to visions of a religious nature and were interested in dream interpretation. Smith's father was also friends with a man named Walters, a traveling magician, vagabond, and fortune-teller. Walters seems to have influenced Smith at an early age. Although it is not known whether his knowledge of trance induction was the cause, as a teenager Smith began to have visions and later was able to "divine things" by reading a stone placed in his hat.

His religious awakening appears to have begun at around the age of fifteen or sixteen. Only some years later did he give a written account of these early episodes, but they were important because they marked the beginning of his charismatic ministry. According to accounts, he first became preoccupied with the state of his soul around age twelve. This developed into a brooding conviction about his sinful nature and, around the year 1821, culminated in an ecstatic vision in which God came to him and forgave him for his sins. Smith dictated the content of this vision on several occasions, the fullest occurring in 1838:

> I . . . retired into the place where I had previously designed to go, having looked around me and finding myself alone, I kneeled down and began to offer up the desires of my heart to God. I had scarcely done so, when immediately I was [seized] upon by some power which entirely overcame me and [had] such astonishing influence over me as to bind my tongue so that I could not speak. Thick darkness gathered around me and it seemed to me for a time as if I were doomed to sud-

den destruction. But exerting all my powers to call upon God to deliver me out of the power of this enemy which had seized upon me, and abandon myself to destruction, not to an imaginary ruin but to the power of some actual being from the unseen world who had such a marvelous power as I had never before felt in any being. Just at this moment of great alarm, I saw a pillar [of] light exactly over my head above the brightness of the sun, which descended gradually until it fell upon me. It no sooner appeared than I found myself delivered from the enemy which held me bound. When the light rested upon me I saw two personages (whose brightness and glory defy all description) standing above me in the air. One of them spake unto me calling me by name and said (pointing to the other) "This is my beloved Son, Hear him." My object in going to enquire of the Lord was to know which of all the sects was right that I might know which to join. No sooner therefore did I get possession of myself so as to be able to speak, than I asked the personages who stood above me in the light, which of all the sects was right, (for at this time it had never entered into my heart that all were wrong) and which I should join. I was answered that I must join none of them, for they were all wrong, and the personage who addressed me said that all their Creeds were an abomination in his sight, that those professors were all corrupt, that "they draw near me with their lips but their hearts are far from me; They teach for doctrines the commandments of men, having a form of Godliness but they deny the power thereof." They again forbade me to join with any of them and many other things did he say unto me which I cannot write at this time. When I came to myself again I found myself lying on [my] back looming up into Heaven.[3]

This first vision was followed by another two years later in which an angel appeared to Smith in his sleep:

A personage appeared at my bedside, standing in the air. . . . He had on a loose robe of the most exquisite whiteness . . . his whole person was glorious beyond description. I was afraid; but the fear soon left me. He called me by name, and said unto me that his name was Moroni; that God had work for me to do; and that my name should be had for good and evil among all nations, kindreds, and tongues.[4]

The angel communicated further to Smith the whereabouts of a holy book written on gold plates, which gave an account of the former inhabitants of the New World and provided information on their true ancestry as one of the lost tribes of Israel. Its primary content was the everlasting gospel delivered by the Savior to the early settlers. With the gold plates were two stones fastened to a breastplate, which were called Urim and Thummim. Considered "seers" in ancient times, the stones could be used for translating the accompanying book. Smith's vision showed him that these godsends could be found buried in a stone box on a small hill near Palmyra. He was given specific instructions, however, not to show these materials to anyone without divine permission. The angel was then surrounded by a shaft of light and ascended to heaven.

Twice more during the course of the night the angel appeared and again the next day when Smith was working with his father in the field. At that time, he was instructed to tell his father what had happened to him. His father in turn told him to follow the angel's commands. Smith went to the designated hill, later called the Hill Cumorah, and found the book and the objects. Only later was he permitted to remove them, but the prohibition against showing them to anyone remained in effect for a much longer period.

After Smith received the plates in 1827, he began a series of sittings in which translations of the book began. With someone else acting as scribe, Smith placed the sacred stones over his eyes, covered his head with a hat, and began dictating. The original text was supposedly compiled by Mormon, the last of the Nephite prophets of the Old Testament and the father of the angel Moroni. Thus it was called the Book of Mormon. It was written in characters that were purportedly from a mix of the Egyptian, Chaldaic, Assyrian, and Arabic languages, but this was never confirmed. Finally, after 116 pages were produced, the transcriber took them to Palymra to arrange for printing. Through some unnamed calamity, however, the manuscript disappeared. This was a major blow, and Smith's angry reaction was predictable.

But Smith recovered from this news when he received a vision that commanded him to translate the same material again. It would now be given to him in a different form. Eventually, he realized that his task was to found a new church. At the end of the translations, just before the book was published, he and another man, Oliver Cowdery, retreated to a holy spot in the woods for prayer and meditation. There, John the Baptist appeared in a vision and initiated them as high priests into the ancient Old Testament order of the Aaronic priesthood. Smith followed this episode with a series of sittings with various people who were shown the gold plates and who later attested that they had seen them.

By the time the Book of Mormon was completed, numerous converts had already been made. By August 1829, there were six elders and seventy members in three different branches. These events were followed by a series of further visions. In the first of these, the group received its formal name, Church of Jesus Christ of Latter-day Saints. In others, the nature of the church hierarchy and the divine law permitting polygamy were revealed. Soon the group had grown in numbers and had settlements in upstate New York, western Pennsylvania, and Ohio's Western Reserve. Even then they were a tightly knit and centrally controlled society with aggressive religious and economic aspirations that must have been attractive to the throngs who came to join their ranks.

In 1830, Smith had another vision in which he foretold that the city of Zion, God's coming Kingdom on Earth, was to be built in Jackson County, Missouri. A settlement was consecrated there, but because of their exclusivity and unusual views, the Mormons were driven out a few years later. From there, the Mormons migrated with an ever-growing number of followers to northwestern Missouri, where they established their own county, built as its new capital the town of Far West, and raised their own militia. But as their numbers swelled so did their social problems. Antagonism with their neighbors over their religious intent to rule the land led to bloodshed and rioting.

Soon they became the object of relentless persecution. The National Guard was called out against them by the governor. Their lands and goods were confiscated; some were killed; and Smith, along with most of the other leaders, was imprisoned.

In 1839, 5,000 disciples made their way to Nauvoo, Illinois, in search of the site where the New Jerusalem was to be erected. The conditions were harsh upon their arrival. But by 1845, it had become the "City Beautiful," with a population of over 11,000, the largest such metropolis in the state.

Violent antagonism developed, however, over such issues as plural marriage, corruption, the establishment of a secret high order within the church hierarchy, and an allegation implicating Smith in the death of the governor of Missouri. Even more contentious than the Mormons' separateness from their neighbors was the fact that they had gone on record claiming they had plans for an empire. They became active in local, state, and national politics, and rumors flew that the Mormons planned to take over several states and amalgamate them into one. In 1844, Smith even became a candidate for president of the United States. But disaster was to follow. After a series of violent clashes with local nonbelievers, the Mormon community was broken up, and nearly all the leaders of Smith's movement were again imprisoned. Smith himself was assassinated along with his brother in Carthage, Illinois, by an angry mob on June 27, 1844. He was only thirty-nine years old.

The Mormon missionary Brigham Young (1801–1877) managed to move the band, however, this time from Illinois to Utah. There, following Smith's vision for how the Holy City should be laid out, Young saw to it that a metropolis in the middle of the Great Salt Lake valley was raised up as the center of the surrounding Mormon communities. This city soon became the guiding light for successive waves of frontier men and women whose personal stories of hardship and hope on the Mormon Trail form part of the most important chronicles of the American experience.[5] In that region of the United States, the Kingdom of Heaven on Earth has not only been preserved to this day, but the number of its adherents has grown to more than 4.5 million. Such growth is partly attributable to the fact that the Mormon community has evolved from a nineteenth-century visionary sect of the Midwestern frontier into a twentieth-century Christian denomination that today puts itself forward as not only conservative, but also mainstream.[6]

The Seventh-Day Adventists

ANOTHER MYSTICAL COMMUNITY with a visionary bent consisted of the Seventh-Day Adventists, led by the prophetess Ellen White. Adventism, although it had affinities with the European millenarian tradition dating back to the medieval period, was most directly an outgrowth of the religious prophesies of the American apocalyptic preacher William Miller.[7] Miller was born in Pittsfield, Massachusetts, in 1782, the later home of Herman Melville. The family moved around between Vermont and New York during Miller's early years. Miller fought in the War of 1812 and afterward became a farmer, a Freemason, and a local politician. After a short excursion into deism, the rational rather than mystical or authoritarian belief in a Christian God, Miller reverted to the opposite pole and became a fervent Baptist. He was largely self-taught, except for transient periods of formal education and some instruction he received in religious subjects from his mother. He appears to have studied the Bible intensely for some fourteen years.

Miller came to believe that the Second Coming was at hand and began preaching this message locally in 1831, gradually extending his trips from New York into New England. He calculated, with reference to symbolism in the Bible, that the thousand-year period of the prophesies was coming to an end and that Christ would soon appear for the Final Judgment, probably sometime between 1843 and 1844.

By 1839, he had preached this idea approximately 800 times, mostly to small congregations. That year, he met and converted Joshua Himes, a Boston minister already engaged in social causes from temperance to the abolition of slavery. Himes turned his attention to Adventism full time and, in partnership with Miller, took over all the advertising and arrangement of lectures. It did not take long before Miller's message was being heard up and down the East Coast, from Maine to Pennsylvania. Millerism, as it came to be called, soon became a social epidemic.

By Miller's own estimate, he had attracted some 50,000 followers as 1843 drew near. According to the most conservative estimate, in all likelihood only 5,000 were hard-core disciples who resonated with his message. According to another commentator, however, "It is possible that upwards of a million others were 'skeptically expectant.'"[8]

Newspapers launched a number of attacks against Miller and his followers, but this only served to heighten public awareness of his teachings and to draw more people to him. By then, the movement had spread to the Midwest and on into the American frontier. It seemed as if the entire nation were gripped with the millennial impulse.

But the day of the event came and went . . . and nothing happened. Miller's response was to remake his calculations. He determined that the first date was just slightly off, so a second date was set: October 22, 1844. But again, the day came and nothing happened. Meanwhile, people had sold their homes and given away their belongings, had said good-bye to their friends, and, after donning snow-white raiment, had climbed to the rooftops and mountain peaks at the midnight hour. Thousands came back down disappointed, many wept, some even went completely mad.

A few stalwarts remained, however. One in particular, Hiram Eden, had retired to a barn to pray with a number of Millerites the morning after what came to be called the "Great Disappointment." Their mission was to plead with God for an explanation. After breakfast, they were passing through a field, and Eden had a vision of heaven. In this vision, he saw the cleansing of the sanctuary as described in the Book of Daniel (8:14), which foretold not the final Resurrection, but Christ's entry into the heavenly sanctuary just prior to the Final Judgment.

This was subsequently interpreted to mean that on October 22, God had ended his ministry to the world and only the faithful who remained inside the sanctuary door would be saved. The idea was now to prepare those who truly believed and were truly ready. This became known in Millerite circles as "the shut door doctrine." It was an explanation that might have appealed to their faith, but one of the main reasons the idea caught on among followers was the influence of a young woman named Ellen White, who appeared with a message she had received in a vision of her own. It confirmed that God had entered the sacred vestibule at the appointed hour and that the Second Coming had not yet arrived.

One of a pair of twin girls, Ellen Harmon White was born in 1827 in Gorham, Maine. Her family was of English ancestry, poor but hard-working, Methodist Episcopal by religious persuasion. She appears to have had a happy and normal childhood until a classmate threw a large stone, hitting her in the face. Her nose was broken, which caused permanent disfigurement, and she remained unconscious for three weeks with a concussion.

Afterward, her life changed dramatically. To her great dismay, she was not able to continue formal schooling. Her disfigured face turned people away or evoked only their pity. White's physical and emotional health was affected as she became increasingly bitter and disappointed over what had befallen her. She fell into a state of morbid introspection.

This episode set the stage for White's spiritual awakening, as she was drawn more deeply into the fervent Christianity of the period. She discovered a discarded scrap of paper announcing the end of the world, in perhaps only thirty years. The idea affected her greatly, and she took the message home to her family and friends. Voraciously, she began to read religious biographies of what she called "immaculate children." She also began to spend greater amounts of time by herself in nature.

Then she heard William Miller preach on February 13, 1840, and was transfixed. A year later, White was led to a Methodist camp meeting in Buxton, Maine, where she experienced a religious conversion: "As I knelt and prayed, suddenly my burden left me and my heart was light."[9] Soon after, she was admitted into the Methodist Church, insisting on baptism by immersion. Trouble followed, however. While attending classes, she refused to acknowledge that she had received sanctification through Methodism, claiming instead that she had been awakened through the inspiration of Miller: "I felt compelled to confess the truth, that it was not through Methodism that my heart had received its new blessing, but by the stirring truths concerning the personal appearing of Jesus. Through them I found peace, joy, and perfect love."[10] This declaration led to her immediate dismissal from the Methodist Church. She confided all her sorrows and perplexities to her mother, who encouraged her to take counsel with a local Adventist preacher. Soon, White turned fully to Miller's teachings.

An equally important factor in her spiritual development had been the increasingly frequent appearance of nighttime dreams and waking visions. She had been prone to these experiences even before her turn to Millerism, but they did not manifest themselves with any intensity until her "first vision." White recounted that, in December of 1844,

> while we were praying the power of God came upon me as I had never felt before. . . . It was not an exciting occasion, and there were but five of us present, all women. . . . I was wrapt in a vision of God's glory, and seemed to be rising higher and higher from the earth, and was shown something of the travels of the Advent people to the holy city.[11]

She saw these people "walking on a straight and narrow path, cast up high above the world." The "midnight cry," referring to the new millennial date of October 22, 1844, was a "bright light set up behind them at the beginning of the path. . . . This light shone all along the path, and gave light for their feet so that they might not stumble." Yet

> some grew weary, and said the city was a great way off, and they expected to have entered it before. Then Jesus would encourage them. . . . Others rashly denied the light behind them, and said that it was not God that had led them out so far. The light behind them went out, leaving their feet in perfect darkness, and they stumbled and lost sight of the mark and of Jesus, and fell off the path down into the dark and wicked world below.[12]

This event was soon followed by another vision confirming the first one. White was attending a meeting in which the shut-door doctrine was being discussed, when suddenly she was gripped with agony and fell off her chair to the floor. In this condition, she recounted that the Lord came to her and affirmed that on October 22, 1844, God had closed the door on nonbelievers in preparation for the Final Event, which had not actually happened yet. Those who believed in this version of events were thus more closely drawn to her.

Through her increased religious activities, White met Joseph Bates, a New England sea captain and ardent follower of Miller who was actively involved in the temperance and antislavery movements. He had broken with the Millerites because he believed that Adventists should honor the Sabbath on Saturday. White confirmed his beliefs in yet another vision that bonded them together even more steadfastly in a common understanding because orthodox Millerites had also rejected those who had their own visions as religious fanatics. Fits, inspired spiritual gifts, and trance states were everywhere in the Millerite fold and constituted a disrupting influence that could not be controlled.

The scholar Ronald Numbers, in his in-depth study of the prophetess, reported that Ellen White's trances came five or ten times a year and would last from a few minutes to several hours.[13] The episodes came unannounced; she might be praying by herself or lecturing to a large audience,

when suddenly, without warning, she would be off in a "deep plunge of glory." Often there were three shouts of "Glory! G-l-o-r-y! G-l-o-r-y!"—the second and third "fainter, but more thrilling than the first, the voice resembling that of one quite a distance from you, and just going out of hearing." Then, unless caught by some alert brother nearby, she slowly sank to the floor in a swoon. After a short time in this deathlike state, new power flowed through her body, and she rose to her feet. On occasion she possessed extraordinary strength, once reportedly holding an eighteen-pound Teale Bible in her outstretched hand for one-half hour.[14]

Numbers goes on to quote from an eyewitness account of White's trances:

She often uttered words singly, and sometimes sentences, which expressed to those about her the nature of the view she was having, either of heaven or of earth. . . . When beholding Jesus our Saviour, she would exclaim in musical tones, low and sweet, "lovely, lovely, lovely," many times, always with the greatest affection. . . . Sometimes she would cross her lips with her finger, meaning that she was not at that time to reveal what she saw, but later a message would perhaps go across the continent to save some individual or church from disaster. . . . When the vision was ended, and she lost sight of the heavenly light, as it were, coming back to the earth once more, she would exclaim with a long drawn sigh, as she took her first natural breath, "D-a-r-k." She was then limp and strengthless, and had to be assisted to her chair.[15]

While these episodes were taking place, Numbers reports that physicians who examined White witnessed a dramatic slowing of her vital functions: Her heart rate would decrease, her breathing would become imperceptible. She could move about, but no one could lift her limbs. The doctors remained skeptical, diagnosing her as a hysteric patient. Believers, however, saw in her visions a confirmation that they were the chosen people.

The woman's extraordinary abilities eventually drew the attention of James White, an ordained Adventist minister from Maine. The two struck up a friendship, and James came quickly to believe that he had a duty to protect Ellen while she was contacting the faithful throughout New England. They began traveling together and were married in 1846. Under less than idyllic circumstances, they began a family (they would eventually have five children), and, in conjunction with Joseph Bates, they launched their ministry. Bates played the role of moral reformer, backed by Ellen's charismatic visions, while James ran the publishing arm of the new church.

Despite the increasing number of new converts, their personal circumstances were strained. This continued until 1855, when Ellen had a vision directing the Adventists to move to Michigan:

The Lord has shown me in vision . . . that God has been opening the way for the spread of present truth in the West. . . . The people of the East have heard the proclamation of the second coming of Christ, and have seen much of the display of the powers of God, and have fallen back into a state of indifference and security where it is almost impossible to reach them at present.[16]

They thus traveled to the little town of Battle Creek, where they established their modest home and printing shop. Other followers, meanwhile, settled in the surrounding area and continued their missionary work. By 1853, Michigan had become one of the strongest Adventist centers in the United States. Soon it became the church's world headquarters, as members expanded operations in order to go forth and preach the Millennial Kingdom to all nations. As in all other matters regarding church policy and behavior, they believed their missionary activity was specifically enjoined by God, who spoke to them through Ellen White, his chosen instrument. At one point she commanded them, "Before the flood, God sent Noah to warn the world, that the people might be led to repentance, and thus escape the threatened destruction. As the time of Christ's appearing draws near, the Lord sends his servants with a warning to the world to prepare for the great event."[17]

This preparation came to involve the cleansing of not only sins, but all aspects of daily living. Reform programs surrounding health, dress, education, and temperance were begun in earnest. Shunning drugs, the Adventists advocated clean foods, exercise, fresh air, and rest. White also produced numerous visions that became the basis of new attire for women. Instead of tight corsets, floor-length dresses, and hoopskirts, which promoted ill health, she designed a loose short skirt, to be worn over accompanying pantaloons, which became known as bloomers. Extensive educational programs were also launched to promote health, clean living, and moral instruction.

The most significant and successful of these Adventist experiments was the Battle Creek Sanitarium. Also known as the Western Health Reform Institute, the facility was the first of a series of worldwide Adventist retreats. At its height, it was a water-cure establishment that provided healthful vegetarian meals, coarse dark breads, vigorous exercise programs, and spiritual education classes. Its most notable superintendent was John Harvey Kellogg.[18] Here was a man who had first earned his medical degree from a questionable institution—the Hygieo-Therapeutic College in New Jersey—but who redeemed himself somewhat in the eyes of the East Coast medical establishment by taking additional medical training at the University of Michigan and Bellevue Hospital Medical School in New

York City. His desire was to bring scientific principles to the Battle Creek Sanitarium, and his successes brought him national recognition.

As a practitioner, Kellogg is completely forgotten today, but his various health-food inventions, such as granola, have become American staples. One of his patients, C. W. Post, today has a cereal named after him, and both Grape Nuts and Rice Krispies are familiar products of their efforts. Kellogg also held the patent on cornflakes, which he tried at one point to sign over to the Adventists, but Ellen White, much to others' later regret, did not want it.

The General Conference of Seventh-Day Adventists was formally organized in May 1863 around 125 churches and 3,500 members. By the time Ellen died in 1915, it had become a worldwide institution. She was even able to travel to societies in Switzerland and Australia. At present, with world headquarters in Washington, D.C., the church membership exceeds five million. We know of them today largely through the recent unfortunate episode in Waco, Texas, when the Adventist group the Branch Davidians, led by the millennialist David Koresh, was mistaken by government law enforcement agencies as a terrorist organization.[19]

Utopianism and the Visionary Tradition

IT HAS ALREADY BEEN MENTIONED THAT, with the exception of a few Dutch, Swedish, and French experiments, the early mystical communities in America were primarily German and English in origin. To this must be added the coda that these communities were just as likely to be led by charismatic women as by men. In fact, it could be said that insofar as the dominant American social institutions at the time represented the patterns set down by European high culture, popular American visionary psychologies were their emotional, intuitive, and experiential counterpoints. As a repressed and often persecuted aspect of a society dominated by masculine forms, the early mystical communities in some ways represented a feminine psychology of the collective unconscious expressed on a national scale.

Further, we cannot help but be impressed by the apparent relationship among asceticism, the induction of trance states, and the appearance of dreams and visions. Traumatic events, environmental hardships, and voluntarily accepted forms of denial can all be conditions that turn the individual toward an opening of the "internal spiritual sense," as Swedenborg called it. Once there has been this opening of the internal sense, one experiences various alternative states of consciousness, visions appear, and dreams take on new meaning. These internal referents then become the guiding force in a person's life, despite all outward adversity. Healing and prophesy also result when visionary experience becomes a community-wide, socially sanctioned event. Such behavior on the part of charismatic leaders almost always promoted visionary experience among the members as well.

This pattern stands in direct contrast to those examples of utopian communalism that became financially successful over the course of American history. Whereas each such community was, in a sense, a case study in the attempt to achieve some perfect relation between spirit and matter, the reigning ideal in Christian contemplation has always been denial of sensory pleasure and material wealth as a prerequisite for experiencing higher spiritual states. Each communal experiment succeeded or failed in reconciling this tension in its own way.

While the Shakers succeeded in business affairs, their population declined largely due to their strict adherence to the doctrine of absolute celibacy. Conversely, the Ephrata Cloister prospered because it was more liberal in the choices offered for sexual reform. But the real source of the Ephratites' prosperity was the business acumen of two brothers. This left everyone else free to pursue forms of spiritual practice that would have been otherwise impossible for an isolated family on the American frontier. The brothers became so successful, however, that they were eventually censured by the rest of the community for becoming so worldly. Curtailing their activities eroded the financial base and eventually led to the demise of the cloister. Meanwhile, the Adventists and Mormons prospered precisely because they drew on otherworldly millennial ideals, but they left the men and women to their own choices with regard to partnering or even provided for an excess of availability. In each case, their approaches promoted sufficient motivation for successful entrepreneurial ventures, especially where self-sacrifice by individuals on a mass scale was required for the sake of the larger spiritual community.

What made the utopian experiments psychological was their emphasis on character development. When, for instance, Sylvester Graham, the inventor of the graham cracker, advocated a diet of coarse grains in the 1830s, he believed that all the organs of the body were linked in a common sympathy so that what one did in one place directly affected the quality of an organ in another. He believed that, in addition to physical interventions, there was the training of the moral faculties to consider. Likewise, in his advocacy of health reforms, he believed in the "intimate relation between the quality of the bread and the moral character of the family." [20]

Indeed, Ellen White's first vision enjoined the faithful not to enter the Kingdom immediately, but to prepare themselves for entrance. This shifted the emphasis of Adventism from the expectation of immediate salvation to an extensive moral and psychological program of self-development. As a result, while Adventists are known throughout the world today for their advocacy of natural foods, at the same time, they are survivalists. Each woman in the community is required to learn preserving, canning, and cooking. Each man is to prepare for the family's safety during the final holocaust. Material readiness and physical health, they believe, are a function of extensive psychological training.

Finally, the diversity of these utopian communities reminds us that spirituality is not the unique province of mainstream denominations. Radically different experiments in religious freedom, from the very beginning, have continued to mark the American landscape. This issue reemerged during the counterculture movement of the 1960s. Was it possible to have a rich inward spiritual life in contemporary America and not belong to any of the mainstream Christian denominations? Thousands answered in the affirmative as extensive social experiments in communal living sprang up and spiritual communities were established on ideals that at first glance may appear foreign to the American mainstream today. Not a few of these experiments were built on the sites of old Native American healing spas or in rural settings that had some historical connection to utopian communities of a previous era. One recent commentator has suggested that the burgeoning concept of co-housing projects for the elderly has received much inspiration from the experimental communes of the 1960s.[21]

Such examples provide us with the most visible signs of continuity between our evolving sense of community today and the older American visionary tradition.

Notes

1. For an overview, see Charles Nordhoff, *The Communistic Societies of the United States from Personal Visit and Observation* (New York: Dover, 1966); or Rosabeth Moss Kanter, *Community and Commitment: Communes and Utopias in Sociological Perspective* (Cambridge, MA: Harvard University Press, 1972).

2. For the Mormons' view of themselves, see *New Mormon Studies,* on CD-ROM [computer file] series *A Comprehensive Resource Library* (Salt Lake City, UT: Smith Research Associates, 1998). For a scholar's view, see Kenneth H. Winn, *Exiles in a Land of Liberty: Mormons in America, 1830–1846* (Chapel Hill: University of North Carolina Press, 1989); or Edwin Brown Firmage and Richard Collin Mangrum, *Zion in the Courts: A Legal History of the Church of Jesus Christ of Latter-day Saints, 1830–1900* (Urbana: University of Illinois Press, 1988). For a comparison with other communities, see Louis J. Kern, *An Ordered Love: Sex Roles and Sexuality in Victorian Utopias: The Shakers, the Mormons, and the Oneida Community* (Chapel Hill: University of North Carolina Press, 1981).

3. Milton V. Backman Jr., *Joseph Smith's First Vision: Confirming Evidences and Contemporary Accounts,* 2nd ed. (Salt Lake City, UT: Bookcraft, 1980), pp. 162–163.

4. Ibid., p. 27.

5. William W. Slaughter, *Trail of Hope: The Story of the Mormon Trail* (Salt Lake City, UT: Shadow Mountain, 1997).

6. Armand L. Mauss, *The Angel and the Beehive: The Mormon Struggle with Assimilation* (Urbana: University of Illinois Press, 1994). See also Roger D. Launius and Linda Thatcher, eds., *Differing Visions: Dissenters in Mormon History* (Urbana and Chicago: University of Illinois Press, 1994).

7. Everett N. Dick, *William Miller and the Advent Crisis* (Berrien Springs, MI: Andrews University Press, 1994).

8. Michael Barkun, *Crucible of the Millennium: The Burned-Over District of New York in the 1840s* (Syracuse, NY: Syracuse University Press, 1986).

9. Quoted in Roy E. Graham, *Ellen G. White: Co-founder of the Seventh-day Adventist Church* (New York: Peter Lang, 1985), p. 19.

10. Ibid., p. 21.

11. Ibid., p. 23.

12. Ibid., p. 24.

13. Ronald Numbers, *Prophetess of Health: A Study of Ellen G. White* (New York: Harper & Row, 1976), p. 18.

14. Ibid.

15. Ibid., p. 19.

16. N. Gordon Thomas, *The Millennial Impulse in Michigan, 1830–1860: The Second-Coming in the Third New England* (Lewiston, NY: Edwin Mellen Press, 1989), p. 86.

17. Ibid., p. 87.

18. Richard W. Schwartz, *John Harvey Kellogg: Father of the Health Food Industry* (Berrien Springs, MI: Andrews University Press, 1995). Other more general works on health foods and fitness include James C. Whorton, *Crusaders for Fitness: The History of American Health Reformers* (Princeton, NJ: Princeton University Press, 1982); and Harvey Green, *Fit for America: Health, Fitness, Sport, and American Society* (New York: Pantheon, 1986).

19. James R. Lewis, ed., *From the Ashes: Making Sense of Waco* (Lanham, MD: Rowman & Littlefield, 1994). See also U.S. Congress, House Committee on Government Reform and Oversight, *Investigation into the Activities of Federal Law Enforcement Agencies Toward the Branch Davidians,* Rept. 13, prepared in conjunction with the Committee on the Judiciary, with additional and dissenting views (Washington, DC: GPO, 1996).

20. Numbers, *Prophetess of Health,* p. 52.

21. A useful collection of essays is John Case and Rosemary C. R. Taylor, eds., *Co-ops, Communes, and Collectives: Experiments in Social Change in the 1960s and 1970s* (New York: Pantheon, 1979).

Chapter Seven

Spiritualism, Theosophy, New Thought, and Christian Science

INCREDIBLE AS IT MAY SEEM TO MODERN READERS, 150 YEARS ago millions of Americans believed that modern science had incontrovertibly established the fact that there was life after death.[1] The chief means by which people understood this to have been established was the mediumistic seance. Here it was believed that spirits of the dead or disembodied entities from some other plane of existence that had never been alive in a physical body would take possession of an entranced or otherwise sensitive subject, called a "medium," and through that person communicate with the living.

Historically, the forms that spirit communication took in the nineteenth century were varied. The principal means were rapping and knocking, automatic speech, automatic writing, displays of floating bodily fluid from the spirit world, table tipping, slate writing, and so on.

These phenomena usually took place within the context of mediumistic circles, the growth and popularity of which represent one of the more interesting chapters in the early history of group psychotherapy.

Seances became the rage, and a flood of literature followed. To answer the increasing public demand for a popular, readable textbook on how to develop a mediumistic circle, Uriah Clark published his *Plain Guide to Spiritualism* in 1863. The work was a summary of his experiments and demonstrations conducted over the preceding eight years, which he intended for "sceptics, inquirers, clergymen, believers, lecturers, mediums, editors, and all who need a thorough guide to the phenomena, science, philosophy, religion, and reforms of modern spiritualism." [2]

Attitude being the prime ingredient, Clark's instructions for the formation of a circle of people desiring to develop their mediumistic powers were as follows:

> Select your company of persons most congenial, harmonious, patient, quiet, persevering, and confidential; the number from three to twenty, with an equal number of each sex; join hands, sing, have music, engage in devout exercises, or keep silence, as shall best accord with the predominant feeling of the circle; seek to put yourselves in sympathy with those whom you would communicate; elevate your thoughts and emotions to the plane they occupy, and, invoking the dominant influences, then let each person freely yield, willing to be an instrument for the manifestations of the spirits under the guidance of the supreme Spirit whose government is over all. [3]

Many of these requirements, Clark tells us, are for convenience, but the main motivation for each person should be to use the circle to test his own capacities. If physical manifestations, like rappings or tippings, are sought, the circle should be formed around a table of suitable size, all hands should be placed on it, and then all participants should wait for at least twenty to thirty minutes. Caution should be taken against anyone perpetuating fraudulent movements, yet the group is to refrain from harboring, even entertaining, any unkind suspicions. Each person should be willing to be questioned and tested if anything is doubted.

If no physical demonstrations are forthcoming, Clark instructed everyone to wait for other forms, like speaking, visions, entrancements, or vibrations. No person should resist whatever impulse or influence may come, unless the conditions are bad and some injury seems likely. People are frequently apprehensive at first, Clark says, but they should not be afraid. "The greatest danger almost invariably ensues from not yielding to the influence but from resisting it. . . . No hesitation or timidity may be felt when persons yield freely with pure and earnest desires for the purest and holiest influences."[4]

As soon as members of the circle begin to receive impressions or communications, if they need further direction, they can ask the spirit whatever questions they please and receive the answer needed. Everything received, however, must be tested by reason, intuition, and common sense, and nothing should be taken on absolute authority. "The highest spirits, seldom, if ever, seek to lead men blindly, or to give particular directions in regard to every step in life, but rather to impart influxes, to enlighten and expand the individual mind and heart, that mortals may receive reliable impressions for their own guidance in all things."[5]

The key here seems to be sympathetic nonresistance. The company should be in harmony with one another, and all should have an open mind about the possibility of communication. This "letting go," allowing anything that arises to flow in, is a suggestion familiar in both hypnosis and classical psychoanalysis. Belief seems to play a major role in the outcome.

Spiritualism as an organized therapeutic and religious movement has traditionally been dated with the "Hydesville Rappings" of March 31, 1848. On that day, the three young Fox sisters first reported unexplained "rappings" in their bedroom, which they soon believed to have come from the spirit of a man once murdered and buried in the cellar of their house. Although the Fox sisters later confessed to fraud, the account of their experiences gained widespread newspaper coverage at the time. They were able to make a career of public speaking, and their many appearances served to heighten public interest in mediumship and the occult.

Soon, as a direct result of the Fox sisters' reported experiences, seances, table tipping, and slate writing became a national phenomenon. Large public demonstrations were common, and a new popular literature on the subject appeared. Medical societies, academic committees, and established church groups then began a counterattack, but by the 1850s, spiritualism as an organized movement could claim as many as a million followers. By the 1890s, the figure had grown to 11 million.[6] Spiritualists were constantly informed by such weekly newspapers as the *Spiritual Telegraph* and the *Banner of Light,* and they attended summer camp revivals by the thousands. They founded such local organizations as the New England Spiritualist Association and the ill-fated national organization known as the Society for the Diffusion of Useful Spiritual Knowledge. The most successful national organization has been the National Spiritualists Association, which was founded in 1893 and is still operating. Its offshoot, the National Colored Spiritualists Association, began in 1929.

Today, spiritualism is an integral part of American folk culture. There are several national federations of spiritualist churches, while psychic fairs and weekend workshops are common. Summer camps, such as Lilly Dale in upstate New York, still exist as remnants of the Hydesville days. Indeed, over the past century, the spiritualist roll call is replete with such famous psychics as Arthur Ford, Minna Crandon, Edgar Cayce, Eileen Garrett, Bishop James Pike, and, more recently, Gina Cerminara and Jane Roberts.

Theosophy

Although "spiritualism" is the name generally given by historians to a distinct movement that developed after the Fox sisters, it is also a generic term sometimes applied to an entire era of mental healing in the nineteenth century. Such usage would be like confusing all forms of mental healing with Christian Science, all of psychotherapy with psychoanalysis, or all of physics with quantum theory. Rather, it is more accurate to define specific schools of thought within a certain period and then let the commonalities and differences emerge from their natural historic roots. Keeping the distinctiveness of the different traditions in mind, a second major institutional organization to appear on the American scene in the second half of the nineteenth century was Theosophy.[7]

Here we have a set of teachings that defined itself as the "Universal Brotherhood of Humanity," which drew on ancient and modern religions, philosophies, and sciences in order to investigate the unexplained laws of nature and the physical powers latent in all human beings. The principal founder and guiding spirit of Theosophy was Helena Petrovna Blavatsky (1831–1891), a well-to-do Russian aristocrat whose independent personality and alleged psychic powers led her early in life to wander alone throughout Asia and the Near East, before she came to the United States in 1874 to defend spiritualism. Traveling to Chittenden, Vermont, she met Colonel Henry Steel Olcott (1832–1907), a lawyer and the agricultural editor of the *New York Times,* who was there attending the seances of the Eddy brothers. Thereafter, Olcott and Blavatsky traveled to Philadelphia to investigate the psychic claims of Mr. and Mrs. Nelson Holmes. They next retired to New York City, where Madame Blavatsky's apartment soon became the most well-known salon for local spiritualists.

The Theosophical Society was officially launched on October 20, 1875, with Olcott as president, Blavatsky as secretary, and William Q. Judge as counsel. Most of the early members were spiritualists interested in Madame Blavatsky's occult powers. Blavatsky, however, soon published her *Isis Unveiled,* which attacked spiritualism on the grounds that the spirits who appeared at American seances were not really departed loved ones but, rather, subhuman entities who permanently inhabit the spirit world, having evolved separately from humans. As an alternative, she presented the outline of a more systematic occult philosophy, which she said she had written under the guidance of ascended masters who had communicated with her from the psychic realms. Anyone, it seemed, could communicate with the dead. But here was someone with a comprehensive philosophy who spoke with authority. Soon Blavatsky became the doyenne of American spiritualists.

Following a vision of what their work was to be—which Blavatsky saw as encompassing more than merely the American scene—Blavatsky and Olcott moved the international headquarters of the Theosophical Society to Adyar, India, in 1879. There, Blavatsky's doctrines became heavily Hinduized. Nurtured by her charismatic utterances and by Olcott's organizational abilities, the society began to spread throughout India and soon was responsible for a major revival in Sanskrit learning. English translations of major religious and philosophical texts were begun, and schools for the preservation of Hindu and Buddhist culture were founded to counter incursions of Christian missionaries. This focus on education had important consequences, among them, methods such as yoga and meditation became more well understood in the English-speaking world.

Although yoga and meditation were known to the transcendentalists in the 1840s, it was not until Blavatsky's Sanskrit revival in India in the latter part of the 1880s that the first mass-produced translations of Patanjali's Yoga Sutras became widely available in the West. The first Theosophical translation, done by Tookeram Tatya, appeared in Bombay in 1885 and was reprinted for American readers in 1889, with a preface by William Q. Judge, head of the New York Lodge.

"Patanjali's Yoga Aphorisms," as they were called, provided the American mental healers with mnemonic instructions and commentary for attaining the ancient Hindu ideal of *samadhi,* or pure consciousness, through the development of intuitive insight. The Aphorisms are divided into four books: the definition of concentration; the means of its attainment; the supernormal powers that accrue to the practitioner as a by-product of the practice; and the characteristics of the highest state of *samadhi,* which is described as the isolation of pure consciousness from inert matter.

Yoga is a powerful tool for physiological self-regulation, as well as for the alteration of one's consciousness. But there is some doubt about how much of this esoteric knowledge the American mental healers actually had at their disposal. A few went to India and studied with meditation and yoga teachers directly. Most, however, would read the Yoga Aphorisms and adopt from it whatever they could understand, usually interpreting it in a Christianized and spiritualist context. Systematic training in the methods of yoga and meditation would have to wait until the mid-1890s, with the arrival in America of the first Hindu swamis.

By 1884, however, a schism had developed within the International Theosophical Society's London group that indicated problems were developing elsewhere. One side followed a Christo-Theosophical orienta-tion, while the other remained true to the Hindu and Buddhist interpre-tation of the Adyar group. At the same time, in Adyar, certain of Madame Blavatsky's letters fell into the hands of Christian missionaries, who publicly accused her of perpetrating fraud with regard to her al-leged occult claims. The incident eventually led to an investigation by the Society for Psychical Research in England, which came to the same con-clusion. Madame Blavatsky resigned her position and retired to Europe for convalescence, where she wrote the definitive bible that most Theosophists follow today, *The Secret Doctrine.*

Meanwhile, in America, Judge had begun *The Path,* an informative publication that soon tripled the American Theosophist membership, so that in 1889, an American section of the Theosophical Society was offi-cially incorporated. At that time, a restructuring of the society was under way in an attempt to gather the nucleus of the most faithful into what was called the "Esoteric Section." This reorganization divided the soci-ety into three groups: the Masters, the Esoteric Section, and the Proba-tioners. Partly as a result of these developments, when Blavatsky died in 1891 and was succeeded by Annie Besant in Britain, in New York William Q. Judge gained most of the power over the organization. This situation lasted several years, until the New York group split from the Adyar headquarters to form an independent Theosophical Society in America. Similar schisms followed in Australia, Europe, and England as the American branch brought many of the Blavatsky lodges around the world under its control.

Judge died in 1896, and that same year, at the annual meeting of the American Theosophical Society, young Katherine Tingley rose before the audience and, through her mediumistic powers, gave a public com-munication from the departed Judge in which he named her as his suc-cessor. Thereafter, she embarked upon an American tour and then traveled abroad to India, where Besant at the world headquarters tried with little effect to launch a counterattack.

Triumphant, Tingley returned to America in 1897 and began a utopian community at Point Loma, California, near San Diego. With the help of wealthy members, she erected Greco-Roman buildings, started a school for esoteric studies, and inaugurated an extensive agricultural program that eventually led to the large-scale cultivation of vegetables, including the avocado, which soon became a major California export. In 1898, Tingley became involved in delivering social services to wounded soldiers in the Spanish-American War, for which she received national recognition and a commendation from President McKinley.

Her utopian experiment reportedly graduated some 2,500 students, but it deteriorated in the late 1920s after her untimely death in an automobile accident while in Europe. The United Lodge of Theosophists had formed in 1909 as a splinter group from Tingley's American domain, and in 1931, upon the one hundredth anniversary of Madame Blavatsky's birth, the United Lodge rejoined the Adyar group under Besant.

Today, the Theosophical Society, in the form reorganized by Besant, maintains lodges and bookstores around the world, many of which are in the United States. At the same time, several offshoots are worth noting. Alice Bailey's Arcane School and Astara are two contemporary examples. Another is anthroposophy, started in 1911 by the Goethe scholar Rudolph Steiner (1861–1925). Yet another influence was Jiddu Krishnamurti, an Indian-born spiritual thinker raised under the aegis of Besant's Royal Order of the Star. Later, as a philosopher and independent lecturer, Krishnamurti had a significant and lasting impact on the American counterculture beginning in the 1930s.

New Thought

ANOTHER MAJOR INSTITUTIONAL DEVELOPMENT within the late-nineteenth-century mental healing movement was New Thought, so called because its practitioners sought to transcend the laws of materialistic science to discover the spiritual laws that govern the mind and the body.[8] Such laws, while not new, were understood to receive fresh application and adaptation. At the same time, the emphasis on thought showed that ideas and images, particularly in their power of suggestion, were a key to health and healing.

New Thought soon became a structural coalition of different mental healing groups that were loosely bound but in agreement on certain principles. Its many strands were a direct outgrowth of Phineas Parkhurst Quimby's healing ministry. The development of New Thought, however, was carried forward not by Quimby, but by several of his more influential patients. Chief among these was Warren Felt Evans (1817–1889), a Methodist minister who came to Portland, Maine, in 1863 to be healed of a chronic physical and mental affliction. Quimby's effect on Evans, it is said, was immediate.

Among other effects, Evans quit the Methodist Church and became a Swedenborgian. Also, healed of his own illness by Quimby, Evans began successfully to treat others. In 1869, he published the first of his many books, *The Mental Cure*. A year later, he opened a sanitarium in Salisbury, Massachusetts, the Evans House, in which he effected numerous cures by applying Quimby's methods. Evans followed this venture in 1872 with the publication of *Mental Medicine* and in 1875 with *Soul and Body*. These, he said, were his preliminary statements that led to the summum bonum of his healing system, *The Divine Law of Cure*. His final works, more philosophical in nature, were *The Primitive Mind Cure* and *Esoteric Christianity and Mental Therapeutics*.[9]

Disease, Evans wrote, was not so much a physical derangement as it was an abnormal condition that arises from wrong thought and wrong belief. The cultivation of right thoughts and beliefs was his major antidote. Philosophically, Evans believed that disease resulted from a disturbance in the spiritual body, which affected the physical body through Swedenborg's law of correspondence. Egotism was thought to be antagonistic to one's inward spiritual nature, as when external sensory desires gain control of one's inner self. Material concerns then predominate over our inner Christ nature. "Matter," Evans wrote, "was only spirit made visible to the mind."[10]

Evans said that he used intuitive or clairvoyant perception to find the cause of sickness in his patients. His method of healing was to disregard the physical body in favor of talking directly from his own spiritual nature to that same dimension within the patient. Thus Evans closely followed Quimby's practices, but to them he added the possibility of "absent treatment"; that is, healing from a distance by projecting thoughts to the absent person's Christ nature. He also introduced the use of "pregnant utterances" or affirmations—the repetition of statements that affirmed and strengthened the person's self-healing capacity. These included such phrases as "peace be with you" and "thy sins are forgiven."

With Quimby's death in 1866, Evans became the first to retail the founder's methods to an eager and devoted public. A controversy eventually developed, however, when Mary Baker Eddy, who had been healed by Quimby in 1863, was later accused by Quimby's disciples of making his ideas over into a system that she published under her own name as Christian Science. Two key figures in this debate were Julius and Annetta Dresser, who had begun their healing ministry in 1882 and published an explication of Quimby's ideas in order to show that Eddy had taken her system from him rather than being divinely inspired, as she had claimed. The controversy flared out of control in 1887, when Dresser published his *True History of Mental Science.*[11] As a result, large numbers of people were drawn into the practice of mental healing that everyone called Christian Science but that had no connection to Eddy. Dresser's wife followed with her own work, *The Philosophy of P. P. Quimby,* in 1895.[12]

In the interim, Eddy had a falling out with a number of her own disciples, many of whom used the Dresser controversy to release themselves from her control and bolt to the side of the more liberal Quimbyites. One such convert, Gladys Hopkins, helped to spread New Thought in San Francisco when she broke with Eddy and began to advocate the use of various scriptures from different world religions, rather than an exclusive focus on the Christian Bible.

By the early 1890s, the term "New Thought" was coming into vogue, especially as it referred to a loose-knit coalition of healers distinct from Eddy's Christian Science. For her own part, Eddy demanded complete obedience to her teachings, with no reinterpretation or changes permitted. Meanwhile, the New Thought practitioners were so liberal and diffuse as to have no central philosophy or standard set of teachings; instead, they held to a rigorous individualism. By this, they meant to put the locus of cure back with the patient and to give the healer wide latitude in interpreting how treatment should be implemented.

One instance of this process was the New Thought technique of inner visualization, or guided mental imagery. Visualization was an essential technique among the mental healers because it appealed to the imagination and awakened the intuitive faculties, which were normally undeveloped in a materialistic cultural climate that promoted only gratification of the senses and the supremacy of the intellect. Mental imagery was the doorway to the realms within.

A good example of its use can be found in Henry Wood's *Ideal Suggestion Through Mental Photography* (1893). Wood was a metaphysical thinker who had written works on political economy and popular spiritual philosophy before publishing his *Ideal Suggestion*. He claimed he was not a healer and did not see patients, but he did assert that his methods were applicable to the treatment of numerous mental and physical diseases, particularly alcoholism and morphine addiction.

The gist of Wood's theory was that all human beings live on the material, psychological, and spiritual planes simultaneously. We confine our attention mostly to the material plane, attributing by our sciences a cause-and-effect relation to that domain only. But neither the body nor the mind really exists independent of its true source, which is the pure shining light of God's love and intelligence in the realm of the spirit. All disease is created by living solely in the material plane and reinforced as such by the definition of each illness as a diagnostic category. Created on the basis of materialistic and rational principles, the use of drugs, surgery, and other medicinal applications logically follows.

But Woods claimed that physical medicine is not the cause of healing. Healing takes place only when we come into the presence of "God's Great Light." We must open our hearts to him, and when this effulgence shines on us, all sins are forgiven and all infirmities disappear. We must make ourselves transparent instead of opaque to this force within us—for it does not merely shine through us, it is actually who we are. If we realize our true nature as infinite strength and love, Wood argued, then we cannot possibly have any enduring relation to weakness, evil, and disorder.

Wood gave a number of practical directions for the technique he called "Ideal Suggestion":

First. Retire each day to a quiet apartment, and be alone in the silence.
　　Second. Assume the most restful position possible, in an easy-chair or otherwise; breathe deeply and rather rapidly for a few moments,

and thoroughly relax the physical body, for by suggestive correspondence this renders it easier for the mind to be passive and receptive.

Third. Bar the door of thought against the external world, and also shut out all physical sensation and imperfection.

Fourth. Rivet the mind upon the "meditation" (left-hand page), and by careful and repeated reading absorb its truth. Then place the "suggestion" (right-hand page) at a suitable distance from the eyes, and fasten them upon it from ten to twenty minutes. Do not merely look upon it, but wholly give yourself up to it, until it fills and overflows the entire consciousness.

Fifth. Close the eyes for twenty to thirty minutes more; behold it with the mind's eye, and let it permeate the whole organism.

Sixth. Call it into the field of mental vision during every wakeful hour of the night.

Finally. If disordered conditions are chronic and tenacious, there need be no discouragement if progress is not rapid, nor if "ups and downs" occur. Absorb the ideals repeatedly, until no longer needed. The cure is not magical, but a natural growth. Ideals will be actualized in due season.[13]

In Wood's text, these instructions are followed by twenty-five meditations, each one on a different left-hand page with a suggestion in large print on each corresponding right-hand page, printed broadside so that the patient could prop up the book at a 90-degree angle and sit staring at the suggestion.

The meditations are inspirational and charismatic in tone, while the suggestions are eminently hopeful. The first meditation, for instance, is the suggestion "God Is Here," and the accompanying text reads:

Man through a careless or mistaken consciousness separates himself from God, and this produces infelicity and dis-ease. Thought confers subjective realism either upon ideal entities or upon seeming bad conditions. What we dwell upon we become, or at least we grow like. Thought must have an outlet, otherwise it stagnates. God is the great normal Reality for it to rest upon. Consciousness must be open to the divine harmony, else it becomes disorderly and abnormal. It takes on character from that to which it links itself,—God, if it be God; change and discord, if materiality. It is therefore easy to be outwardly and morally correct and yet be *un*-Godly. The highest human consciousness is that of God, and is this, "Godliness which is great gain." To change from a controlling self-consciousness to a ruling God-consciousness, is to find harmony and health. The vision must be clarified so as to behold God everywhere, within and without, as all Life, all Love, and All in All. Discord cannot long abide the divine companionship. Take the name, and through the medium of the outer eye engrave it on the tablet of the inner consciousness.[14]

Other suggestions include "Pain Is Friendly," "I Am Not This Body," and "I Will Be Healed."

The point is that the healer remains sufficiently flexible to adapt the visualizations to the needs of the patients, while the patients can achieve a general sense of well-being, regardless of their particular malady. With the exception of the reference to a divine higher power, no particular theory is invoked, although Christianity, Theosophy, and New Thought are the obvious influences on Wood's writings.

Such liberal mixing at the individual level allowed a number of different mental healing organizations eventually to collaborate together, and in 1899, the first convocation of eclectics, the International New Thought Convention, was held in Hartford, Connecticut. Another gathering was held the same year in Boston. Both were based, it was claimed, on the philosophy of practical idealism, the religion of spiritual development that leads to a conscious oneness with God, and the science that has for its foundation the universality of love and law. According to the charter of the New Thought movement, there was no hampering creed, no personal dogmas, no forms or ceremonials, and no need for destructive methods. The organization described itself as tolerant, optimistic, and constructive. None other than Richard Clarke Cabot, a physician at the Massachusetts General Hospital, and Josiah Royce, a Harvard philosopher, spoke at the annual meeting in Boston in 1907. In 1908, these meetings were incorporated as the International New Thought Alliance.

Branches of this group today include such healing systems as Ernest Holmes's Divine Science and the Unity School of Christianity.[15] Perhaps more well known is the work of the New Thought practitioner Ralph Waldo Trine, whose *In Tune with the Infinite* has been in print for almost 100 years.[16]

Christian Science

AS THE AMERICAN RELIGIOUS SCHOLAR J. Stillson Judah has so aptly put it, the ideas and methods of Mesmer, Davis, Swedenborg, Emerson, Quimby, and the various Hindu teachers mingled to form a cultural ethos that stood apart from orthodox science and religion. But it was the genius behind Christian Science who welded these opposing traditions into a totally unique American institution that persists today as an influential cultural force.

Mary Baker Eddy (1821–1910), the founder of Christian Science, was born in Bow, New Hampshire, and raised in a strict Congregationalist environment.[17] Though a devout Christian, she later wrote of her deep internal struggle to accept certain Congregationalist tenets. She also reported hearing voices at an early age that were distinctly religious in character. She married George Washington Glover in 1843, but this happy union was terminated only a year later when Glover died of yellow fever. She lived with her family until 1853, during which time she became associated with various spiritualist and Unitarian groups then flourishing. Throughout this period, she suffered from bouts of spasms and nervous prostration. In 1853, she married Daniel Patterson, a dentist and homeopathic physician, but they later divorced.

In October 1863, after several attempts to contact Phineas Parkhurst Quimby, she traveled to Portland, Maine, to be treated by him personally. She arrived, it is reported, in a condition of extreme feebleness, but when she left to return to her home, then in Tilton, New Hampshire, she was in good health. She later wrote of her miraculous healing at Quimby's hands, praising him as one who "rolls away the stone from the sepulcher of error, and health is the resurrection."

She returned to visit Quimby in 1864 "for enlightenment," she said, during which time she read and edited parts of his writings on mental healing and worked with his patients and disciples. Quimby died in 1866, and that same year, Mary, then recently divorced, had a serious fall on the ice. According to the doctor who was called, she sustained a spinal dislocation. Semiconscious and initially in great pain, she was taken to a nearby house, but against her doctor's orders she soon had herself removed to her own home. She refused to take her prescribed medicine, having no faith in it, she said, and chose instead to have only friends and church members around her. At one point, alone with only her Bible, she turned to one of the healing episodes of Jesus, and she later wrote that his words began to flood into her thoughts: "I am the way, the truth, and the life. No man can come unto the Father, but by me." She was suddenly filled with the conviction that her life was in God and that at that moment she was healed. The core of her realization was that faith in matter was in error. "Mind is all, matter nothing" became her watchword.

Returning to the company of her friends, unaided and apparently well, she created some surprise. When the doctor visited, his reaction was one of genuine alarm to see her up and mobile, since he had expected complete debility and permanent loss of the use of her legs. His reaction so affected her that she immediately collapsed in sudden weakness again, but she regained her former strength as soon as he had departed. Continuing to vacillate between health and prostration, she soon wrote to Julius Dresser, asking for his help to heal her permanently. Dresser declined, however, on the grounds that he was unable and unworthy to fill the late Quimby's role and that, in any event, he was now employed as a newspaperman in Maine. Having recourse only to her own inner powers and sustained only by her Bible, she resolved to place herself solely in God's hands. By these means, she achieved the regeneration she sought. Christian Science dates its beginnings from this experience.

Between 1870 and 1875, she traveled extensively throughout New England, teaching, writing, and healing others. In 1875, she published her first edition of *Science and Health,* her enduring statement to an unenlightened world enmeshed in the sins of materialism.[18] The book was also her immediate answer to various students and patients who had differed with her over the previous nine years, bringing court litigation and frequent newspaper controversy. In this work, she self-consciously proclaimed her system as different from mesmerism, spiritualism, and other forms of healing then in fashion, advocating instead the absolute healing power of God alone.

Her life continued to flourish, both personally and professionally. In 1877, she married Asa Eddy, and in August 1879, she was granted a charter by the state of Massachusetts to create the Church of Christ Scientist with headquarters in Boston. She followed in 1881 by forming the Massachusetts Metaphysical College, which taught pathology, therapeutics, moral science, and metaphysics according to her teachings. By 1883, Eddy's prestige considerably widened with the inaugural publication of the *Christian Science Journal.* Missionary work around the United States expanded, and numerous churches were founded. Her organization had grown large enough by 1886 that the National Christian Science Association was formed.

The immediate problems Eddy faced, however, were two-pronged. First was the issue of the public controversy with the Dressers over how much of her teachings she had plagiarized from Quimby. Second was the constant threat that practitioners in the various churches were diluting her teachings with everything from Hindu monism to what she later called "malicious animal magnetism." While the Quimby imbroglio raged, she handled her revisionist followers by dissolving her Boston church in 1896. She reconstituted her ministry around the idea of a mother church—one church to which all other smaller and newer congregations answered, instead of a loose-knit confederation of churches over which she could exert little control. Individual sermons were forbidden, and no free interpretation was permitted. The Bible was read as the standard source, followed by relevant passages from *Science and Health* as commentary. In this way, her book became the official pastor in each church and the continuity and centrality of her teachings as revealed by God were ensured.

One measure of Eddy's success is the fact that *Science and Health* had sold more than 91,000 copies by 1895. Another indication of the contemporary viability of her ideas is the worldwide acclaim still accorded the *Christian Science Monitor.* One might expect a one-sided, narrow, and extremist position from a church known for its complete rejection of scientific medicine and all its principles, yet what the Christian Scientists have produced is a newspaper lauded for its objectivity and fairness in reporting international events.

Surely, Eddy's life was the embodiment of the divine principle espoused by the American mental healing churches—that to be a success in the spiritual world is also to be a success in the material one. A charismatic personality with a successful healing message, she was also a shrewd businesswoman in an age when women in business, let alone in medicine and religion, could expect to achieve little. In fact, it is probably fair to say that, as compared to the vicissitudes Freud encountered in keeping his own teachings pure and the plethora of psychoanalytic variants that have arisen since his death, Eddy was eminently more successful in launching, as well as preserving, her therapeutic healing ministry.

Notes

1. A slightly inaccurate and derisive attempt at a history of spiritualism is Peter Washington, *Madame Blavatsky's Baboon: A History of the Mystics, Mediums, and Misfits Who Brought Spiritualism to New York* (New York: Schocken Books, 1995). An outstanding scholarly presentation of the same subject is Ann Braude, *Radical Spirits: Spiritualism and Women's Rights in Nineteenth-Century America* (Boston: Beacon Press, 1989). An informative collection of essays from the same period is Howard Kerr and Charles L. Crow, eds., *The Occult in America: New Historical Perspectives* (Urbana: University of Illinois Press, 1983). Two standard reference works are: J. Stillson Judah, *The History and Philosophy of the Metaphysical Movements in America* (Philadelphia: Westminster Press, 1967); and Robert Laurence Moore, *In Search of White Crows: Spiritualism, Parapsychology, and American Culture* (New York: Oxford University Press, 1977). A history by a nineteenth-century spiritualist is Emma Hardinge Brittan, *Nineteenth Century Miracles: Or, Spirits and Their Work in Every Country of the Earth* (New York: Arno Press, 1976). For a regional study, see Gail Thain Parker, *Mind Cure in New England: From the Civil War to World War I* (Hanover, NH: University Press of New England, 1973).

2. Uriah Clark, *Plain Guide to Spiritualism* (Boston: W. White & Co., 1863).

3. Ibid., p. 172.

4. Ibid., p. 173.

5. Ibid., p. 174.

6. Judah, *History and Philosophy.*

7. Michael Gomes, *The Dawning of the Theosophical Movement* (Wheaton, IL: Theosophical Publishing House, 1987). See also Michael Gomes, *Theosophy in the Nineteenth Century: An Annotated Bibliography* (New York: Garland, 1994). For scholarly views, see Bruce F. Campbell, *Ancient Wisdom Revived: A History of the Theosophical Movement* (Berkeley: University of California Press, 1980); and K. Paul Johnson, *The Masters Revealed: Madame Blavatsky and the Myth of the Great White Lodge* (Albany: State University of New York Press, 1994). For a sympathetic view by a spiritualist, see S. L. Cranston, *HPB: The Extraordinary Life and Influence of Helena Blavatsky, Founder of the Modern Theosophical* (New York: G. P. Putnam's Sons, 1993).

8. The standard history is Charles S. Braden, *Spirits in Rebellion: The Rise and Development of New Thought* (Dallas: Southern Methodist University Press, 1963).

9. W. F. Evans, *Mental Medicine* (Boston: H. H. Carter, 1872); *Soul and Body* (Boston: Colby & Rich, 1875); *The Divine Law of Cure* (Boston: H. H. Carter, 1881); *The Primitive Mind Cure* (Boston: H. H. Carter, 1885); and *Esoteric Christianity and Mental Therapeutics* (Boston: H. H. Carter & Kerrick, 1886).

10. Quoted in Judah, *History and Philosophy,* pp. 160–168.

11. Julius A. Dresser, *The True History of Mental Science: The Facts Concerning the Discovery of Mental Healing* (Boston: Ellis, 1899).

12. Annetta G. Dresser, *The Philosophy of P. P. Quimby, with Selections from His Manuscripts and a Sketch of His Life* (Boston: Ellis, 1895). See also Phineas Parkhurst Quimby, *The Quimby Manuscripts,* ed. Horatio W. Dresser (New York: Thomas Y. Crowell, 1921).

13. Henry Wood, *Ideal Suggestion Through Mental Photography: A Restorative System for Home and Private Use, Preceded by a Study of the Laws of Mental Healing* (Boston: Lee & Shepard, 1893), pp. 107–108.

14. Ibid., p. 110.

15. James Dillet Freeman, *The Story of Unity* (Lee's Summit, MO: Unity School of Christianity, 1954); see also T. E. Witherspoon, *Myrtle Fillmore, Mother of Unity* (Unity Village, MO: Unity Books, 1977).

16. Ralph Waldo Trine, *In Tune with the Infinite: Or, Fullness of Peace, Power, and Plenty* (New York: Thomas Y. Crowell, 1897). For Trine's influence on Henry Ford, see Ralph Waldo Trine, *The Power That Wins: Henry Ford and Ralph Waldo Trine in an Intimate Talk on Life, the Inner Things, the Things of the Mind and Spirit, and the Inner Powers and Forces That Make for Achievement* (Indianapolis: Bobbs-Merrill, 1929).

17. There is no dearth of biographies on Mary Baker Eddy: Georgine Milmine, *The Life of Mary Baker G. Eddy and the History of Christian Science* (Lincoln: University of Nebraska Press, 1993); Robert Peel, *Mary Baker Eddy: The Years of Authority* (New York: Holt, Rinehart & Winston, 1977); Julius Silberger, *Mary Baker Eddy: An Interpretive Biography of the Founder of Christian Science* (Boston: Little, Brown, 1980); Norman Beasley, *The Cross and the Crown: The History of Christian Science* (New York: Duell, Sloan & Pearce, 1952); and Mark Twain, *Christian Science* (Buffalo, NY: Prometheus Books, 1986).

18. Mary Baker Eddy, *Science and Health, with a Key to the Scriptures* (Boston: Christian Science Publishing Co., 1875).

Chapter Eight

Psychical Research, Scientific Psychotherapy, and the Psychology of Religion

ON FEBRUARY 9, 1886, PROFESSOR WILLIAM JAMES OF HARVARD University, acting as official agent of the American Society for Psychical Research and head of the society's Committee on Hypnotism, began yet another of his by then frequent experiments with the medium Leonora Piper, the wife of a common tailor and the healthy mother of two children. He had been investigating her powers for the past year.[1] With Piper's prior consent, James began talking in soothing tones to induce a light hypnotic trance. After a couple of minutes, her eyes began to close. James then moved his hands several times in an upward motion in front of her body, instructing her to open her eyes. Her trance was deep, however, and he found he could hardly recall her to consciousness. Finally, she awakened from this sleeplike trance into a state of waking trance consciousness. She was able to report that she felt so weak that she could hardly move or speak.

James then tried several of the usual tests. He pricked her arm with a small needle, but she appeared to feel nothing. She could not seem to clench her fist on command. When he raised his hand to scratch his nose, she raised her hand to scratch her nose. When James pulled on his earlobe, she pulled on hers. James even made a small incision in her left wrist that remained open but did not bleed. All the while, she kept trying to fall into a state of sleep once again. Finally, James impressed upon her that she should not fall asleep but should remain awake and guess cards with him before he awakened her from the trance altogether. James flipped through a deck of playing cards as Piper called out the numbers and the suits without seeing them, and he separated the hits and the misses into piles. James observed that she was always able to guess at the cards as rapidly as he could draw them from the deck.

Finally, he brought her out of the trance. The instant she was awake, the small incision in her wrist began to ooze blood.[2] Later, James reported that she had named more cards correctly than would have been expected. Upon being asked about the procedure, Piper remarked that she did not actually see the cards but simply named whichever ones came into her mind.

Thus began an important episode in the annals of psychical research and in the history of scientific psychotherapy. It was important for psychical research because Piper was soon to become the first paid and most well-studied subject in the early history of the parapsychological experiment. It was important for psychology because, under the aegis of the first organized professional society in America devoted to the experimental study of the mind-body problem, James had empirically demonstrated the induction of a true altered state of consciousness different from sleep and normal wakefulness, all the phenomena of which he later showed could be replicated under controlled laboratory conditions. And it was important for psychophysiology in that, although no conclusive evidence for the existence of the supernormal had yet been found, it was abundantly clear that in this altered state the human organism had remarkable powers of control over normally involuntary bodily processes and perhaps even access to heightened powers of perception, memory, attention, and cognition.

James's experiments were part of a larger burgeoning effort to make sense of public phenomena that had reached almost epidemic proportions by the 1880s. The situation in Boston was emblematic. Magnetic healers, phrenologists, herbalists, aura readers, and mediums represented a large transient population that went in and out of the city giving forecasts of business, health, and personal relationships to all who would subscribe. As part of a vast network, local spiritualist groups and lecture bureaus dotted the national landscape to handle engagements. A slew of wildcat newspapers devoted exclusively to spiritualist topics arose to keep people informed about these engagements.

The most long lived of these periodicals nationally was the *Banner of Light,* published in Boston from 1857 to 1907. Advertising itself as "the oldest journal in the world devoted to spiritual philosophy" and "a first-class family newspaper," the *Banner* was issued as an eight-page weekly by Colby & Rich, publishers and proprietors, aided by "a large corps of able writers." It contained a literary department, reports on spiritual lectures, a section of original essays, editorials, a "spirit message" department, a section reporting on spiritual phenomena, and "contributions from the most talented writers in the world." In addition, for those who subscribed by mail, the publishers offered a mail-order catalog of "spiritual, progressive, reformatory, and miscellaneous books" from England and America.

Another example of the flourishing state of the times in Boston can be seen in a directory made available to the public by the New England Eclectic Bureau, which specialized in providing lecturers and test mediums to spiritualist societies.[3] The directory included a calendar with names and addresses, listing a dozen spiritual seances daily. It gave the location of spiritualist churches and newspapers, of bookstores, and of mail-order houses specializing in occult and spiritualist literature.

The directory also contained advertising for more than seventy inspirational healers; trance lecturers; practitioners who treated with "soul-currents"; astrologists specializing in Chaldaic and Egyptian systems; doctors offering pure vegetable preparations, massage, vapor baths, the laying on of hands, and electrical therapy; and mediums who would diagnose and cure illness, as well as conduct developing circles and cast natal charts.

It showed that practitioners worked out of their homes, rented storefronts and lecture halls, and advertised out of local hotels for all manner of activity. L. Barnicot, electromagnopath, lecturer, and psychometrist of 125 Tremont Street, Boston, for instance, advertised that he treated all general diseases with success, especially such nervous affections as paralysis, insomnia, and constipation, giving particular attention, he said, to ladies and children. He could diagnose without information from the patient and even on the basis of a written letter accompanied by a lock of hair. Abbie N. Burnham, public lecturer and test medium of Chandler Street, announced that she was available to "attend funerals." Dr. W. A. Hale, C.M.D., of 46 Russell Street, Charlestown, advertised himself as a clairvoyant physician and surgeon. The Boston Health Foods and Glen Mills Agency, at 40 Boylston Street, sold specially handled cereal products under the banner "To think well, breathe well, and eat well, is to live well." Dr. J. B. Cherry's Botanic Drug Store, 157 Shawmut Avenue, offered to remove tapeworms in three hours ("No fee asked unless the entire worm, with head, is expelled"). Lomis F. Jones, of 17 East Canton Street, offered spirit portraits in crayon. Dr. Stansbury, who had offices in both Boston and San Francisco, advertised the Elixir of Life Tonic and Nervine for all nervous debility in both sexes; Sea-Moss Hair Tonic, which promoted hair growth and prevented both dandruff and premature graying; and Wild-Fire Liniment, fully guaranteed for man or beast. A list was even included of more than a dozen occult bed-and-breakfast arrangements, the editors announcing to all visitors to Boston where to find "pleasant rooms and harmonious surroundings, at reasonable rates."

The decade of the 1880s was one of booming development for the mental healing community in Boston. What had previously been a variegated network of individual experiments in the supernatural soon became a collective social phenomenon. Finally, in September of 1885, the spiritualists of Boston got their own church, named the First Spiritualist Temple. Erected by Marcellus Ayer at a cost of $250,000, the temple was located on the corner of Newbury and Exeter Streets in Boston's fashionable Back

Bay. It was a large brownstone and granite building of Romanesque style, completely heated by steam. It contained ten public rooms (with seating capacities from 100 to 1,300), which were used for library, lecture, school, and seance purposes, and these also included additional office, class, and reception spaces. Run by the Spiritual Fraternity, the temple held regular programs each week, including a Sunday morning service, followed by a children's school, Sunday evening lectures, Wednesday evening socials, and a Friday meeting for women. Through the First Spiritualist Temple, humans could be in constant communication with the spirit world; miraculous healings were proclaimed a regular occurrence; higher consciousness seemed almost at hand.

But there were plenty of skeptics, as well. In some cases, local citizens took the law into their own hands to investigate mediums who claimed to bring the dead back to life. Hannah V. Ross, for instance, assisted by her husband, Charles, advertised widely between 1883 and 1887 that she was able to produce "full-form materializations"—not just a voice in a disembodied head. The *Banner of Light* reported on one of her sittings, held on December 27, 1886, which had been attended by sixteen distinguished ladies and gentlemen, some of whom had been regular attendees at Mrs. Ross's seances before. On that occasion, the *Banner* reported:

> Mr. Brackett's [deceased] niece, Bertha, came; she was quite strong, and passed around the room, vivaciously greeting all in her characteristically pleasant way. Mr. B. said, "You are not quite as tall as you are at some other seances." She replied, "I come here just as I am in spirit-life; in my feelings and actions I am, and always expect to be, a child." The appearance of Bertha attracted much attention. She is a most singular embodiment of youthful beauty and child-like affection.

A week later, according to the *New York Times,* a party of concerned citizens disrupted the proceedings at one of Mrs. Ross's materializations, which were held in an almost completely darkened room. It had been agreed that at a certain moment, each member of the party should seize one of the "spirits," as well as the medium and her husband. A moment or two before the signal was given, one of the party was conversing with a materialized spirit. The young man seized the shadow by the hand and with a firm grip yanked it into the middle of the room. The light was turned on, and a stalwart man seized Mr. Ross in his arms just as that gentleman pulled his revolver. Others securely held Mrs. Ross and grabbed several "spooks" in a cabinet. Close investigation showed four boys and a little girl inside the cabinet and an ingenious mechanical contrivance that operated a hidden door.[4]

Members of the lay public were not the only ones interested in settling the question of spiritualism. By the 1860s and 1870s, vituperative criticism of both spiritualists and mental healers had begun to spew forth from the pen of an increasing number of physicians, educators, and lawyers. Commissions were organized to investigate the claims of the occult. In 1857, for instance, Henry Lawrence Eustis, a professor of engineering at Harvard, brought Frederick Willis, a divinity student, before the faculty and accused him of fraud. Willis was charged with cheating while conducting seances with Harvard faculty and students, and he was expelled, although he strenuously protested his innocence. Willis was taken in by the well-known Unitarian minister and ardent abolitionist Thomas Wentworth Higginson, who publicly testified to his genuineness as a medium. Soon the editor of a local Boston newspaper devised a scheme to boost circulation, offering $500 to any medium who would submit to investigation by a distinguished group of Harvard professors, made up of Benjamin Peirce, Louis Agassiz, E. N. Horsford, and B. A. Gould. Famous mediums were paraded in, including the Davenport brothers and Kate Fox, and numerous seances were held, but the results were inconclusive. Newspapers reported phenomena that appeared, both real and contrived. No money was ever paid, and the Harvard professors never published a report of their findings—only a warning against the contaminating influence of spirit communication, which, they said, "surely tends to lessen the truth of men and the purity of women." In the end, the commission and the public controversy that surrounded it served to further legitimize, rather than quell, the activities of the spiritualists because of the frenzy of attention.[5]

In Philadelphia, a similar situation developed. An ardent devotee of spiritualism gave the University of Pennsylvania an endowed chair in philosophy on the condition that the university trustees convene a panel

to investigate impartially spiritual phenomena.[6] Named after its bene-
factor, the Seybert Commission for Investigating Modern Spiritualism
was made up of such distinguished figures as Professor George Fuller-
ton; William Pepper, the university provost; and Silas Weir Mitchell, the
famous neurologist. They gave their report in May 1887, covering only
an investigation of local evidence. The commission had undertaken a
study of slate writing—in which spirits write a communication on one of
the two slates screwed together and held out of sight by a medium sitting
at a table. They investigated several professional mediums, although they
lamented their inability to attract any amateurs who had spontaneously
manifested this capacity. They also investigated the phenomenon of
spirit rapping. The final estimate of the commission was that all who
came before them were either proven fraudulent or, even if genuine,
were incapable of eliciting the desired effects at the time of the commission's scrutiny. Subsequently, the report served only to confirm the opinions of the medical men and increase the ire of the mental healers.

Mainstream medicine, too, provided skeptics. The youthful Oliver
Wendell Holmes Sr., who later became a professor of anatomy and physiology at Harvard and the famed "poet at the breakfast table," had written
on *Homeopathy and Its Kindred Delusions* in 1842.[7] Homeopaths, and those
who advocated treatment by that system, he likened to past believers in
such delusions as the "Royal Touch" for scrofula, weapon salve, tar water,
and the infamous case of Perkin's tractors. A spate of sophisticated rejoin-
ders to Holmes's essay by distinguished homeopaths followed. By 1850,
however, Holmes had softened his judgment somewhat when appointed
to a committee to review expulsion of a member from the exclusively allopathic Massachusetts Medical Society for homeopathic leanings.[8]

The noted New York neurologist William Alexander Hammond, former surgeon general and a founder of the American Neurological Association, launched his own attack on the mental healers in an essay he
contributed to the *North American Review* in 1870, in which he explained
alleged psychic phenomena by the laws of science. A committed materialist, Hammond had little patience for explanations other than the physiological, so that his position was to analyze spiritualism by referring to
all such manifestations as "symptoms of psychopathology." His essay was

soon reprinted in book form and then, in 1876, expanded into a large volume, in which he stated that belief in the supernatural was one of the essential causes of mental illness.[9]

The American Society for Psychical Research

THE FIRST SYSTEMATIC AND IN-DEPTH ATTEMPT to investigate the claims of spiritualists and mental healers began after 1885 in Boston with the founding of the American Society for Psychical Research.[10] The society was launched through influential members of the American Association for the Advancement of Science; its first meetings were held in the prestigious quarters of the American Academy of Arts and Sciences; and its original research committees were all chaired by distinguished Harvard professors in science, medicine, and philosophy.

The main work of the society was to apply modern techniques of scientific investigation to the claims of spiritualism and mental healing. Whereas the organizers left the question open as to whether they would be able to marshal evidence for the existence of the supernatural, they did expect to uncover what they called any underlying and consistent "laws of mental action." In this regard, the work of the committees was particularly instructive.

The Committee on Thought Transference, for example, led by the research physiologist Henry Pickering Bowditch, then also dean of Harvard Medical School, sent out circulars and public notices asking any "sensitives" or mediums to come forth, but the committee did not receive a single reply. It concluded that "in this community, those who profess to believe in the genuineness of the phenomena of 'mind-reading' are not at present disposed to subject their convictions to the test of scientific experiment."[11]

Another aspect of the committee's work, however, lay in the commitment to a rigorous application of statistical methods. Two major projects were undertaken. One was a collation done by E. C. Pickering and Charles Peirce of responses to a circular that attempted to measure thought transference, as gauged by the relative number of right and wrong guesses made by respondents to independently described events. In this case, the "event" consisted of words or diagrams in an envelope, the content of which was known only to the experimenters. A total of 210 subjects gave 10,650 separate judgments. The results suggested that thought transference was not a common trait in the population tested but that scattered individuals showed remarkable talents probably worth further study.

The second project was undertaken by Professor Pickering alone, who had worked on an analysis of recorded observations of star magnitudes. A large amount of laboratory observations existed that could be submitted to statistical analysis, and Pickering was interested in testing for the existence of thought transference between recorder and observer. If thought transference existed here, he reasoned, then a serious error might be present in many scientific investigations. But in the end, his reexamination of stellar observations found no such effect.[12]

Of greater consequence for future developments in scientific psychotherapy was the society's Committee on Hypnotism, led by William James and his cohorts: James Jackson Putnam, head of the Outpatient Department for Nervous and Mental Diseases at the Massachusetts General Hospital, and Morton Prince, assistant physician for nervous and mental diseases at the Boston City Hospital. Charged with the experimental investigation of all aspects of hypnotic phenomena, James had fitted up a psychological laboratory at the Lawrence Scientific School, in Cambridge, which was essentially a research facility at the university. Here, James commandeered Harvard undergraduates as his first subjects and carried on extensive studies in hypnosis, crystal gazing, and automatic writing.

We have a most instructive account of James's hypnotic activities reported in the journal *Science*. James was described as entrancing one of his subjects, Governeur M. Charnochan, a Harvard student, before the society's membership at a meeting on January 12, 1886:

> The meeting closed with some remarkable experiments by Dr. William James, who mesmerized Mr. Carnegie [Charnochan], one of the committee on hypnotism. While the latter was in the trance, Dr. James told him he could not see the chairman, with the effect of rendering him blind to that officer. Placing a prism in front of Mr. Carnegie's eye, so as to produce two images on his retina, Dr. James asked what he saw. The

answer showed that he saw only one chairman, and therefore remained blind to one of the two images. This is believed to be quite a new fact in hypnotism. To show that although the subject adopts any suggestions made to him as to his sensory images, no matter how false the suggestion, yet he has extreme delicacy of perception, the following experiment was made: the subject was made to see an imaginary photograph of President Cleveland on a blank sheet of paper; the photograph was made, in the subject's vision, to leave the sheet of paper and travel around the room; behind Mr. Carnegie's back the paper was turned upside down; the photograph was now made to seem to Mr. Carnegie to return to the paper, which was handed to him; he immediately turned it about to its previous position. Thus an hypnotic subject can be made to believe in a sensation which is unreal, and yet can distinguish between two ends of a blank piece of paper.[13]

This technique was to become an important tool in the development of scientific psychotherapy precisely because it was a way to artificially expose in the laboratory a host of phenomena that normally lay outside the field of conscious awareness. For the first time, investigators had the means to scientifically manipulate hidden mental processes and, by so doing, to verify the reality of the subconscious.

Further, the Committee on Hypnotism was soon to reinforce the use of hypnotism as a diagnostic and therapeutic agent by the subsequent work of Putnam and Prince in the local outpatient departments of two of Boston's most prestigious hospitals. As hypnotism revealed more about how certain symptoms could be controlled by subconscious ideas, it became a valuable aid in the diagnosis and treatment of true organic injury to muscles, because hysterical paralysis almost always could be alleviated under hypnosis whereas paralysis from organic causes could not. And once the difference between functional and organic disturbances became important in therapeutic interventions in the hospitals, hypnotism then became an acceptable topic in the instruction of medical students as well.

James not only led the research on hypnotism, but he also headed the Committee to Investigate Mediumistic Phenomena. In the opening months, it had been widely circulated that the society was interested in investigating genuine mediums, but no responses had been forthcoming. Then, in the fall of 1885, James made what has been judged one of the most momentous discoveries in the early annals of psychical research when he came upon the aforementioned Leonora Evelina Simonds Piper, a "sensitive" who exhibited apparently genuine clairvoyant powers while entranced.

Born in Nashua, New Hampshire, in 1859 into an English family of Congregationalist descent, Leonora Simonds was raised in Methuen, Massachusetts, and married William R. Piper of Boston in 1881. They moved to Boston shortly after their marriage and began to have children.[14]

Mrs. Piper belonged to a family that was free from a history of nervous maladies. During her childhood, however, she suffered occasional episodes where she lost consciousness and had visionlike experiences in which she appeared to have knowledge of distant events. Until sometime between 1882 and 1883, she enjoyed otherwise perfect health. At that time, she developed a tumor, which followed an accidental blow from a hammer, and she feared cancer. Her husband's parents advised her to seek medical consultation with a medium, so to oblige them, she went to see a blind man, J. R. Cocke. Cocke first advertised himself as an unconsciously entranced musical medium. He helped develop mediumship in others, gave magnetic treatments and free medical exams, and did psychometric readings from a lock of hair sent to him in the mail. Later calling himself Dr. Cocke, he also claimed he was assisted by powerful and intelligent spirits who endeavored to bring the best influences to those in his care. In particular, he claimed to be controlled by a French doctor named Finny.

Here, in one of Cocke's circles, Mrs. Piper had her first trance experience. Later, in another group meeting, she entered into a deep trance and received her first spirit communication. This occurred on a Sunday evening at Cocke's home in 1884. Cocke, already in a clairvoyant condition, began moving around the circle, placing his hands on the head of each person in turn. When he reached Piper, hardly had he put his hands on her when her body went into a paroxysm of chills. She saw in front of her "a flood of light in which many strange faces appeared," while "a hand seemed to pass to and fro" before her face. She then rose from her chair and, unaided, walked to a table in the center of the room where there was some writing material. Picking up the pencil and paper, she wrote hurriedly for a few minutes. When she had finished, she handed the paper to a member of the circle and returned to her seat. To the utter shock of the person receiving the note, it was a message from a deceased son.[15]

After this public display, Piper received numerous requests for sittings, one of which came from Elizabeth Gibbens, the mother-in-law of William James. Gibbens's housemaid gossiped with James's housemaid about the matter, and James himself became involved. James was initially skeptical but became quickly convinced of Piper's extraordinary powers after a sitting had been arranged for him and his wife. James had also sent his sons around to Piper's neighborhood, and the boys returned with news that she was a perfectly normal mother and well thought of by her neighbors. James introduced Mrs. Piper to the American Society for Psychical Research, saw to it that she received some remuneration for her efforts as a subject of investigation, and, for the next eighteen months, personally arranged her sittings. Eventually, a Frenchman she called "Dr. Phenuit" was to emerge as her first "control." Later, she would be taken over by the spirit of a then recently departed young man, George Pellew, and after him by a band of three spirits. Finally, after 1905, she became a conduit for the departed spirit of Richard Hodgson, one of the society's investigators.

From the beginning, almost everyone of any consequence in Cambridge and Boston held a seance with Piper: Bowditch, Pickering, Putnam, Prince, Mitchell, President Eliot of Harvard, even Charles Sanders Peirce. She soon became the most extensively studied medium of the era, although others were investigated as well. Stenographers were hired, verbatim reports collected, and much traveling undertaken. Eventually, the cost of these reports would strain the society to its limit, but the great historical value of the transcripts is that they are the earliest and most complete records of the interchange between a scientific observer and a subject in a somnambulistic state. The transition to the fifty-minute psychotherapeutic hour, where the physician would place the patient in a similar state to recall repressed or forgotten memories, was not far off. But detailed records that included the entire subject-experimenter exchange would not appear in the American literature until after 1910.

Piper became what James called the "white crow," a metaphor he took from the logical syllogism "All crows are black. Therefore, if I see a crow, it will be black." A single exception, however, such as the reported existence of a white crow, destroys the universality of the general rule.[16] For James, Piper destroyed the most cherished objections of reductionistic science and medicine to the investigation of inner phenomena. Physicians were reluctant to admit the reality of mediumship, preferring to deem it either artful shamming or a symptom of psychopathology. Yet here was a healthy mother who could spontaneously enter these states and return again to lead a regular life.

Thus, the naturally occurring trances of mediums and the ability to replicate them under hypnosis opened an entirely new field of inquiry in physiological psychology, because they suggested ways in which cognitive ideas could be translated into both pathological emotions and physical symptoms. Once the pathology of the emotions became an object of scientific scrutiny, psychology could at last expand beyond the sterile measurement of the senses and the introspective analysis of consciousness to at last embrace the problem of motivation within its purview. In the beginning, all the scientific psychologists could do was ask "what?" and respond with description. Now, with the advent of new hypnotic techniques, there was a "how." Thought and action were governed by vast forces in the subconscious.

Finally, the relation of the mediumistic trance to the artificially induced state of hypnosis set the stage for a close association between abnormal psychology and psychical research, a combined effort that eventually came to be known as "experimental psychopathology." This conceptual association lasted for more than a quarter of a century and caused psychical research to be equated with experimental psychology in the eyes of the general public in America.

The Society's Findings

Although the psychical researchers were unable to discover any evidence for the reality of life after death, they made significant contributions to a modern dynamic psychology of the unconscious—"depth psychology," as it has also been called, the theoretical framework underlying almost all contemporary techniques of psychotherapy.

In the first place, investigation of mental healers established the reality of the unconscious. There are states of possible experience beyond the condition in which we normally find ourselves on a daily basis, and there does seem to be a barrier that we are able to continually maintain that keeps these states hidden from view. But under certain circumstances, such as shock, fatigue, and physical illness, these alternate realities make themselves known to the normal everyday waking state, making it seem as if an invasion from below has taken place. New thoughts flood into the field of awareness. Moods change. Thoughts, words, and actions are affected. Meanwhile, others may notice the differences even when, at first, the affected individual herself does not see them.

The investigation of mental healers also revealed a number of useful techniques for gaining access to unconscious states. The most widely studied was light hypnosis. One could possibly make the subject go into a deep unconscious trance and be completely forgetful of what happened afterward. But researchers found that if they kept subjects under light hypnosis, it was possible to remain in constant communication with them. Hypnosis therefore became regarded as both a technique and a state. Researchers used the technique of hypnotic induction to alter their subjects' state of consciousness. At the same time, whenever subjects were found able to go into altered states by various means on their own—whatever the subjects themselves might call their experiences— the researchers came to refer to all such states as "hypnotic."

Another technique that psychical researchers borrowed from mental healers was that of crystal gazing. Seemingly a variation on the induced hypnotic trance, the technique involved staring at a source of light that has been reflected off a shiny surface. Recall that the Concord transcendentalists such as Thoreau would induce a meditative trance by sitting near a riverbank or by Walden Pond looking at the reflection of the sun off the surface of the water. To enter their healing trances, spiritualists used crystals hung in the sunlight. Medical doctors found that asking a patient to look at any source of light reflected off the surface of a glass of water was sufficient to induce a dissociation, or splitting, of consciousness.

Yet another technique psychical researchers appropriated was automatic writing. In this technique, an experimental subject seated at a table in the laboratory was put into a light trance. A pencil was then put in the subject's hand and a screen placed on the table between her eyes and the paper. The hypnotic trance would create a dissociated condition, so that the hand could be asked questions and could write answers independently of a conversation that might be taking place between the experimenter and the subject. In this way, information not normally available to the subject in the waking state could be made available to the experimenter through the subject's unconscious.

What the generic characteristics of these techniques really were soon became obvious to the experimenters. The very first prerequisite was the ability to relax. This meant that the subject was completely at ease with the experimenter, in a state analogous to the relief a sick person feels in the presence of a trusted healer expecting to be cured in some way. Eventually, the subject was asked to sit or lie down to reduce muscle tension. Instructions then guided the subject into a progressive condition of physical relaxation of the body. Mental relaxation and inward calmness naturally seemed to follow.

Second, in all these techniques, psychical researchers were aware that some means had to be employed to carry the subject's attention over the threshold of waking consciousness and into the unconscious. Hypnotic induction was one means. Other means included crystal gazing, systematic forms of breath control, and the reliving of certain life experiences, including accidents and illness. The point was that, once the subject was completely relaxed, physically and mentally, it was then possible to induce a transition from the normal everyday waking state into the hypnotic condition.

Finally, it was apparent to the psychical researchers that, once the hypnotic trance had been induced in a willing subject, the entire contents of the person's world of internal mental images became available. Their hope was that the secrets of dreams might be unlocked. Religious visions could be understood. The hallucinations of the insane might now become more manageable. Discovering the nature of these images held below the surface of the mind and mastering the art of substituting one for another became a primary interest for a small group of Boston physicians, philosophers, psychologists, and clergymen that came to be known as the so-called Boston School of Psychopathology.

The International Psychotherapeutic Scene

TO TAKE THE CLAIMS OF SPIRITUALISTS and mental healers seriously, the investigators of the American Society for Psychical Research succeeded in applying the most advanced techniques of scientific investigation then known to a study of the paranormal. Though they failed to show any evidence for the reality of life after death, they were able to articulate a variety of theories about unconscious mental life in general and to abstract out of the welter of techniques used by the clairvoyants and mediums a handful of tested methods appropriate to the diagnosis and treatment of functional disorders of the nervous system that had no underlying pathology.

The ruling dictum of medicine up to that time was that there could be no form of mental illness without some underlying organic disturbance, such as a lesion or tumor. Increasingly, however, physicians were seeing physical symptoms with no such underlying evidence of organic disturbance. These included fainting, dizziness, paralysis of limbs, epileptic-like attacks, vomiting, nausea, and intestinal episodes, in addition to exhaustion, nervousness, and melancholia, or what we would call today depression. The label neuroses was given to the presentation of such symptoms, the identification of which led to such new medical diagnoses as neurasthenia, hysteria, and what came to be called "multiple personality." Their origin could be found in the aftermath of traumatic shock, such as war wounds; they appeared with increasing frequency as a result of train wrecks, where passengers escaped physical harm but experienced deep emotional pain and fear. Eventually, their origin would be traced to even more ephemeral sources, such as prolonged psychological conflict, usually of a sexual nature. The fact that psychological conflict could lead to actual physical symptoms came to be known as the psychogenic hypothesis. The origin of the physical symptom, in other words, instead of a lesion, could be the result of a buried idea. Since the origin of the physical symptom was psychological, the new investigators reasoned that, by inducing a hypnotic trance, the hidden idea could be discovered and either banished or replaced with a less malignant thought. When they did so, they found the offending symptoms would disappear. This process involved interacting with the patient, listening to his or her personal life story, and talking with them in response. Hence, the field of psychotherapy was born.

Psychology and psychiatry as academic professions were slow to acknowledge these developments. In fact, in an attempt to define themselves as legitimate sciences, they found numerous ways to deny all claims regarding the reality of the unconscious. Beginning in the 1880s, psychology in American universities looked toward the experimental laboratories of Germany for their study of higher mental processes of reasoning and sensation, while asylum psychiatry continued to focus on the biological basis of mental illness and problems of diagnosis and classification. Investigation of such phenomena as hysteria and mediumship was initially left to psychical researchers and to a budding new class of specialists in medicine called neurologists.

Internationally, research into the dynamic origins of neuroses centered in France, particularly on the work of Jean-Martin Charcot at the Salpêtrière in Paris, a sprawling hospital for the insane holding mostly women with incurable disorders. Charcot began experimenting with hypnosis and discovered that physical symptoms could be induced and removed in his hysteric patients by hypnotic suggestion alone. He developed some neurological theories about hypnosis that were challenged by Hyppolyte Bernheim at the medical school in Nancy, and a furious argument developed that drew international attention to the phenomenon of psychogenesis. Isolated researchers in Austria, Germany, the Netherlands, Sweden, Poland, Russia, and Italy soon appeared who were interested in investigating the French claims, Josef Breuer and the young Sigmund Freud among them. But to the west of France, a loose-knit international psychotherapeutic alliance developed that was focused on the work of the French investigators but that was diffused throughout the research committees of the Society for Psychical Research in England and the American Society for Psychical Research and was further reinforced by continued investigations of mediums in countries such as Switzerland.

The model of consciousness used to explain such processes as psychogenesis was dissociation theory—the idea that the buried thought was a split-off fragment of the waking state that had become dissociated from the larger worldview of the person. Consciousness, however, was conceived as a plurality of states ranging from the pathological to the transcendent, with normal everyday waking consciousness being somewhere in the middle and only one state out of many. Meanwhile, within this international psychotherapeutic alliance, there was also an emphasis on the growth-oriented dimension of personality. Personality had a higher, transcendent side to it that the therapist could appeal to in the patient's recovery from illness. Positing a transcendent dimension to personality also created the conditions for a psychology of health that identified psychic experiences and religious visions as evidence of superior functioning, rather than as signs of mental illness, as medical doctors wanted to claim.

For approximately a forty-year period, between 1880 and 1920, efforts were made by investigators to construct a cross-cultural comparative psychology of the subconscious, using the entranced medium as the subject most appropriate to generate the basic data of this new science. Within this international alliance, the so-called Boston School of Psychopathology played a major role in defining the growth-oriented dimension of personality. This involved articulating the role of spiritual experience in the development of character and establishing an appeal to the higher and more morally intact side of personality as the standard for psychotherapeutic treatment.

The Boston School of Psychopathology

THE BOSTON SCHOOL OF PSYCHOPATHOLOGY was made up of an informal knot of investigators including William James, James Jackson Putnam, Richard Clarke Cabot, and Morton Prince, many of whom had direct ties either by birth or by upbringing with the intuitive psychology of character formation bequeathed to them by Emerson and the Concord transcendentalists.[17] Indeed, several of these investigators, such as James and Putnam, saw themselves as direct heirs of this intellectual tradition. These younger investigators, however, were all reared in a much more scientific and Darwinian environment than their predecessors and hence were charged with refashioning the transcendentalist legacy into the more rigorous scientific dictates of the age.

Therefore, the prehistory of the Boston School of Psychopathology begins in 1859 with early debates over the theory of natural selection when Darwin's ideas were first introduced into the United States. As a young medical student, William James was a member of the most influential Darwinian circle in America. While others took up the details of evolution of plants and animals, James was interested in the problem of consciousness—how our conscious choices affect the social and biological evolution of the species; how an abundance of creative thoughts sets the stage for more innovative selection of the most adaptive ones; and how the minds of creative American geniuses work. Citing Emerson and others, James said that their most important trait was that they think not logically, but by analogy.

James had already been exposed to the automatic writing of mediums as a young teenager traveling in England. At the time that he was studying consciousness within the context of Darwinian theory, he was also writing reviews of A. A. Liebeault's theories of hypnosis (later father of the Nancy School under Bernheim) and chastising scientists for not taking the claims of spiritualists seriously. In his 1868 review of Epps Sargent's *Planchette: The Despair of Science,* James maintained that psychic phenomena were destined to change the very shape of science in the future.

The prehistory of the Boston School of Psychopathology also includes the interdependent founding of experimental laboratories in physiology, neuropathology, and psychology at Harvard beginning in the mid-1870s. These endeavors eventually involved testing the claims of mental healers with hypnosis under controlled laboratory conditions using Harvard undergraduates as subjects. From these researches, clinicians such as Putnam and Prince were then justified in applying psychotherapeutic methods to the treatment of patients at both the Massachusetts General Hospital and the Boston City Hospital on a wide scale.

Soon, graduate-level courses on experimental psychopathology were developed as a new field of specialization. Courses sprang up at Clark University, Harvard, and elsewhere. Particularly at Harvard, an informal interlocking curriculum emerged among psychiatry, psychology, and neuropathology that eventually came to include faculty and students from the philosophy department and the Divinity School.

In 1894, James himself was responsible for introducing the psychotherapeutic work of Breuer and Freud to the American psychological public and for retailing the hypnotic work of such French neurologists as Pierre Janet to English-speaking audiences. Moreover, James's point was to show that here was corroboration from both French and German sources for the assertion that American mental healers had been practicing sound methods of psychotherapy all along. He followed with a historic series of public lectures for the Lowell Institute on Exceptional Mental States in 1896, an exposition of dynamic theories of the subconscious both individually and in the social sphere, and in 1898, he successfully championed the rejection of a medical licensing bill that would have required all mental healers to hold a license signed by general practitioners in order to see patients.

The true psychotherapeutic explosion, however, occurred nationwide after 1900, with Boston as its epicenter. Cases of multiple personality were studied for both cause and treatment. Hundreds of patients were being treated each year in the outpatient clinics of local hospitals with psychotherapeutic methods of suggestion, persuasion, light hypnosis, and dream analysis, and with regimes such as social milieu therapy. The historical evidence shows that group psychotherapy began with the class treatment of tuberculosis patients in 1905, first at the Emmanuel Church and then at the Massachusetts General Hospital and elsewhere. At some local hospitals, individual methods of one-to-one psychotherapy were compared in primitive clinical trials for their effectiveness; medical social service was launched; and the professions of psychiatric social work and occupational therapy were founded. Even philosophers such as Josiah Royce saw patients in a psychotherapeutic context, while Cabot, an internist and physician, entertained a psychology of character development.[18]

The Psychology of Religion

THE DRAMATIC EXPANSION of psychotherapy in America after 1900 was particularly quickened by several significant events associated with the acknowledgment that spirituality played a key role in a person's mental health. The first of these was publication of William James's Gifford Lectures on Natural Religion, titled *The Varieties of Religious Experience* (1902). In this work, James focused not on the history of the different denominations or an exposition of doctrinal creeds, but on personal accounts of how people experienced religious phenomena across cultures. The heart of religion is always centered within the interior life of the individual, he said. It is to be known by an exploration of subconscious states of awareness, for there is ample evidence, James maintained, that an understanding of subconscious processes is the doorway to the opening of ultimately transforming experiences that he called mystical. Mystical experiences lie at the heart of all faith traditions, but we hardly know how to regard them, because they are so different from the normal everyday waking state—although, paradoxically, states of mystical awakening, James emphasized, may be the very source of the discursive intellect. Comparing these states to one another and judging which is more authentic is pointless, he concluded, for their true test is always how they enhance the moral and aesthetic aspects of daily functioning. We cannot offhandedly dismiss even the claims of any religion, including those of spiritualists and mental healers, if by their beliefs they contribute to making the world a better place to live.

James's book was widely read in America and abroad and helped define an entirely new area of study that came to be known as the psychology of religion.[19] Although we cannot go into the fate of the psychology of religion as an academic field of study within the universities, one of the most important developments in the field during this period was the Emmanuel movement, an experiment launched by collaborating physicians, psychologists, and clergymen in 1906 to fuse modern scientific psychotherapy with the Christian teachings of moral character development.

The Emmanuel movement began in 1906 when Boston physicians Richard Clarke Cabot, Isador Coriat, and James Jackson Putnam joined with the Episcopal priest Elwood Worcester and his assistant, Samuel McComb, to give weekly lectures on the influence of the mind on the body at Worcester's Emmanuel Church. When they announced at the end of the series that they would hold a clinic and see any interested patients, the next morning almost 200 people were waiting to be seen. The clinic was continued, and soon the church offices and vestry began to resemble the crowded outpatient department at the Massachusetts General Hospital.

In addition to the regular church services, psychotherapeutic meetings held at the Emmanuel Church twice a week drew upwards of 500 people. These were public discussions on the mental and emotional elements in the treatment of disease. There were also smaller group psychotherapy sessions for tuberculosis patients, no bigger than twenty-five persons. Each patient was seen first by one of four neurologists present before patients were seen individually or in groups. In the mornings, office meetings were held by the ministers, called moral clinics, which were followed by house calls in the afternoons.

The movement began in the Emmanuel Church and then spread to surrounding churches in Boston's fashionable Back Bay and to several of the local hospitals. By 1909, it had spread across the United States and had even reached cities in Europe, causing psychotherapeutic practices to be taken up by ministers of various denominations. Books and newspaper articles began to appear in a great flood, and university courses on the subject abounded, in which joint courses were designed for ministers and physicians. At one point, mail-order courses were even made available. W. B. Parker, James's former student, brought out *Psychotherapy,* a home study course of readings that immediately went into two editions and that contained papers by Royce, Cabot, Putnam, Worcester, and others.

In 1909, attacks began on the movement, from Christian business organizations that claimed it was nothing but Christian Science and from medical societies that maintained that ministers were practicing medicine without training or licensing. Cabot and Worcester, the two key leaders of the movement, moved immediately to quell the criticism by shutting down the operations at the church, refusing newspaper interviews, and curtailing all activity except a small, private practice with individuals, which each one kept going without announcing that fact. Within the year, the Emmanuel movement had ceased to be a topic of discussion, and the general sense that there was some kind of international network combining religion and medicine through psychology had dissipated. Yet religion had been duly inoculated. Protestant ministers continued widely to support the new psychotherapeutic ideas for purposes of both individual rehabilitation and group transformation.

The hiatus was only temporary, however, as Cabot and Worcester were to play a major role in the 1920s in fostering the career of Anton Biosen, who later became a co-founder of the clinical pastoral education movement in the United States, which combines psychology and psychotherapy with pastoral counseling and places ministers in clinical settings—an integral component of nearly every divinity school program in the United States today.[20]

As a final word about the Emmanuel movement, a bare indication of how all these historical forces came together can be demonstrated by a single small incident:

At one point, Worcester successfully intervened in the case of a conversion reaction. A young architect had been working outside too long on a construction project in very cold weather. He arrived indoors, freezing cold, in a state of near collapse. The next morning, his right arm was completely paralyzed, and his right knee was drawn up near his chin in an exaggerated and fixed position where it could not be moved by the patient or a physician. By the time Worcester visited the case, two toes had been amputated due to gangrene, partly because of poor circulation from the bizarre position of the leg. Worcester recounted the man's mental state as "the spiritual condition of a mad dog," cursing God for abandoning him and the priest for thinking he could help him.

Worcester visited him twice, the first time talking about the difference between faith and reason and the importance of preparing oneself with the expectation of being healed. On his second visit, Worcester reminded the man about God's infinite capacity for forgiveness and then instructed him in some simple techniques in deep relaxation. The man fell into a deep hypnotic sleep. Worcester then began to talk with him, commanding that he move the paralyzed arm, whereupon the man, still entranced, moved his paralyzed arm by offering to shake hands. Worcester suggested a deeper state of hypnosis and commanded the man to move his rigid leg. The man protested that it would hurt, but Worcester assured him there would be no pain. Next, Worcester gently straightened the man's leg out and placed it slowly down next to the other one. Worcester then summoned the doctor and the nurse waiting in the other room. A few days later, the man was able to walk normally and was pronounced cured.[21]

Here we have a classic case of a traumatic shock—namely, overexposure to the cold—being converted to a physical symptom, the paralysis, or freezing, of a limb. The physician of physical medicine who attended this patient had only physical remedies to suggest, such as amputation, but only as a reaction to the prolonged effect of the trauma. In contrast, Worcester's intervention was psychological in nature. But before he employed it, he had to counter the patient's reluctance, which he did, not by converting him to a point of view, but by suggesting in his presence what was needed: hope, faith, the attitude of expectation, the higher emotion of forgiveness, and so on. The hypnotic relaxation technique was then administered under these conditions, which had the desired salutary results.

On a much larger scale, this small example, and the course of the Emmanuel movement itself, suggests a number of historical conclusions about the entire era.

In the first place, an interdisciplinary effort of scientists, philosophers, and clergymen to test objectively the claims of spiritualists and mental healers in the 1880s led to the discovery of dynamic principles of subconscious life that were subject to repeatable control in a laboratory environment. This, in turn, allowed neurologists and other clinicians to apply these principles in hospital settings to the treatment of an increasing number of patients suffering from functional disorders of the nervous system, or what came to be more technically called the ambulatory psychoneuroses. The urge toward moral and aesthetic personal goals could be a means to harness a patient's will to live, and in this way, psychological and emotional factors associated with any illness or injury could be harnessed in service of healing.

Taking such cases beyond the realm of illness, investigators also began to look at the possibility of a healthy, growth-oriented dimension to human personality through the general study of spiritual experience. The moral and aesthetic dimensions of personality, seen to be the basis for the shaping of character, were then defined by an objective study of the highest states of spiritual consciousness. The development of character, the practice of ethical behavior, and even sound mental and physical health were seen in light of the depth and breadth of a person's interior experience and not merely based on outwardly imposed rule-bound behavior.

Second, there appear to be some interesting parallels between mediumistic trance states investigated by psychical researchers and cases of multiple personality studied by medical psychologists. Both appear to be an example of dissociation, in which a person might exhibit more than one state of consciousness simultaneously. Both permit unexpressed or previously undeveloped sides to a person's personality to find expression. Both allow the individual to speak in a variety of different voices regardless of gender and age differences—a male can speak as a female, while a woman is permitted to speak as a man, and both can speak as a child or an elderly person. Although there is as yet no resolution on whether these are distinctly other personalities speaking through the person or genuine multiples of the same person, one is clearly considered a case of mental illness, while the other suggests more voluntary access to such capacities.

Finally, there is the interesting observation that, while spiritualists and mental healers had been involved in an exploration of higher states of consciousness all along and had always been conversant in techniques for doing so, mainstream Protestant Christians could get the message only once science had investigated the phenomena and declared them genuine. This may be as much a commentary on different levels of culture as it is a statement about the objective science of investigating anomalous events.

The scientific method has played an enormous part in defining the culture of modern mainstream American society, so much so that the scientific point of view has seeped into everyone's lives and, in many cases, has become the unquestioned way in which it is now assumed that we should take the world. The reality of the situation is that the visionary tradition (as well as a wide range of non-Anglo-Saxon ethnic traditions) has always taken the world quite differently as a true alternative tradition to mainstream culture. The development of psychotherapy at the end of the nineteenth century was one way in which the influence of the visionary counterculture penetrated the pervading popular culture, even though it made it only partway into the hard sciences themselves. No better example of this can be found than the introduction of psychoanalysis into mainstream American social thought, which tended to mask an even more potent trend occurring simultaneously in the visionary counterculture: the renewed introduction of Asian ideas into the West, but now on a wider and more unprecedented scale than before.

Notes

1. W. James, "Notes on Echolalia in Mrs. Piper (1886)," reprinted in F. H. Burkhardt, F. Bowers, and I. Skrupskelis, eds., *The Collected Works of William James: Essays in Psychical Research* (Cambridge, MA: Harvard University Press, 1986), p. 19.

2. Described by Ignas Skrupskelis in ibid., p. 408 n. 38.13.

3. New England Eclectic Bureau, *Directory* (n.p., 1891); courtesy of the archives of the Spiritual Fraternity, Brookline, MA.

4. Quoted by Skrupskelis in Burkhardt, Bowers, and Skrupskelis, eds., *Collected Works of William James: Essays in Psychical Research,* p. 402.

5. Robert Laurence Moore, *In Search of White Crows: Spiritualism, Parapsychology, and American Culture* (New York: Oxford University Press, 1977), p. 34. See also Allen Putnam, *Post-Mortem Confessions: Being Letters Written Through a Mortal's Hand by Spirits Who, When in Mortal, Were Officers of Harvard College* (Boston: Countway Medical Library Rare Books; originally published Boston: Colby & Rich, 1886).

6. Seybert Commission, *Preliminary Report of the Commission Appointed by the University of Pennsylvania to Investigate Modern Spiritualism* (Philadelphia: J. B. Lippincott, 1887).

7. Oliver Wendell Holmes Sr., *Homeopathy and Its Kindred Delusions* (Boston: W. D. Ticknor, 1842). See also E. H. Clarke, *Visions: A Study of False Sight (Pseudopia),* with an introduction by O. W. Holmes (Boston: Osgood & Co., 1878).

8. Martin Kaufman, *Homeopathy in America: The Rise and Fall of a Medical Heresy* (Baltimore: Johns Hopkins University Press, 1971), pp. 55–58.

9. Published in book form as W. A. Hammond, *The Physics and Physiology of Spiritualism* (New York: Appleton, 1872), and explained as *Spiritualism and Allied Causes and Conditions of Nervous Derangement* (New York: G. P. Putnam's Sons, 1876).

10. E. I. Taylor, "Psychotherapy, Harvard, and the American Society for Psychical Research, 1884–1889," in *Proceedings of the Twenty-eighth Annual Convention of the Parapsychological Association* (Medford, MA: Tufts University, August 15, 1985), pp. 319–346; E. I. Taylor, "The American Society for Psychical Research, 1884–1889,"

in D. Radin and N. Weiner, eds., *Annual Review in Parapsychology* (Secaucus, NJ: Secaucus Press, 1986).

11. *Proceedings of the American Society for Psychical Research,* 1:1–4 (July 1885–March 1889): 7.

12. Recent investigations at the Princeton Anomalies Research Laboratory suggest that, depending on feedback and intention, the consciousness of normal subjects may exert more of an influence over the operation of machinery than has previously been supposed. See Robert G. Jahn and Brenda Dunne, *Margins of Reality: The Role of Consciousness in the Physical World* (San Diego: Harcourt Brace Jovanovich, 1987).

13. The account is Skrupskelis's in Burkhardt, Bowers, and Skrupskelis, eds., *Collected Works of William James: Essays in Psychical Research,* p. 383.

14. See M. Sage, *Mrs. Piper and the Society for Psychical Research,* trans. and abridged by Noralie Robertson, with a preface by Sir Oliver Lodge (New York: Scott-Thaw Co, 1904); Gardner Murphy, "Leonora Evelina Simonds Piper," in *Notable American Women,* vol. 3 (Cambridge, MA: Harvard University Press, 1971), pp. 73–75; and Skrupskelis's notes in Burkhardt, Bowers, and Skrupskelis, eds., *Collected Works of William James: Essays in Psychical Research,* pp. 394–400.

15. Adapted from Skrupskelis's notes in Burkhardt, Bowers, and Skrupskelis, eds., *Collected Works of William James: Essays in Psychical Research,* p. 398.

16. See, for instance, Moore, *In Search of White Crows.*

17. E. I. Taylor, "The Boston School of Psychotherapy: Science, Healing, and Consciousness in Nineteenth Century New England." These were the unpublished Lowell Lectures of 1982, delivered at the Boston Public Library for the Lowell Institute, in cooperation with the Massachusetts Medical Society and the Boston Medical Library.

18. E. I. Taylor, "Louville Eugene Emerson: Psychotherapy, Harvard, and the Early Boston Scene," *Harvard Medical Alumni Bulletin,* 56:2 (1982): 42–46; and E. I. Taylor, "On the First Use of 'Psychoanalysis' at the Massachusetts General Hospital, 1903–1905," *Journal of the History of Medicine and Allied Sciences,* 43:4 (1988): 447–471.

19. E. I. Taylor, "Psychology of Religion and Asian Studies: The William James Legacy," *Journal of Transpersonal Psychology,* 10:1 (1978): 66–79; and E. I. Taylor, *William James on Consciousness Beyond the Margin* (Princeton, NJ: Princeton University Press, 1996).

20. E. Brooks Holifield, *A History of Pastoral Care in America: From Salvation to Self-Realization* (Nashville: Abingdon, 1983).

21. Sanford Gifford, *The Emmanuel Movement: The Origins of Group Treatment and the Assault on Lay Therapy* (Boston: Countway Medical Library, 1997), pp. 71–71.

Chapter Nine

When the Swamis Came to America

ON SEPTEMBER 11, 1893, SWAMI VIVEKANANDA, A YOUNG HINDU monk of the Ramakrishna order, rose before an audience of 4,000 people in Chicago, Illinois, many of whom were delegates of non-Western religions, and began an oration that was destined to become a decisive event in the history of the American visionary tradition. Dressed in a yellow turban and red mendicant's robes, erect in stature, radiating poise and confidence, and with great eloquence of speech, he immediately captured everyone's attention. "Sisters and brothers of America," he began—only to be interrupted by peals of applause that lasted several minutes.

In his message, he emphasized first that the religions of India were not new, but actually quite ancient. Moreover, the greatest gift India had to offer the world was the twofold teaching of its intense spirituality and its widespread toleration of all faiths. In India, he said, persecuted religions from around the world have been welcomed, just as the most extreme forms of religiosity have been permitted. All religions are accepted as true and universal. So he said, "As different streams having their sources in different places all mingle their water in the sea, so, O Lord, the different paths which men take through different tendencies, various though they appear, crooked or straight, all lead to Thee."[1]

He pointed out that sectarianism, bigotry, and fanaticism had long possessed the Earth. The past had been filled with violence and blood. Individuals, nations, and entire civilizations had disappeared because of these forces, and they had retarded the advancement of humanity. He fervently hoped for an end to all narrow-mindedness, all uncharitable feelings among people, and all persecution by the pen and the sword.

The audience was electrified. And over the course of the next two weeks, as he continued to speak and enthrall them, they would rise repeatedly in standing ovations.

The occasion for the first of Vivekananda's several remarkable presentations was the World's Parliament of Religions, part of the World's Columbian Exposition of 1893.[2] The exposition was held to celebrate the four hundredth anniversary of the discovery of the New World, and it was also meant to be a showcase of scientific progress and technical invention in the nineteenth century. But the proceedings of the parliament turned out to be its most remarkable result. Originally conceived by Charles C. Bonney, a lawyer and ardent Swedenborgian, the parliament was part of a series of congresses held at the fair on subjects as diverse as women, music, engineering, agriculture, temperance, commerce, finance, and religion.

The parliament went on for seventeen days, with sessions from morning until night. The opening meeting was presided over by Cardinal James Gibbons, archbishop of Baltimore. Other speakers included Rabbi Gustav Gottheil, later a founder of the Federation of American Zionists; the Most Reverend Dionysios Latas, archbishop of Zante; and the Reverend Olimpia Brown, one of the first women to be ordained a Unitarian Universalist minister in America. Judge J. S. Hanna spoke on Christian Science; scholars such as C. H. Toy from Harvard, William Wilkinson from the University of Chicago, and Professor F. Max Mueller, a German philologist from Oxford University, spoke on the academic study of religion; Elder Daniel Offord of New Lebanon, New

York, spoke on the Shakers; and the well-known Boston minister Edward Everett Hale delivered a talk on Unitarianism.

Representatives came from Catholic, Jewish, and Protestant organizations. These included Pentecostals, Evangelicals, advocates of the social gospel, both Conservative and Reform Judaism, the Eastern Orthodox Church, numerous Protestant missionaries, scholars in comparative religions, and staunch advocates for the place of women in religion.

Of the 200 official delegates, the largest number from foreign countries came from India and Japan. Among the Japanese delegation was the venerable Zen master Soyen Shaku, whose paper had been translated by his young disciple, Daisetz Taitaro Suzuki. Confucianism, Taoism, Jainism, Zoroastrianism, and, to a limited degree, Islam were represented as well.

No one spoke for the Native American Indian, however. Most of the tribal religions of the world had no delegates, and only Irish Catholics were represented. The Sultan of Turkey refused to send delegates or to become involved in any of the planning. The general assembly of the Presbyterian Church refused to come as well. There were a few tirades in the conservative press about the monstrous absurdities of false faiths of the world that were permitted to speak. Even at the congress, there was a great deal of Christian triumphalism. But despite these controversies, the voices for harmony and reconciliation prevailed. Pluralism and ecumenical dialogue were by far the larger messages, and the meetings were judged a smashing success.

Vivekananda turned out to be the darling of the congress. This was chiefly because of a discrepancy between what the Christians expected and the subsequent mood of the meetings that Vivekananda captured so well. Sub rosa, hidden in the minds of many who planned the event, was the goal that such a congress would show once and for all the superiority of Christianity over all other religions. But so many articulate, thoughtful, and pious members of non-Christian faiths showed up that the unspoken Christian agenda was quickly swept aside.

Vivekananda rose to the occasion and, in largely extemporaneous speeches, not only extolled the unacknowledged gifts of his own tradition, but under the banner of the harmony of religions, he continually reemphasized the gifts of the other delegates. Inspired by his talks, several speakers flung away previously prepared speeches and rose to talk passionately to these issues and their implications. Not the least of these, debated throughout the parliament, was Christian missionary incursion into non-Western countries and the consistent failure of these emissaries of Christianity to acknowledge the legitimacy of native beliefs. The force of the arguments presented had the effect of significantly altering the debate over missionary activity in some quarters for almost two decades.

Vivekananda had quickly become a spokesperson for the disenfranchised, and audiences thronged to hear him. Realizing this, the organizers rearranged the schedule, announcing that he would speak but not telling the time. The gimmick was to always put him on at the end. As a result, because people came early and stayed late, the less engaging presentations were assured listeners.

Afterward, Vivekananda left Chicago in a state of exaltation. He toured the United States, lecturing at such places as Harvard University. He gathered devoted crowds around him, mostly women. He taught meditation and yoga at Sarah Farmer's Greenacre School in Portsmouth, New Hampshire; he presented at Mrs. Ole Bull's conferences on comparative religions in Cambridge, Massachusetts; and in the wake of these successes, he founded numerous Vedanta Societies in America that exist to this day.

The influence of the parliament has been variously assessed.[3] Some attendees viewed it as the religious event of the century. Historians have subsequently decided that it elevated religious dialogue in ways still being felt today. The parliament, they believe, reinforced not only the interaction among denominations, but also the interfaith discussion of beliefs and values. It set the stage for the discussion of religious pluralism in the modern world, and it is recognized as an important landmark in the current proliferation of multiculturalism. It is also clear that the event infused new life into the fledgling academic field of comparative religions.

Its most significant effect, however, was less obvious. For the first time, the various religious ideas of Asia were presented to American audiences by Asians themselves. This trend, the import of which was not immediately understood, was to continue and would later have important consequences in the American counterculture during the second half of the twentieth century.

The Americanization of Asian Ideas

EVEN BEFORE THE AMERICAN REVOLUTION, ideas about Eastern meditative traditions began seeping into American popular culture through the various sects of European occult Christianity that transplanted themselves to such new settlements as Germantown and Ephrata in Pennsylvania. The early framers of the Declaration of Independence and the U.S. Constitution were influenced by teachings from mystical Sufism and the Jewish Kabbalah through their membership in secret fraternities such as the Rosicrucians and the Freemasons.

Asian ideas then came pouring in during the era of the transcendentalists, especially between the 1840s and the 1880s, largely influencing the American traditions of spiritualism, Theosophy, and mental healing. The Hindu conception of "Brahman" was reformulated by Ralph Waldo Emerson into the New England vision of God as the Over-Soul, while Henry David Thoreau's ideas on civil disobedience arose out of his reading of Hindu scriptures on meditation, yoga, and nonviolence. At the same time, spiritualists—those who believed that science had established communication with the dead through the medium of the group seance—also dabbled in Asian ideas. Madame Blavatsky, co-founder of the International Theosophical Society, is usually credited with introducing Hindu conceptions of discarnate entities into American spiritualist circles. In this context, the Theosophists also translated Hindu texts on meditation and for the first time made them available in popular form to English-speaking audiences. Similarly, New Thought practitioners—followers of Phineas Parkhurst Quimby—also included such meditation techniques as guided visualizations and mantras in their healing regimes.

In general, by the late nineteenth century, Americans appropriated Asian ideas to fit their own optimistic, pragmatic, and eclectic understanding of inner experience. This usually meant adapting ideas such as reincarnation and karma into a very liberal and heavily Christianized but nevertheless secular psychology of character development that was closer to the philosophy of transcendentalism than to the doctrines of any of the Christian denominations. Today, the same standard for interpreting Asian ideas persists, but in the form of a neotranscendentalist, Jungian, and countercultural definition of higher consciousness.[4]

The World's Parliament of Religions increased Western awareness of meditation because, as mentioned, this was the first time that Western audiences on American soil received Asian spiritual teachings from Asians themselves. Thereafter, in addition to Vivekananda's missionary activities, Anagarika Dharmapala lectured at Harvard on Theravada Buddhist meditation in 1904; Abdul-Baha followed with a 235-day tour of the United States teaching the Islamic principles of Bahai, and Soyen Shaku toured in 1907 teaching Zen and the principles of Mahayana Buddhism.

By then, comparative religions had caught on as an academic field of inquiry in the universities. Following the Sacred Books of the East Series, edited by F. Max Mueller, and major translations of the Theravada scriptures by the Pali Text Society in England, the Harvard Oriental Series appeared after 1900 under the editorship of Charles Rockwell Lanman. Throughout Europe and the British Empire, a renaissance of interest in Asian cultures was growing.

During the 1920s, American popular culture was introduced to the meditative practices of the Hindu yogi Paramahansa Yogananda. G. I. Gurdjieff, the White Russian mystic, toured the United States in 1924 and spread his gospel of movement, meditation, and consciousness. A young Hindu trained in Theosophy named Jiddu Krishnamurti had been touring the United States around that same time. Settling in southern California in the 1940s, Krishnamurti would soon be joined by English émigrés fleeing the war in Europe, such as Christopher Isherwood, Gerald Heard, and Aldous Huxley, who were writers and themselves practitioners of the Asian meditative arts.

During World War II, Huxley, Heard, and others became disciples of the meditation teacher Swami Prabhavananda, helped found the Vedanta Society of Southern California, produced such influential books as *Vedanta for the West,* and assisted in the popular dissemination of texts such as the Hindu Upanishads and the Yoga Sutras. Meanwhile, on the East Coast, Swami Akhilananda, situated in Boston, frequently met with leading university intellectuals in psychology, philosophy, and religion, including Gordon Allport, Peter Bertocci, William Ernest Hocking, and George Hunston Williams. One product of this liaison was Akhilananda's *Hindu Psychology* (1946), a text on the philosophy and psychology of Vedantic meditation, with an introduction by Allport.

Another momentous event introducing Asian ideas to the West was the arrival in 1941 of Heinrich Zimmer, an Indologist and Sanskrit scholar who had been a friend and confidant of Carl Jung. Zimmer brought the young Joseph Campbell, a comparative mythologist and folklorist, to the attention of the newly formed Bollingen Foundation. Subsequently, the foundation produced the English translation of Jung's collected works, as well as numerous books by Zimmer, which Campbell edited, among other titles. Perhaps the most influential product of this endeavor was the Bollingen edition of the *I Ching,* or the Chinese Book of Changes. The *I Ching* was a Taoist oracle in book form revered in Chinese religious history as one of the four great Confucian classics. Translated by Richard Wilhelm and with a preface by Jung, the work has enjoyed immense popularity since its first U.S. publication in 1947.

The 1950s represented a major expansion of interest in both meditation and Asian philosophy. Frederick Spiegelberg, a professor of comparative religions at Stanford, opened the California Institute of Asian Studies in 1951, which highlighted the work of the modern Hindu mystic and social reformer Sri Aurobindo Ghose. Alan Watts, an aficionado of Zen and Episcopalian minister, soon joined the faculty and, within a few years, produced such best-selling books as *Psychotherapy East and West* and *The Way of Zen.*

It was also during this time that Michael Murphy first came under the influence of Spiegelberg, was introduced to the teachings of Sri Aurobindo, and began the practice of meditation. With the assistance of Watts, Huxley, Abraham Maslow, Willis Harman, George Leonard, and others, Murphy would soon collaborate with Richard Price to launch the Esalen Institute, which quickly became the world's premier growth center for human potential.

Also during the early 1950s, with the help of Watts, a remarkable man came from Japan to California and introduced Zen to a new generation of Americans. He was D. T. Suzuki.

Suzuki and American Zen

Daisetz Taitaro Suzuki was born in Kanazawa, an area north of Tokyo, in 1870 into a family of Rinzai Zen lineage.[5] His father was an impoverished physician who died when Suzuki was six. Because of strained circumstances, his mother had to take in boarders, and Suzuki was forced to work at an early age. Nevertheless, he was an avid reader and taught himself English by reading books. When he finished his schooling, he became a teacher in a small fishing village until his mother died, when he moved to Tokyo and began taking classes at Tokyo Imperial University. He entered Zen training at this time under Setsumon Roshi and began with koan training under the master Kosen. Thereafter, under Soyen Shaku, Suzuki lived the strict life of a novice for four years at the Engakuji monastery, although he remained a lay disciple. During this period, Suzuki also came under the influence of Kitaro Nishida, a Japanese thinker well versed in German idealist philosophy, whom Suzuki was later to introduce to the writings of William James.[6]

Throughout the course of his training, Suzuki undertook the first of his many translation projects, rendering Paul Carus's *Gospel of Buddhism* into Japanese. Another effort, small but with large consequences, was his English translation of Soyen Shaku's speech for the 1893 World's Parliament of Religions. As a result, Suzuki was invited by Carus, one of the organizers of the parliament, to come to the United States, where he was to undertake the translation of Chinese and Japanese texts for Carus's business enterprise, the Open Court Publishing Company.

Carus, born in Germany in 1852 and raised in a family of distinguished scholars, took his doctorate from Tübingen in 1876 and afterward emigrated to the United States. He had by then worked his way through a period of intense religious skepticism, arriving at the position of rational idealism, in which he believed science would reveal God's intended world order and that immortality meant the survival merely of one's influence. He was a thoroughgoing monist who believed in the possible unity of all world religions.

Carus became the editor of *Open Court,* a journal devoted to the establishment of religion and ethics on a scientific basis. Soon after, he began editing the *Monist,* which promoted more technical articles on the science of religion and the religion of science. Eventually, his successes led to the aforementioned Open Court Publishing Company, which reprinted classics in philosophy and issued in accessible form contemporary works by scientists and philosophers such as George Boole, Alfred Binet, Théodule-Armand Ribot, and Ernst Mach.

By the mid-1890s, Carus had become an indefatigable defender of Buddhism. Through the translation of Buddhist and Taoist texts he had commissioned from Suzuki, he was able to launch counterattacks against both Christian apologists and Sanskrit scholars whom he believed missed the substance by concentrating too much on the mere external form of Buddhist thought.

Meanwhile, the invitation from Carus seems to have precipitated a crisis in Suzuki's Zen practice, which had become very intense in his four-year struggle to fathom his koan, *Mu,* meaning "no-thing." Just before he left, according to his teachers, Suzuki experienced self-realization. In honor of this occasion, his teacher, Soyen Shaku, gave him the name Daisetz, meaning "great simplicity." Years later, one commentator recounts, the ever self-effacing Suzuki would translate this as "great stupidity." His awakening would continue to deepen during his first years in America.

Suzuki arrived in San Francisco in February 1897, and after some immigration delays, he was able to proceed on to La Salle, Illinois. There, he was given a place in Carus's large house, where, in addition to his translating duties, which included the study of Sanskrit grammar, he chopped wood, carried water, carted earth, shopped for food, and did some of the cooking. His first project for Carus was an English rendering of the Tao-te Ching, the Chinese classic attributed to Lao-tzu, followed by Ashvaghosha's *Awakening of Faith in the Mahayana.* Suzuki also engaged in all aspects of the publishing business, including typing, proofreading, editing, and photography. Furthermore, he began work on his first book, perhaps one of the most influential for American readers, his *Outlines of Mahayana Buddhism,* which treated the mystical aspects of Buddhism before it came to Japan. In all, Suzuki spent almost eleven years working for Carus, during which time several notable events occurred that must have assisted him greatly in his later Americanization of Zen.

First, Suzuki came into contact with the philosophy of American pragmatism variously espoused by William James and Charles Sanders Peirce. James and Carus were correspondents, and Peirce had published a pioneering series of cosmological essays in Carus's journal in the early 1890s that expanded pragmatism from a mere rule of logic to a full-fledged metaphysics. Pragmatism, in James's hands, having been greatly influenced by the older Swedenborgian and transcendentalist literary traditions, was emblematic of an entire era of progressivism in America. Based on the idea that beliefs are to be tested not by their sources, but by their consequences, pragmatism was optimistic, growth-oriented, eclectic, and centered on the contribution that each individual makes to a healthy, functioning, and evolving society. It was also the first uniquely American philosophy to have international consequences. Suzuki's introduction to this philosophical outlook at the turn of the century was to provide him a key that would give his ideas entrance into popular American visionary psychology.

In addition, writing to Nishida just after the publication of *The Varieties of Religious Experience* (1902), Suzuki began to introduce his teacher to Jamesian philosophy. There is clear evidence that James's essay "A World of Pure Experience" (1904), which was a cornerstone of his own metaphysics of radical empiricism, was read by Nishida. Nishida, in turn, incorporated James's ideas into *Zen no kenkyu* (1911), a treatise on pure experience that marked a new era in modern Japanese philosophy (James responded to it somewhat critically). By his own reading of James, Suzuki was inspired to initiate conversations with Westerners on the subject of religious experience.

Second, Soyen Shaku returned to the United States for a nine-month visit, and he and Suzuki set off across the country by train in 1906. They visited Carus in Illinois, had a reunion with other friends Soyen Shaku had made when he had first come to the World's Parliament of Religions, saw Niagara Falls, and toured New York City. Along the way, Soyen Shaku lectured on the principles of Mahayana Buddhism, probably the first public lectures given to Americans on the subject, since, aside from Soyen Shaku's own lecture, the parliament of religions had introduced only the Hinayana or earliest form of Buddhist teaching. During these travels, Suzuki must have paid close attention to the response of American audiences and shaped his own ideas accordingly.

Third, Suzuki married an American woman in 1911. Beatrice Erskine Lane was a Radcliffe graduate and a Theosophist who had been a student of William James, Josiah Royce, and George Herbert Palmer. She had come to Radcliffe from Newark, New Jersey, and prepared at the Cambridge Latin School before entering Radcliffe in 1894. One of her classmates was Gertrude Stein. After her graduation in 1898, Lane proceeded to New York, where she earned her master's and a certificate in social work in 1908 from Columbia University. She married Suzuki in Japan, in 1911, and together they had one son, Paul. Her influence on Suzuki was both loving and profound, and he was devoted to her until her death in 1939. She helped him tirelessly with his translations and must have been instrumental in interpreting for him the American way of life. Her own work, *Mahayana Buddhism* (1938), was published in London the year before she died. She was considered important enough by Japanese scholars that a biography was written of her, although it has yet to be translated into English.

Finally, in these early years, Suzuki also embarked upon a detailed study of Emanuel Swedenborg, seeing much in the Swedish seer's writings that he must have found compatible with various aspects of Buddhist thought. By grasping Swedenborgian ideas, Suzuki gained access to the earlier tradition of folk psychology upon which the American visionary tradition of the nineteenth century was based.

The project ostensibly started when the Swedenborg Foundation in London contacted the Japanese embassy and asked for a competent translator to render Swedenborg into Japanese. The embassy suggested Suzuki, who, by way of London and Paris, had returned to Japan in 1908. Suzuki agreed and, in due time, translated Swedenborg's *Divine Love and Wisdom, Divine Providence, Heaven and Hell,* and *The Heavenly Doctrines.*

Suzuki also turned up at the International Swedenborg Congress as an official delegate when it was held in London in 1910, along with other Swedenborgian notables such as the novelist Henry James. Letters residing at the Swedenborg Society in London indicate that Suzuki also agreed to produce at least one biographical sketch of Swedenborg as a separate little volume in order to promote the sale of the longer, more technical works throughout Japan. In 1914, Suzuki was one of the three men who officially launched the Japanese Swedenborg Society, which from then on oversaw the publication and distribution of Swedenborg's works in Japan.

With the exception of occasional trips to England and Europe to spend time with other Buddhist scholars, Suzuki appears to have remained in Japan until he moved back to the United States in 1950. During that time, he was first a professor of English at Tokyo Imperial University, then a professor of English at Gakushin, and, until 1940, a professor of English and Buddhist philosophy at Otani University in Kyoto. During the war, Suzuki went into religious retreat after he became a critic of Japanese militaristic policies and came under surveillance by Japanese police.

Suzuki published extensively on the nature of Zen as well. His *Essays in Zen Buddhism,* first published in 1927, went through several editions and is still in print. He wrote a history of early Chinese philosophy; published a translation of the Lankavatara Sutra, one of the Chinese Buddhist texts upon which Zen teaching is based; and composed an introduction and a manual to Zen, as well as an account of a Buddhist monk's life. In addition to some half dozen other works on philosophy and practice, he penned an important statement concerning the influence of Zen on Japanese culture.

Suzuki continued to develop numerous contacts in the West. His *Introduction to Zen Buddhism,* for instance, first published by the Eastern Buddhist Society in 1934, was edited by Christmas Humphries and contained a foreword by Jung. Huxley read his work; Watts considered him his teacher.

In 1949, Suzuki went to Hawaii for a year before arriving in California to teach at Claremont Graduate School in Pasadena. After another year on the West Coast, he came to New York and began to lecture in churches and private homes. Funds were raised through a wealthy businessman, Cornelius Crane, whose company manufactured bathroom fixtures and who endowed a lecture series for Suzuki at Columbia on the stipulation that the talks be open to the public. By these means, the neo-Freudians Erich Fromm and Karen Horney found their way to Suzuki's side, as did other budding adepts such as Philip Kapleau. According to the Buddhist writer Rick Fields, these lectures formed the seed for Zen's flourishing in the 1950s. Crane, for his part, also set up the Zen Studies Society to encourage Suzuki's work, the purpose of which was to introduce the cultural, spiritual, and educational aspects of Zen to the West.

Suzuki's fortunes began to change rapidly. He officially became a visiting professor at Columbia University in 1955. Articles about him began appearing in *Christian Century,* the *Guardian,* the *Journal of Religion,* the *Nation,* and the *New York Times.* His books were analyzed in the *Saturday Review* and the *Times Literary Supplement.* He was interviewed on television and appeared in *Vogue,* and in 1957, a profile of him appeared in the *New Yorker.* In this article, he was praised as the most celebrated and most eloquent international commentator on a branch of Buddhism practiced by millions of people.

Now began the most important period of his influence on the American visionary tradition. Many of his previous works were reprinted and widely read. He published *Mysticism: Christian and Buddhist: The Eastern and Western Way* and contributed to Fromm's *Zen Buddhism and Psychoanalysis,* the product of a historic meeting held in Cuernavaca, Mexico, on the relation of Zen to modern depth psychology. His influence was felt in the world of jazz, in the music of John Cage, and in literature; he influenced such lights of the younger generation as J. D. Salinger and Jack Kerouac, the poets Allen Ginsberg and Gary Snyder, and the Trappist contemplative writer Thomas Merton.

In 1957, Suzuki moved to Cambridge, Massachusetts, where he fell in with a distinguished group of educators and practitioners led by Elsie and John Mitchell. They had begun a library that eventually reached 20,000 volumes and maintained Zen sitting practice in a small converted area of their house. Finally, the group incorporated in 1959 as the Cambridge Buddhist Association, which continues to exist today. Suzuki, meanwhile, returned to Japan in the early 1960s. He died in Kamakura in 1966, while sitting at his desk, still writing at the age of ninety-six.

The Dalai Lama

THERE HAVE BEEN MANY Asian spiritual teachers who have come to the United States and gained a following in the folk culture—Kirpal

Singh, Bhaktivedanta Swami Prabhupada, Maharishi Mahesh Yogi, Guru Maharaj Ji, Swami Satchitananda, Chogyam Trungpa, Thich Nhat Hanh, Lama Anagarika Govinda, Aanada Moi Ma, Swami Muktinanda, Guru Mai, and others. One of the reasons for this was the Communist invasion of Asia, which drove many spiritual teachers to the West. Another reason was the receptivity of Western audiences to the message of Eastern religions, which is generally projective, oriented toward self-knowledge, mythic, visionary with regard to a dynamic language of inner experience, and, indeed, a counterpoint to the Western rationalist tradition. There is also a tendency in various traditions such as the Sufis of Islam or the yogis of Hinduism toward mysticism, the cultivation of intuitive insight, and a focus on the unitive experience.

Almost paradoxically, these expressions are at once both psychology and religion as we normatively define those terms. Vedantic Hinduism describes the relation between the individual self and Atman, also called Brahman or the supreme self, as totally one. The statement is religious because it is a claim about ultimate reality, but the language is all psychology—the language of the self. Protestants can relate to the idea of the supreme Brahman, because the concept is just like their monistic, Judeo-Christian conception of one God. Buddhism, on the other hand, is a nontheistic religion. It posits no supreme deity, no enduring self behind the world of appearances, and no absolute principle of any kind. All that Buddha ever claimed was to have a way to release us from suffering—namely, through an examination of our own consciousness. Thus, Buddhist teachings have everything to do with the mind. They are preeminently a religious psychology that speaks to personality transformed from a state of ignorance to one of enlightenment.

Such ideas have always appealed to communities of the Western visionary tradition. In the case of the modern counterculture, however, there is a clear stratification reflecting personality style and social level. Most Westerners know of Asian cultures through either Vedantic Hinduism or Zen, as these are the most readily accessible doorways into Asian culture because they are the most prominent and most readily understandable of the religious systems, depending on what enters the West through India or through Japan. Non-Western forms of yoga and med-

itation or more esoteric forms of Buddhism or Taoism originally attracted a different more entrepreneurial kind of Westerner.

Whereas Madame Blavatsky immersed herself in the culture of Hindu
monism, it is less well known that Henry Steel Olcott championed Theravada Buddhism. The Hindu temples on the plains in India were always
more accessible to Westerners than the monasteries of the Himalayas,
just as the Zen temples in Japan were more readily penetrable than the
remote mountain shrines of Shinto.

By the time of the American counterculture movement of the 1960s,
these differences had become more pronounced. Singing missionaries of
the Hare Krishna church would take anyone in under their wing, even
burnt-out methamphetamine addicts. The followers of Maharishi Mahesh Yogi, in contrast, tended to be college-educated, folk-music types
who smoked marijuana and perhaps had tried LSD once or twice. Heav-
ier psychedelic drug users comprised yet another type, one whose visions
had been so intense that they were not just followers of a particular tradition transplanted to the United States, but became ordained monks
and nuns and spent years in foreign countries mastering difficult texts in
non-Western languages and achieving deep levels of meditation with the
best of the other advanced but native students.

Today, beyond Zen, there is a significant cultural movement among
young Jewish intellectuals and people who hold middle-level corporate
management positions to be involved in Vipassana, or insight meditation. Similarly, one is not just a practitioner of transcendental meditation;
one is an initiator, or has been designated as an advanced graduate of the
Sidhi program—those who are more adept at the practices than even
regular meditation teachers.

Having said this, it is also true at the moment that perhaps no Asian
teacher is more influential in the American counterculture movement
than Tenzin Gyatso, the fourteenth Dalai Lama, head of the Gelugpa
sect of Buddhism, and spiritual leader of Tibet, who, with 118,000 of his
people, was driven into exile by the Chinese Communist invasion of his
country in 1950.[7]

The Dalai Lama was born July 6, 1935 under the name Lhamo
Thondup, in Taktser, situated in far northeastern Tibet, in the province of

Amdo. He was the youngest child of a farming family that leased land to grow crops and raise animals. At age three, based upon certain oracular tests that were supervised by senior Tibetan monks, he was designated as the incarnation of the thirteenth Dalai Lama, representing the lineage leading back to Avalokiteshvara, the Bodhisattva of Compassion. After passing all the required tests, even at that young age, he was renamed Tenzin Gyatso and taken to Lhasa, the capital, to be prepared as the leader of the Tibetan people. For the next twenty-three years, he was given the rigorous training of a Buddhist monk. He became adept at meditation and learned and eventually mastered the intricacies of technical Buddhist philosophy to the level of what we in the West would call the doctorate. Meanwhile, he lived a life of relative seclusion, although he had playmates and occasionally saw his family. His teachers taught him all aspects of Tibetan art and culture, and they also schooled him in the affairs of statecraft, as he was both the spiritual and temporal ruler of Tibet.

At the same time, Gyatso had periodic contact with Western culture. The English government had given him a motorcar, which had been disassembled and carried piece by piece over the Himalayas, where it was reassembled but kept in a garage because Tibet had no roads. He was particularly fascinated with Western inventions and had such items as a telescope and a generator-powered movie projector. One of his tutors for a number of years was the Austrian mountain climber Heinrich Harrer, who had escaped from an English prisoner of war camp in India in 1941 and fled up into Tibet to avoid capture, remaining there after the war until the Chinese invasion. These events were the subject of the recent popular American movie *Seven Years in Tibet*.

The People's Republic of China began its takeover of Tibet in 1949. The Chinese claimed that imperialist forces from the West had infiltrated Tibet and that, in any case, Tibet was suffering from a thousand years of a feudal monarchy. Calling it a "peaceful liberation," the Chinese marched 80,000 soldiers across the Tibetan border. The Dalai Lama, at age fifteen, was quickly advanced to his majority and took over the direct control of six million followers on the eve of what looked like war. He immediately sent out delegations around the world asking for support, but the call went unheeded. He then made preparations to flee to India after the Chinese had overrun all of western Tibet.

At the Tibetan border, just as he was about to cross into India, to his complete astonishment, he heard over the radio that the Chinese announced they had signed a peace agreement with the Tibetan government to incorporate Tibet into the Chinese motherland. This was a propaganda ruse, as he had the official state seals with him and had signed no such agreement. A Chinese delegation approached him and threatened that there would be more bloodshed if he did not return to Lhasa. Without a standing army, with no hope of international help, and believing in absolute nonviolence as a devout Buddhist, he returned to a capital city occupied with foreign troops, where there were extensive food shortages, increasing hardships, and the imprisonment of his people.

In 1954, the Dalai Lama traveled to China himself in an attempt to gain a reprieve for his country. He met with Chou En-lai and Mao Tsetung, attended numerous meetings, and was given a wide-ranging tour of the Chinese interior. He was not permitted to have any contact with the Chinese people, however, and he soon found out that the Chinese press had been misrepresenting his visit as the complete capitulation of Tibet to the Chinese cause. Also, it soon became apparent to him that the Chinese were bent on the complete eradication of religion in Tibet and that he was to be a virtual prisoner in his own country.

Meanwhile, a Tibetan resistance movement had developed in the mountains and had carried off a number of successful raids against the Chinese. In retaliation, the Chinese began aerial bombardment of the Tibetan monasteries, monks and nuns were rounded up and tortured, and conditions became more difficult for the Tibetan people.

After a brief visit to meet with Jawaharlal Nehru in India, the Dalai Lama's situation became more difficult in Lhasa. In March 1959 at a major Buddhist festival attended by thousands of Tibetans, it appeared obvious that the Chinese were about to take him prisoner. Although he evaded directly being seized, he received word that the palace he was staying in would be attacked openly the next day. That night, in disguise, he managed to leave the city with his entourage. Intending to flee permanently, he headed once again for India, where eventually 118,000 men, women, and children followed him into exile.

The Dalai Lama was welcomed by the Indian government, who permitted the Tibetans to settle in Dharamsala, a Himalayan hill station in the northwest of India. Eventually, land was set aside in south India for the increasing tide of Tibetan refugees, and today, there are more than forty settlements throughout India, settlements of 1,000 Tibetans in both Switzerland and Bhutan, and settlements in Canada and the United States as well.

At first, the refugees fared poorly. Many elderly died on the way, and many more succumbed to disease, exhaustion, and altitude differences once they arrived in India. This also created a large orphan population. Nevertheless, the Tibetans set up schools, small crafts businesses, and a government-in-exile, which is now run by a democratically elected body of representatives, while the Dalai Lama has retained his position as spiritual ruler.

Human rights violations in Tibet continue to be among the most serious in the world. The Chinese Communists have launched a program to annihilate Tibetan culture. Temples have been looted and converted to granaries, and monasteries have been bombed. Millions of Chinese have now immigrated into Tibet, creating a two-tiered social class and making Tibetans a deprived minority in their own country. The group Asia Watch has documented the continuing arrest and torture of monks and nuns and instances where Tibetan women have been forced to undergo abortions against their will and simultaneously submit to sterilization. There is also evidence of infanticide, where newborn Tibetan babies have been killed by injection.

At the same time, China has turned Tibet into the largest nuclear arsenal in the world, stationing nuclear missiles throughout the Himalayas. It has practiced systematic deforestation of the mountains and has also made Tibet the world's largest dump site for nuclear waste. Moreover, Chinese goods that are now flooding into the American markets, such as toys, textiles, and clothing, are the products of state-run industries staffed by slave labor, which includes Tibetan prisoners of conscience.

Nevertheless, after almost forty years away from Tibet, the Tibetans have been attempting to regain their homeland through nonviolent means. With this outlook in mind, and with the aim of teaching Buddhist philosophy to a growing number of younger Americans, the Dalai Lama came to the United States on several occasions in the late 1970s and early 1980s. As a result, on the political front, ninety-one members of the U.S. Congress signed a letter to the president of the People's Republic of China expressing support for direct talks between the Chinese government and the Dalai Lama's representatives.

Then, on September 21, 1987, the Dalai Lama presented his plan for Tibet to the Human Rights Caucus of the Congress in Washington, D.C. There he proposed that China open negotiations right away with the Tibetan government-in-exile to transform Tibet into the Earth's largest wilderness preserve and nuclear free zone, dedicated to human rights and world peace. Here we have in one statement the spiritual aspirations of the Tibetan people and also the core vision of the alternative reality tradition in the West: nonviolence, religious freedom for all beings, the preservation of the Earth, and the end of nuclear proliferation. Subsequently, honoring his nonviolent commitment to this effort, the Dalai Lama was awarded the Nobel Peace Prize in 1989.

While all this was going on, Tibet's spiritual leader continued to have a growing impact on the American counterculture. The backdrop for this influence was that, since the 1960s, Buddhism in all its forms, from Zen and Vipassana to Mahamudra, has spread in the United States to such an extent that an entirely new phase of its history can now be defined as uniquely American. Today, regardless of what its detractors may claim, there is presently being written an entirely new chapter in the history of world Buddhism, one that is defined by the spread of Buddhism in America. In this regard, to more than one generation of young Americans, the Dalai Lama is considered a world spiritual leader and an inspiring personality even to people who are not specifically followers of his teachings. Celebrities such as Richard Gere and the Beastie Boys have been directly associated with the Buddhist influence. More recently, an entire new generation of younger people has been introduced to the Dalai Lama and the Tibetan cause by way of cable television broadcasts of several Concerts for a Free Tibet.

To underscore the significance of Tibet for the contemporary counterculture, in 1989 an effort was begun by a small group of Americans around a young man, Edward Bednar, a practicing Catholic and also a Buddhist meditator, to initiate legislation in the Congress to bring Ti-

betan refugees to the United States. The Tibetan request was finally in-
serted in the Omnibus Immigration Bill of 1990, sponsored by Senator
Ted Kennedy and Reprentative Barney Frank and supported by Jesse
Helms. Through this legislation, a thousand visas were issued to stateless
Tibetans. Essentially, the bill designated the incoming Tibetans as immigrants who would qualify for U.S. citizenship; they would not be designated as refugees, thus avoiding a potential political argument with
congressional supporters of China, for refugees receive financial support
while immigrants do not. Consequently, Bednar assembled a board of di-
rectors and founded a nonprofit group called the Tibetan-U.S. Resettlement Project, made up of American friends of Tibet who raised money,
generated housing and job opportunities, and arranged for health care
for the 1,000 Tibetans who were destined to come.

Bednar and the Resettlement Project worked in conjunction with the
Office of Tibet in New York City and the Dalai Lama's personal representative, Rinchen Darlo, to establish twenty-one cluster sites around the
United States where the incoming Tibetans would be able to live and
work together, preserving the ideals of Tibetan language and culture
while they learned to assimilate to American society. Some of these sites
are presently established in New York City; in Boston and Amherst,
Massachusetts; in Hartford, Connecticut; in Austin, Texas; in Salt Lake
City, Utah; in San Francisco; and (the largest) in Saint Paul, Minnesota.

On the diplomatic side, for the first time in the history of U.S. foreign
policy, the U.S. State Department began direct negotiations with the Tibetan government-in-exile in India, and Tibetans coming into the United
States were not declared Chinese citizens but were officially registered as
displaced persons. On the receiving end, one of the biggest supporters of
the Resettlement Project has been the New York Association for New
Americans (NYANA). This is essentially a Jewish service organization
that was established just after World War II to help survivors of the concentration camps come to the United States. Since then, NYANA has assisted Jewish populations all over the world in immigrating to America.

At the time when the Tibetans were just about to come over, NYANA
was geared up to assist what it expected would be a large wave of Jews
emigrating from the Soviet Union, but this influx was delayed. As a re-

sult, NYANA offered to lend its considerable resources to resettling Tibetans instead. It took over all aspects of the New York City cluster site, established the headquarters of the national Tibetan-U.S. Resettlement Project in its offices in lower Manhattan, and played a major role in the success of the project.

When the Immigration Act was passed, a deadline for all those wishing to be resettled had been set at September 1993. All 1,000 Tibetans arrived a full three months before the deadline and began their new lives as members of American society. Since then, the Tibetan-U.S. Resettlement Project has formally disbanded, as its initial job was completed, and it reformed around the Tibetan Community Assistance Project, a nonprofit group of American supporters working in conjunction with Tibetans to achieve family reunification. This means that by the first few years of the twenty-first century, more than 2,000 dependents of the 1,000 Tibetans who have already arrived will be coming to the United States to rejoin their families. The United States will then have the largest community of exiled Tibetans in the world outside of India.

Although there are many different lines of Asian spiritual practice now going on, Tibetan Buddhism is perhaps the most influential. This is because the folk culture has generally fostered a widespread sense of *bhakti,* or devotion to spiritual teachings in whatever form they may come. Consequently, regardless of a person's individual practice, there is extensive sympathy within the American psychotherapeutic counterculture for both the Dalai Lama's teachings and the Tibetan cause.

The question of why, however, is an important one, because it involves the fusion of two great streams of concern in the visionary tradition into a single unified ethic; namely, freedom of religious expression as a basic human right. Within the American visionary tradition, these influences have always been implicitly associated together as something uniquely American. It has only been recently that such an ethic has been extended to other cultures and applied on a global scale, where each situation is more difficult and more complex and less likely to be influenced by what is perceived as a more parochial American agenda.

As well, within the American visionary tradition itself, interest in Asian spiritual teachings of higher consciousness has often been divorced from the actual plight of Asian immigrants. But this situation has also changed dramatically just since the late 1980s. If the Tibetan cause has produced anything, it is the fusion of these two concerns together in the collective psyche of the visionary shadow culture. Thus, in the same way that the women's movement, the black civil rights movement, or the anti-Vietnam demonstrations were the causes thought worth championing in the 1960s, the new political agenda of the visionary tradition in the twenty-first century may well be an international movement toward religious freedom and human rights in which Tibet holds an important key.

On the other hand, the question that is most freqently asked by skeptics is, But why Tibet? What is so special about Tibetans? They are not the only Buddhist community in America to have experienced repression. Certainly the Cambodians have fared just as badly, if not worse. Ten times more Jews and Slavs were annihilated by the Nazis during World War II; why should we be concerned with the fate of such a small population of foreigners? Perhaps the Chinese were right to have just only recently ended a feudalism that reflected life in the eighth century A.D.

The answer may at first appear quite idealistic, but my sense as a historian and philosopher of the subject suggests that the single most important reason that Tibet represents the epitome of Asian spiritual contributions to Western thought is because, when the Buddhists taught that we can evolve into a higher state of consciousness, the Tibetans took them seriously and, by elevating Buddhist teachings to the level of a national religion, became the first culture on Earth to self-consciously renounce violence in all its forms as the goal of social evolution.

One thinks of freedom of religious expression as quite natural to pursue in the context of American culture. This is, after all, the meaning of a democratic way of life, and democracy is what the Tibetans have come to learn and to incorporate back into their own culture. At the same time, the newcomers themselves have come as ambassadors of Tibet, bringing with them a deep and intense spiritual message for the modern world. The visionaries of the American shadow culture have heard it, even though now they may be only just beginning to understand its more far-reaching implications. Thus, to understand the history of Asian ideas in the West is to comprehend the present plight of the Tibetans, and to have some sense of what their contemporary practice of Buddhism is all about is to have a key to the heart of present-day American folk psychology.

However, we have rushed far ahead of our story, as more than a half century of events still had to take place to prepare the way for these more current developments.

Notes

1. Quoted in Elva Nelson, *Vivekananda and His Swamis in Boston and Vicinity* (Boston: Ramakrishna Vedanta Society, 1992), pp. 151–152. See also E. I. Taylor, "Swami Vivekananda and William James," *Prabuddha Bharata: Journal of the Ramakrishna Society* (Calcutta), 91 (September 1986): 374–385; E. I. Taylor, "The Transcendent Experience," *Prabuddha Bharata,* 100 (February–March 1995): 434–443; and E. I. Taylor, "Sriyogirajmahagurusat Sarvagatananda-ji," in C. Mehta, ed., *The Lamplighter: Swami Sarvagatananda in the West: Fortieth Anniversary Tribute to the Ministry of Swami Sarvagatananda* (Boston and Salem, NH: Ramakrishna Vedanta Society/Frugal Printer, 1996), pp. 141–144.

2. Adapted from Carl T. Jackson, *Oriental Religions and American Thought: Nineteenth Century Explorations* (Westport, CT: Greenwood, 1981), pp. 243–262. See also E. I. Taylor, "Review of Carl Jackson's *Oriental Religions in Nineteenth Century American Thought,*" *Journal of Transpersonal Psychology,* 14:2 (1982): 184–186.

3. Richard Seager, *The Dawn of Religious Pluralism: Voices from the World's Parliament of Religions, 1893* (La Salle, IL: Open Court, 1993).

4. E. I. Taylor, *An Annotated Bibliography in Classical Eastern Psychology* (Dallas: Essene Press, 1973); E. I. Taylor, "Asian Interpretations: Transcending the Stream of Consciousness," in K. Pope and J. Singer, eds., *The Stream of Consciousness: Scientific Investigations into the Flow of Human Experience* (New York: Plenum, 1978), pp. 31–54, reprinted in J. Pickering and M. Skinner, eds., *From Sentience to Symbol: Readings on Consciousness* (London: Harvester-Wheatsheaf; Toronto: University of Toronto Press, 1990); E. I. Taylor, "Psychology of Religion and Asian Studies: The William James Legacy," *Journal of Transpersonal Psychology,* 10:1 (1978): 66–79; E. I. Taylor, "Contemporary Interest in Classical Eastern Psychology," in A. Paranjpe, D. Ho, and R. Rieber, eds., *Asian Contributions to Psychology* (New York: Praeger, 1988), pp. 79–122; E. I. Taylor, "Mortality and Self-Realization," in J. MacMahon, ed., *Psychic Phenomena and Near-Death Experiences* (New York: Parapsychology Foundation, 1995), pp. 86–107; and E. I. Taylor, ed., *The Physical and Psychological*

Effects of Meditation: A Review of Contemporary Research with a Comprehensive Bibliography, 1931–1996, 2nd ed. (Sausalito, CA: Institute of Noetic Sciences, 1997).

5. The following section relies on Rick Fields, *How the Swans Came to the Lake: A Narrative History of Buddhism in America,* 1st ed. (Boulder, CO: Shambhala, 1981), but also draws from the archives of the Swedenborg Society in London, courtesy of Nancy Dawson and Les Stone, "Deitsetz Suzuki," in the *Contemporary Authors* series. See also E. I. Taylor, "Swedenborgian Influences on American Pragmatism: The Case of D. T. Suzuki," *Studia Swedenborgiana,* 9:2 (1994): 1–20.

6. William R. LaFleur, "Between America and Japan: The Case of Daisetsu Tietaro Suzuki," in R. S. Elwood, ed., *Zen in American Life and Letters* (Malibu, CA: Undena Publications, 1987), pp. 67–88.

7. Biographical details adapted from Tenzin Gyatso, *Freedom in Exile: Autobiography of the Dalai Lama* (New York: HarperCollins, 1990). See also the chapter "Healing Personalities" in E. I. Taylor, *A Psychology of Spiritual Healing* (West Chester, PA: Chrysalis Books, 1997).

Chapter Ten

The Americanization of Jung and Freud

THE SCENE IS CLARK UNIVERSITY, SEPTEMBER 7, 1909. THE PLACE is a large lecture hall of the main university building. Celebrities in psychology, psychiatry, philosophy, and education from Europe and America, along with graduate students and faculty, have just taken their seats. The event is the twentieth anniversary celebration of the founding of the school. Clark's president, G. Stanley Hall, has invited the Viennese neurologist Sigmund Freud to come to America and, before receiving an honorary doctorate, to deliver five lectures on the new theory of psychoanalysis.[1] After the appropriate introductions, Freud rises and begins speaking without notes in his native German, still the lingua franca of the academic elite in America.

Over the course of the next five days, Freud outlined the historical origins of psychoanalysis, which at that time he attributed to his partner, Josef Breuer (Freud later claimed this distinction was wholly his own), and he presented the psychogenic hypothesis as the origin of hysterical symptoms—that psychic trauma improperly integrated into one's conscious worldview can convert to the physical symptoms of neurosis. Freud explained the dynamic mechanisms at work that cause a patient to resist revealing unconscious contents, and he also described the means by which traumatic events are repressed in the unconscious in the first place. He described his method of free association and gave numerous examples of how the unconscious accidentally breaks into the field of waking awareness through jokes, slips of the tongue, and what is remembered of dreams. He lectured on the central role of sexuality in normal and neurotic development, and finally, he elucidated the dynamics of the accidental transference of feelings for the parent onto the therapist by the patient. The resolution of this mistake, Freud concluded, was the standard for success in therapy, since it represented a resolution of long-buried unconscious conflicts with one's parents. Then, beyond therapy, was sublimation—a redirecting of instinctual impulses such as immediate sexual gratification into more socially acceptable channels, the product of which Freud called "culture."

Carl Gustav Jung, a young Swiss psychiatrist, spoke after Freud a few days later. His subject was the diagnostic association test—the results of research that showed how people can have very emotional reactions to the presentation of a list of simple words. Their reactions, he posited, are often consistent enough to reveal hidden unconscious complexes controlling behavior from just below the surface of consciousness.

Historians are fond of going into great detail about the importance of Freud's visit to America for the effect it had on launching psychoanalysis as an international movement, for the function it served in elevating Freud to the level of Copernicus and Darwin, and for its impact on transforming American psychology and psychiatry. Yet Jung's lectures remain largely unnoticed, as he has always been seen as a mere acolyte of Freud, a dissident who eventually broke from the fold, and a man whose career was lived out in Freud's shadow.[2]

From the standpoint of an American visionary psychology, these perceptions are, of course, incorrect. Freud was not the most important figure at the conference, although contemporary accounts still maintain that he was. If one goes back and looks at the actual program of lectures at Clark or the extent of the newspaper coverage of Freud's visit, for instance, we find that Herbert Spencer Jennings was, in fact, much more popular and that the only two newspaper interviews with Freud had been either arranged by Hall or written by himself personally. So there was no spontaneous outpouring of public recognition of Freud, and though those who came as professionals were certainly interested in his theories, the reactions were decidedly mixed.

As for Jung, he had come from a completely different psychological lineage.[3] He had been raised in a religious household in which his father, a clergyman, occasionally ministered to patients in asylums, while his mother was prone to mediumistic trances. As a young medical student, Jung had surveyed the literature in psychiatry and, with regard to the interior life, was puzzled to find little in the psychiatric literature on the dynamic nature of consciousness. He located such discussions only in the writings of occultists and philosophers from a previous era, such as Du Prel, Pasavant, and Swedenborg.[4] His dissertation, "The Psychology and Pathology of Occult Phenomena," was a study of the medium Helene Prieswerk, and it was thus linked to a handful of other single-case studies that had characterized the work of neurologists and psychical researchers involved in an international psychotherapeutic alliance in the latter half of the nineteenth century among French, Swiss, British, and American scholars.

Once he had obtained his doctorate in medicine and had begun an assistantship at the Burghölzli Asylum in Zurich under Eugen Bleuler, Jung surveyed the European and American scene and found that all the pioneers in psychical research such as William James and F. W. H. Myers were just passing from the landscape. He studied unsuccessfully with Pierre Janet in Paris during the winter of 1903 and, by 1906, ended up corresponding with Freud in Vienna, whose controversial theories about dream symbolism and the sexual basis of neuroses were just then becoming known.

Jung was already recognized internationally in his own right, however, because of his studies in word association. This work registered the probable origin of psychological disturbances in consciousness, to which Jung added accompanying psychophysiological measures of emotion. Indeed, through the Swiss-born pathologist Adolf Meyer, then running asylums in the state of New York, Jung's work had been introduced the year before in the American psychological literature.[5] Thus, Jung was already well known to American professionals in the field of psychotherapeutics before he met Freud and before Freud's innovative ideas were a topic of discussion in the United States.

One reason for Jung's popularity was that psychopathologists and mental healers were persistently drawn to any scientific evidence that gave their subject matter credibility. Jung's researches provided substantial corroboration for developing theories about the unconscious, about the psychophysiology of the mind-body problem, and about the probable unconscious origin of dream symbols. Another reason was that there had been a long-standing and deep connection between Swiss and American psychology already established through Auguste Forel, a Swiss neuropathologist and previous superintendent of the Burghölzli Asylum who had been a corresponding member of several local Boston medical societies since the 1880s. Forel was also interested in hypnosis, which he introduced into the asylum in the 1890s and which he used on both the patients and the staff. When Forel stepped down as superintendent of the Burghölzli, he saw to it that he was replaced by one of his best students, Eugen Bleuler, who became Jung's supervisor at the hospital in 1900. Bleuler permitted Jung to administer word association tests to psychotic patients, and encouraged Jung in his first reading of Freud's work. Adolf Meyer, the man who introduced Jung's earliest researches to the American psychological community, was also an older student of Forel's, so that Jung's researches entered American psychotherapeutic circles through this earlier Swiss connection and not through later association with psychoanalysis.[6]

Overall, then, the picture emerging of Jung here paints him as part of a much different and much earlier set of connections to American culture than one based on his later association with Freud. And Jung's intellectual lineage in the field of psychopathology linked him more closely with the late-nineteenth-century psychologies of transcendence than with the type of psychology Freud represented. During his years communicating with Freud, however, Jung did develop the method of symbolism beyond that of any other psychological theorist, applying it not only to an analysis of dreams and hallucinations, but eventually to myths and visions of all world cultures and to the problems in symbolism that Jung discovered in the more esoteric sciences, such as alchemy. This method of symbolism, extrapolated to far more than Freud's theory of neurosis, is Jung's real contribution to psychoanalysis. Much else that is encountered in Jung's theories—the psychogenic hypothesis, the comparative study of trance states, the investigation of mediums, the idea of a collective reservoir of consciousness, even the theory of psychological types—can largely be attributed to the earlier French-Swiss-English-American alliance.

Moreover, Jung's first face-to-face meeting with Freud, which took place in Vienna in 1907, lasted thirteen hours. In that first encounter, everything in which Jung was interested was made known to Freud, including Jung's penchant for mediumship, clairvoyance, telepathy, and synchronous events. In other words, Freud heard nothing new at the end of their relationship in 1912 that he had not already known about Jung's work from the beginning of their communication in 1907. By the end, the relationship had grown complicated, but there were no surprising revelations; Freud had made Jung his heir apparent but could not abide by Jung's overt redefinition of his theories, which Jung had by then made openly and in print.

A not insignificant fact for the present discussion is that, once they began corresponding on a regular basis and Jung became known internationally as a spokesperson for Freud's ideas, most of the major American physicians who became influenced by psychoanalysis approached Freud in Vienna by first going through Jung and Bleuler in Zurich.[7] These physicians included Frederick Peterson, August Hoch, William Alanson White, Smith Ely Jelliffe, and A. A. Brill, among others. Therefore, even though Brill went on to become the earliest translator of Freud's work into English and Jelliffe and White went on to launch the first American psychoanalytic journal, *Psychoanalytic Review,* whatever psychoanalysis was in Freud's hands, it was always Jung's interpretation that became the first retailed version presented to Americans, at least until World War I.

The Americanization of Psychoanalysis

TO UNDERSTAND THE AMERICANIZATION of Freud's ideas, one has to remember that, in addition to the historical Jungian filter through which they all passed, there is a gender bias, as well as a sociocultural bias, to consider. All the major early figures in psychoanalysis operating in the United States were males (the few women pioneers in America—Karen Horney, Greta Bibring, Helena Deutsch—came later)[8] while the early Jungians were mostly women, chief among them Beatrice Hinkle, Constance Long, Eleanor Bertine, Esther Harding, and Kristine Mann.[9]

This was because Freud's was preeminently a masculine psychology. In his writings, he emphasized the Oedipus complex, which was applied to gender identification in young boys, much more so than the parallel Electra complex in young girls. Moreover, psychoanalysis always allied itself in the United States with physicians, and before the 1920s, there were few women in the medical profession. In the early days of psychoanalysis, then, women were excluded from its inner circle, although they did make up the bulk of Freud's patients.

Conversely, Jung surrounded himself with women. The intelligent, the rich, and the beautiful were attracted to him. He took many of them as patients, some as friends, and a few as lovers. Furthermore, his psychology accounted for the feminine psyche—as the undeveloped half of the male personality, as the devouring demon, and as the Divine Mother, but more important, in whatever form she appeared, she was instrumental in the spiritual evolution of the whole person.[10] Naturally, then, the Freudian view of depth psychology was quite different from the Jungian view insofar as the type of American clientele each attracted.

From a sociocultural standpoint, there were at least three levels of audience who received the teachings of depth psychology in the tradition of Freud and Jung in American culture. The most obvious and primitive level of understanding was that of the American lay public, who read the daily newspapers and pulp magazines, who had never heard of Freud, let alone Jung, and who were being introduced to Freudian ideas for the first time via mainstream avenues. They simply had to take Freud as he was interpreted to them by others or as he was made available to them in translation.

Between 1912 and 1916, articles on psychoanalysis were beginning to appear in such popular publications as *Ladies Home Journal* and *Good Housekeeping,* and Freud was becoming a household word, though only in terms of the most basic of his ideas.[11] The primary emphasis in the popular literature was on the interpretation of dreams and unconscious mechanisms at work in psychic life, such as slips of the tongue and forgetfulness. Whereas the sexual hypothesis would come later and would at first be too controversial for comfortable digestion, at least the general public was becoming acquainted with such terms as the "id," the "ego," and the "superego," as well as with the dream as an expression of an unconscious wish.

On a slightly more sophisticated plane were Freud's interpreters— usually physicians and psychologists, but they were soon joined by literary and artistic types, by liberal clergymen, by journalists, and by successfully treated patients. This group tended to be educated, middle to upper class, intellectually oriented, and highly verbal, since the "talking cure" was a primarily verbal practice. Before World War II, this level of audience included such figures as the social critic Walter Lippmann; Boston and New York physicians like James Jackson Putnam, Isador Coriat, Jelliffe, and Brill; and Washington psychiatrist William Alanson White. By the 1930s, others could be counted among this group, such as Franz Alexander, who ran the Chicago Institute for Psychoanalysis after 1931; Erik Erikson, who came to the United States after 1933; Karen Horney and Erich Fromm, both neo-Freudians; Gordon Allport, academic psychologist; the writer Anaïs Nin; and the psychiatrist Karl Menninger. All together, this tier comprised the most objective interpreters of Freud's ideas, professionals who followed the development of his theories, discussed his ideas among themselves, fought the battles for professional recognition, and interpreted psychoanalysis to public audiences.

For Freud's most avid lay readers, psychoanalysis was the source of all culture. One's sexual life not only became a matter of record in the doctor-patient relationship, but for those more liberal artists and writers who saw themselves as an integral part of modernism, psychoanalysis also meant freedom to express one's unconscious impulses in art, literature, and film, as well as in social relationships. No idea about psychosexual stages of development was too shocking to be discussed.[12]

Many of these were in the third group, individuals of the visionary tradition whose inner experiences have always been more profound and much deeper than the American cultural institutions to which they belonged could articulate. These individuals either freely mixed the new ideas of Freud and Jung with their liberal Christian, transcendentalist, occult, or esoteric worldviews, or else they had no need of Freud, because their Catholicism, or their yoga, their meditation, their Rosicrucianism, Theosophy, or Christian Science, or whatever persuasion, provided them with everything and more that Freud and Jung offered about the possibilities of interior exploration.

Within this group, Ralph Waldo Trine and Napolean Hill wrote inspirational best-sellers based on New Thought; Frank Buchman, originator of the Oxford Group, out of which came Alcoholics Anonymous, developed a worldwide charismatic and psychospiritual ministry without mentioning a word of Freud; and Edgar Cayce, Arthur Ford, and Eileen Garrett became well-known psychics whose writing about interior states of consciousness had nothing to do with psychoanalysis. Similarly, the endeavors of the astrologer Evangeline Adams and of the writers Thomas Merton and Aldous Huxley dealt with interior planes sans the influence of psychoanalysis. Such figures lived through the Freudian era but had access to altered states of consciousness more dynamic than the ones described in Freud's system.

This distinction among audience levels is important to keep in mind because the histories of psychology and psychiatry as written tend to present a different story than the histories of psychoanalysis written by psychoanalysts themselves or by popularizers of Freud's ideas. The histories of psychology and psychiatry tend to be the histories of these disciplines as sciences, and since the status of psychoanalysis as a science has always remained questionable, these are the histories that mention psychoanalysis, if at all, most unfavorably.[13]

Histories written by psychoanalysts themselves or by those who know of their interior experience only through psychoanalysis have tended to be hagiographic—that is, lauding Freud sometimes to the level of sainthood. These writers are absolutely convinced that Freud had a tremendous impact on modern culture, that Freud discovered the unconscious, and that psychoanalysis as a secular form of self-knowledge was the first ideology to replace formal religion.

Both formal and popular social histories of psychological schools completely ignore the fact that there remained underground a flourishing alternative reality tradition, the devotees of which often took up the psychological language of Freud but used it to describe spiritual kinds of experiences completely denied to the normative interpreters of mainstream American culture. Such experiences were interpreted in terms of the id, the ego, and the superego, but when it came to talking about the unconscious generally—what it was, where it was, how deep it was—the tendency was always to superimpose on Freud's language a neotranscendentalist, Jamesian, Bergsonian, and Jungian definition of higher consciousness that Freud never intended. It is my contention that psychoanalysis became truly Americanized once it was interpreted at this level and transmitted in this form.

We can point to numerous historical examples of how this came about: Some of the keenest early supporters of psychoanalysis were the religious psychotherapies such as the Emmanuel movement. Elwood Worcester praised Freud on many occasions, incorporated his ideas about sexuality and the defense mechanisms into his books and articles, but clearly mixed Freudian metaphors with those of the Christian scheme of salvation. To these, especially in the 1920s, Worcester also added a heavy dose of laboratory-based psychical research, believing all three were compatible. Here was a significant reinterpretation of what Freud had intended.[14]

Freud made his opposition to this view quite clear when interviewed by Adlebert Albrecht after the Clark University conference in 1909:

When I think that there are many physicians who have been studying modern methods of psychotherapy for decades and who yet practice it only with the greatest caution, this undertaking of a few men without medical, or with very superficial medical training, seems to me at the very least of questionable good. I can easily understand that this combination of church and psychotherapy appeals to the public, for the public has always had a certain weakness for everything that savors of mysteries and the mysterious, and these it probably suspects behind psychotherapy, which, in reality has nothing, absolutely nothing mysterious about it.[15]

James Jackson Putnam's reinterpretation of psychoanalysis is another case in point.[16] As previously noted, Putnam had originally helped launch the Emmanuel movement but had distanced himself from it and had become one of its most trenchant critics by 1909. As one of the leading elder statesmen in American neurology at the time, he turned out to be, according to Ernest Jones, the "biggest catch" for psychoanalysis as a result of the Clark conference. Thereafter, Putnam tirelessly championed Freud's ideas both in America and abroad and kept up an important correspondence with Freud himself.

But when we look into the nature of their exchange and into the various articles he composed in service of the movement, the one idea that stands out is Putnam's staunch advocacy of a philosophy for psychoanalysis. By this he meant that, whereas Freud claimed psychoanalysis was scientific and therefore value free and not based on any philosophy, Putnam, following James, believed that all systems of thought are always based on philosophical presuppositions of some kind. Psychoanalysis, he said, needed to be aware of its implied philosophy, which Putnam interpreted as healing and character development.

This issue came out in Putnam's letters to Freud, when Putnam explained that one cannot simply get a patient to sublimate instinctual impulses of a sexual nature just because it was a scientific principle that they should do so. There always had to be a reason why a person tried to strive to become something more, and this Putnam said comes about through an appeal to ideals, goals, and values. Freud interpreted this as altogether too Protestant an explanation, but he encouraged Putnam to keep on writing nevertheless. Putnam's further elaboration on these themes made it clear that he was talking about striving to realize a higher consciousness that he could interpret only in transcendentalist, Jamesian, and Bergsonian terms.

Putnam transmitted this legacy to others in the Boston School of Psychopathology, among them L. Eugene Emerson, the first clinical psychologist at the Massachusetts General Hospital in 1911, who practiced a modified form of Freudian and Jungian analysis. Emerson inherited Putnam's psychotherapeutic patients after 1917, when Putnam died, and went on himself to write articles advocating the same position. The most significant of these in terms of this discussion was a piece he published in 1933 titled "Emerson and Freud: A Study in Contrasts," a comparison of transcendentalist and Freudian ideas.[17]

Another case study for the Americanization of psychoanalysis comes from Smith Ely Jelliffe and William Alanson White. Here were physicians who had followed the psychotherapeutic movement closely and had already made important contributions before they jointly launched the *Psychoanalytic Review* in 1913. Jelliffe and White had been the translators of Paul DuBois's *Psychic Treatment of Nervous Disorders* (1905), the first text in the English language to present psychotherapeutics in the context of the diagnostic categories of physical medicine, hence making the new medical psychology accessible to the general practitioner. Jelliffe, originally a chemist interested in natural plant substances, and White, a physician interested in the new subject of environmental factors in mental illness, both brought a perspective to the *Psychoanalytic Review* more liberal than Freud's own orthodox views. In 1917, Jelliffe had also translated into English Herbert Silberer's *Problems of Mysticism and Its Symbolism*. This was a remarkable text applying psychoanalysis to the interpretation of alchemy,[18] a work that appeared long before Jung pursued the same subject. The question of Silberer's apparent suicide over Freud's rejection of the book remains unsettled, however.

Another significant influence on the reinterpretation of Freud to American audiences was the Frenchman Henri Bergson, who toured the United States in 1912 to the acclaim of thousands, including Teddy Roosevelt and Walter Lippmann.[19] Bergson had established a warm friendship with William James beginning in 1905, and James had begun to spread the gospel of Bergson to English-speaking audiences immediately thereafter. James had arranged for Bergson's *Creative Evolution* to be translated into English, and Bergson likewise arranged the translation of James's works into French after James died in 1910. While James was still alive, their correspondence bustled with comparisons between their respective theories. Sounding very Jamesian, the French philosopher and scientist lectured authoritatively on the stream of consciousness and the relation of matter to memory in a way that transfixed American audiences. He had read Freud and borrowed from his dream theories, meanwhile preaching a beneficent subconscious and the existence of a life force that guided evolution, which he called the "élan vital," an idea that American audiences thought Freud had used as well.

On the popular front, artists, writers, and actors began reading Freud's works and books about psychoanalysis. A flood of articles began appearing in women's magazines; novels and plays were produced with Freudian themes. Radical intellectuals disillusioned with Western capitalist culture took up Marx in protest against the oppressors of the masses and read Freud as a declaration of their liberation from outmoded sexual constraints of the nineteenth century. Harry Emerson Fosdick, the popular New York preacher, read him, as did Norman Vincent Peale, author of *How to Win Friends and Influence People.* Freud's ideas were also important in the work of Jacob Mareno, founder of a new form of theater and psychotherapy called psychodrama, and they were central to the teachings of the man who controlled the attention of American mothers with newborns for fifty years, Dr. Benjamin Spock.

But the earliest popularizers of Freudian theories after the religious psychotherapists were the New York intellectuals. Max Eastman, for example, was a New York writer and editor of *The Masses,* a liberal publication that freely mixed Freud and Jung and advocated fun, truth, and beauty, along with feminism, freedom, and revolution.[20] Originally, Eastman had come from a New England Congregationalist family that had been raised on Fletcherism, deep breathing, and raw foods. He attended Columbia University, where he came under the influence of John Dewey, the great American philosopher of pragmatism who himself was a practitioner of the Alexander movement technique. Eventually making his way into the New York literary scene, Eastman was a man who moved comfortably between uptown mainstream society and the bohemian set in Greenwich Village. At one point, he became worried about committing adultery and decided to see an analyst; he was referred to Jelliffe by Jung's disciple Beatrice Hinkle, whom Eastman had met in a New Thought sanitarium. Eastman read every book he could get his hands on about Freud's theories and became in his own words a kind of "amateur specialist in mental healing."[21] He was a patient of Brill's as well, but he eventually left analysis unsatisfied that his neurosis could be cured by that method.

Mabel Dodge was another example of a young radical interested in psychoanalysis.[22] The sometime partner of D. H. Lawrence and the eventual wife of the Taos Native American Tony Luhan, Dodge came from a wealthy family in Buffalo, New York. She was interested in everything liberal, involved herself in literature and the arts, became immersed in radical political causes like sexual emancipation, traveled extensively, wrote books, and ultimately settled in Taos, New Mexico. She was first psychoanalyzed in New York in 1914, when she went to see Jelliffe over a "jealousy complex" that had developed over her lover's flirtation with another woman. Later, she became a patient of Brill, who only denigrated her belief in an inner power and criticized her for having a Jehovah complex. However, in order to balance things out, during this analysis she was also a patient of Emma Curtis Hopkins, an independent New Thought practitioner who had originally been a disciple of Mary Baker Eddy.[23]

In 1923, Andre Tridon lectured in defense of psychoanalysis to 500 members of the National Opera Club, providing another example of how Freud's ideas were able to flourish in the context of the shadow culture. The event was billed as a "psychic tea." In the name of the new freedoms ushered in by modernism, the chairwoman held up the ideal of the "unclad flapper," urging all members to "throw off" their "corsets" and "learn wonderful things."[24] Tridon's talk attempted to portray psychoanalysis as sound science that treated nervous diseases, not a means of carrying on a lewd conversation with a decent woman. Although some in the audience no doubt appreciated his message, he was followed on the agenda by a speaker who photographed spirits.

The American Jung

THERE CAN BE LITTLE DOUBT that the concept of America meant different things to Freud and Jung, although it is equally true that without the large American reception of their ideas, without American patients and American money to buy American editions of their works, there likely would have been no Freud and no Jung. Jung dreamed about going to America, and once he visited, he returned again and again; Freud came only once and swore he would never return.[25]

Jung had begun his study of English around 1890 as a schoolboy in Basel. He spent two months in London as a postgraduate doctor of medicine practicing the language and thereafter collected numerous English-speaking students and patients. Physicians such as Frederick Peterson, August Hoch, and Brill came from America to work at the Burghölzli Asylum, and through these American contacts, Jung was called in to consult such rich American patients as Stanley McCormick, a schizophrenic who had been at the McLean Hospital between 1905 and 1907. Most likely through this connection to McCormick, Harold Fowler McCormick and Edith Rockefeller McCormick also came to consult with Jung in 1909. In 1913, at the suggestion of Putnam, Jung accepted Fanny Bowditch as a patient, the daughter of the late Henry Pickering Bowditch, who, we will recall, was the dean of the Harvard Medical School and William James's close friend.

Jung's first trip to the United States was in 1909, when he traveled with Freud and Sándor Ferenczi to speak at Clark University. One of the highlights of this journey was that he got to meet William James, during which time they discussed their mutual interest in psychical research. He spent a month afterward traveling to Worcester, Niagara Falls, the Adirondacks, and back to New York City. He returned to the United States again in March 1910 and passed through New York en route to Chicago, where he was to consult with the McCormicks. He had hastily arranged this particular trip and delayed telling Freud, who was most annoyed to find out that he had gone. When he finally did write, Jung told Freud that one of the items on his agenda had been to pay another visit to James.

Sometime during one of these trips, Jung first met Beatrice M. Hinkle, a Californian who had been commissioner of health in San Francisco before coming to New York in 1905. She opened a psychotherapeutic clinic at Cornell Medical College in 1908. In 1911, she went to Zurich and worked with Jung, who referred to her as an "American charmer," and by 1913, she was back in New York at work on the first English-language translation of Jung's *Psychology of the Unconscious.*

Jung traveled again to the United States in September 1912. Jelliffe had arranged for him to lecture at Fordham University, where he presented his own reinterpretation of psychoanalysis, which, when printed as *Symbols of Transformation,* led to the final break with Freud. Numerous people who attended were significantly influenced by these talks, among them L. Eugene Emerson.

While he was in New York, Jung also held seminars for psychiatrists at Bellevue Hospital, Wards Island, and the New York Academy of Medicine. These events were newsworthy enough for the *New York Times* to print a feature story on Jung, complete with a photograph.

Jung returned to America yet again in the spring of 1913, when he again lectured in New York City. After this, he did not return for another twelve years. During this interlude, a Jung circle began to develop. There was, of course, Hinkle, who always remained somewhat of an outsider to the groups that subsequently developed. A more enduring relationship developed among Constance Long, a London analyst who had just emigrated to New York, and two women, Eleanor Bertine and Kristine Mann, both medical graduates of Cornell. Bertine and Mann traveled to Zurich in the 1920s and attended Jung's first seminars in England, where they met Esther Harding, who followed them back to New York to establish an analytic practice.

Other Jungian analysts from America also appeared on the scene at this time. One was Frances G. Wickes, who, after her analysis with Jung in Zurich, set up her practice in New York apart from these others. Another was Elizabeth Whitney, from San Francisco, who studied with Jung in the mid-1920s. When she began her practice in 1928, she was likely the first Jungian in California.

In 1924, Jung returned to the United States on a whirlwind trip financed by two American friends, Fowler McCormick, Edith's son, and George Porter. He went to Chicago, the Grand Canyon, the Taos Pueblo in New Mexico, New Orleans, and Washington, D.C. He spent just one day in New York, lecturing on racial psychology and the morphology of skulls to a seminar that convened at Mann's apartment.

By then, his *Psychological Types* (1922) had appeared, and most of the major ideas for which he is now known had become common currency. Hinkle's *Psychology of the Unconscious* had been a mass-market success, having been reviewed in newspapers across the nation, and just as everyone was talking about Freud, they were also talking about Jung. Freud was known for his psychosexual stages of development, the Oedipus complex, and his secular trinity of the id, the ego, and the superego. Jung was known for his idea of the unconscious complexes, for the conception of the archetypes and the collective unconscious, and for establishing the goal of his kind of therapy as individuation—the struggle between the ego and the self for control of personality and the eventual supremacy of selfhood in the holistic evolution of the individual. The concrete living out of Jung's myth of individuation became the focus of several creative relationships during this period, one of which developed between Christiana Morgan and Henry A. Murray.

Murray and Morgan

ALSO AT THIS TIME, Jung met two important figures in the history of Jungian psychology in America: Henry A. Murray, physician, biochemist, Melville scholar, and personality theorist; and Christiana Morgan, lay analyst, psychonaut, paramour, and artist extraordinaire.

Murray had come to psychology with a background in embryology and biochemistry and left the field completely transformed through his scientific and clinical study of personality. He accomplished this by constructing a personological system that was at once eclectic, pragmatic, and holistic. Based as much on William James, Herman Melville, and nineteenth-century American literature as on European depth psychology and L. J. Henderson's blood grid work in physical chemistry, the goal of personology was to measure the component parts of the whole through a battery of assessments that produced an in-depth biography of the individual. Through this work, Murray defined the direction of personality theory in American psychology for a generation. His name is synonymous with the Thematic Apperception Test, the most widely used instrument in clinical practice for decades. He developed the assessment procedures for the OSS during World War II; he helped introduce depth psychology to American literary criticism; he was a key player in bringing psychoanalysis into academic psychology; and he was the foremost exponent after James of psychology as a person-centered science, despite the rigid dictates of the reductionistic age in which he worked.

Morgan, on the other hand, was a highly intelligent, well-connected, beautiful woman from a Boston Brahmin family on her mother's side and scientific medicine on her father's. After training in nursing and art school, she turned her attention to the practice of psychotherapy and the process of personality transformation. Her trance visions unlocked the deepest recesses of her femininity and launched her on an inward journey toward self-actualization that became the main point of her life, and she did this long before the modern women's movement gave widespread credibility to such an endeavor. She so inspired Jung that his method of active imagination was immeasurably quickened, and her notebooks formed the basis of Jung's Vision Seminars. She was the primary motivating force behind the Harvard Psychological Clinic under Murray; she was the principal author of the Thematic Apperception Test, in that she herself painted half the pictures; and she was the inspiration behind Murray's Melville biography, as well as the sounding board for Murray's understanding of personality in the dyadic relationship.

So far, history has judged this pair as simply two people who embarked upon a highly erotic, intellectual, and religious quest for forty years while they were both married to someone else. But the real issue is discerning what resulted from this relationship. Lives were certainly shattered, projects left unfinished, goals unrealized. Their journey was not without pain and sorrow. Morgan was not permitted to actualize her transformative visions and emerge as her own independent soul, because she chose instead to follow Jung's advice and live through the less relevant aspirations of the powerful men in her life. Murray, brilliant, penetrating, but mercurial, consistently fled the scene either to get away from Morgan or to abandon his psychological work at her bidding. They were both guilty of being too rich, too privileged, too narcissistic, and too absorbed in the overblown spiritual importance of their essentially illicit relationship.

Nevertheless, they were experimenters in personal freedom before its time. They risked the existential dangers of standing perilously outside the bounds of acceptable lifestyles in order to peer over a horizon that few, except perhaps the Tantric adepts of yoga, are permitted to view. They believed, however rightly or wrongly, that they were participating in a holy experiment—the spiritual integration and transcendence of opposites.

Partly through Murray's influence, Jung was able to return again to America in 1936. At that time, he received an honorary doctorate from Harvard University on the occasion of its three hundredth anniversary, along with other notables in psychology, such as Jean Piaget and Pierre Janet. In his speech, Jung gave an overview of his psychology as it had developed up to that point and praised only one American as a major influence on his thinking: William James. The talk was little remembered, helped into obscurity by the fact that Harvard printed it under the authorship of "Charles Gustav Jung."

A year later, when Murray was traveling through Vienna, he got an unexpected summons to see Sigmund Freud. In the substance of the conversation, Freud wanted to know why Harvard hadn't offered him an honorary degree. Murray explained that Harvard never offered an honorary degree unless it was absolutely sure that the recipient would come to the university to accept it, and Freud had always said that after his visit in 1909 to Clark, he would never set foot in America again. The university officials had even gone to some lengths to interview two of Freud's closest disciples, Erik Erikson and Hans Sachs, both of whom were in Boston during the planning of the festivities. Erikson had been working for Murray in the Harvard Psychological Clinic and for Stanley Cobb in psychiatry at the Harvard Medical School, while Sachs was the senior training analyst at the Boston Psychoanalytic Society. Both of them assured the Harvard people that Freud remained adamant about not coming to America, so the university never made the offer. Freud accepted Murray's explanation, then asked, "But why Jung?" Murray answered simply, because he was the next on the list.

After the Harvard trip, Jung returned to the States once more to give the Terry Lectures at Yale on psychology and religion. In addition to other lectures and seminars given at that time, he met with Mr. and Mrs. Paul Mellon, who came a year later to Zurich, attended Jung's seminars, and then returned again to undergo analysis. Subsequently, they funded the Bollingen Foundation, which produced the English-language version of Jung's collected works through Princeton University Press.

After the Yale trip, Jung never again came to the New World. Nevertheless, his work continued to have an influence. Numerous Jungians fled Europe and settled in the United States because of the war, and beginning in the 1940s, Jungian groups began to convene, several of which later developed into full-fledged training institutes. Jungian journals, such as *Spring,* started to appear.

Despite the fact that he loved America, Jung remained somewhat bitter toward the country to the end of his life because it had cast him so totally in the shadow of Freud, when, as has been suggested, he was really the only twentieth-century psychologist of the older dissociation school to take up the methods of unconscious symbolism. Rightly, however, his archetypal theories have been Americanized and continue to have strong vitality among the various counterculture psychotherapies of transcendence, long after psychoanalysis has ceased to be a moving influence in that domain.

The True Era of Psychoanalysis

WHEREAS FREUDIAN IDEAS HAD BEEN CIRCULATING in certain pockets of American culture for decades, it was not until the 1930s that we can speak of the era of psychoanalysis proper. This delay occurred because psychoanalysis rode in on the coattails of the older intuitive psychology of character formation originally derived from the transcendentalists that had been revamped into a uniquely American dynamic psychology of the subconscious in the hands of people like William James, James Jackson Putnam, and other researchers associated with the so-called Boston School of Psychopathology. This older tradition persisted until about the 1920s, when the psychotherapeutic focus in American culture slowly began to shift from Boston to New York, Baltimore, and Washington, D.C., and to the new readers of psychoanalysis. Also at this time, the first of the psychoanalytic training institutes was established. The New York Psychoanalytic Institute remained the most orthodox and loyal to the Viennese model. Chicago, Boston, and other American cities soon followed suit.

But this was also a time of numerous renditions of psychoanalysis. The analytic émigrés began pouring into the United States by the mid-1930s, and one informal but highly influential group responsible for the widespread reinterpretation and dissemination of psychoanalysis throughout American culture was already under way. This group, the Zodiak Club, hovered around the American psychiatrist Harry Stack Sullivan beginning in 1931.[26] Through Sullivan and the Zodiak Club, psychoanalysis found its way into various avenues of the social sciences related to psychology and psychiatry, particularly sociology, anthropology, and linguistics. Beyond these boundaries, several personalities constellating around Sullivan, including Erich Fromm and Karen Horney, applied their version of psychoanalytic ideas to such contemporary problems as gender issues, totalitarianism, the meaning of love and freedom, and the fate of modern civilization. Through their best-selling books, depth psychology in the Freudian mold found able interpreters who by their very deviations served to elevate psychoanalysis to the status of a cultural phenomenon in the West.[27]

The Zodiak Club first convened during Prohibition, when Sullivan, Clara Thompson, William Silverberg, and a few others began meeting in a New York speakeasy on Monday evenings for dinner, drinks, and discussion of psychiatry, mainly Freud's ideas. The three had known one another from time they had spent in Baltimore, where Thompson had founded what was then called the Miracle Club, because patients seemed to miraculously get better after their cases were discussed by the group.

According to one biographer, the newly reconvened New York circle was named the Zodiak Club on a whim by Sullivan. Every member was required to represent themselves through the symbol of some appropriate animal, the exact reason for which remains unknown. Sullivan became a horse; Thompson became a puma; Silverberg, a gazelle. Later, others were to join this group, including Horney, Fromm, Ruth Benedict, Margaret Mead, Ralph Linton, and Edward Sapir. In all, the Zodiak Club became a convergence of intellectual influences from Chicago, New York, New Haven, and Washington, linking some of the best minds in the social and behavioral sciences from those environments. For the dozen or so years that it lasted, its members produced some remarkable cultural benchmarks, not the least of which were a few national best-sellers, including Horney's *The Neurotic Personality of Our Time* (1937) and Fromm's *Escape from Freedom* (1941).

As for the group's internal dynamics, while Sullivan's stature and ideas dominated, he himself also evolved as the discussions became more theoretical. Thompson was his devoted follower, but she also introduced him to orthodox psychoanalysis and feminine psychology. In a certain sense, she was just as much at the center of the group as the more conspicuous Sullivan. Horney, another important woman in the group, appreciated Sullivan's ideas, but her psychology was already well formed from her contact with Freud before her membership in the club. Fromm, in contrast, continued to go through large changes from all quarters. But overall, everyone operated more or less as independent entities. Each had his or her own positions, and there seems to have been more interaction and cross-fertilization than competition. Ideas and insights were aired and discussed, then each person applied the result in his or her own domain. Occasionally, some mutual project would emerge. One of the big issues they discussed, for instance, was female sexuality, which led to a collaboration between Thompson and Horney and an altogether new psychoanalytic interpretation of women.

After Freud's death in 1939, psychoanalysis in America had a curious fate, as analysts in the more orthodox institutes valiantly but unsuccessfully attempted to keep Freud's teachings true to their original form at the same time that psychoanalysis was rapidly being adapted to more pragmatic, pluralistic, and optimistic ideals unique to the American scene. Freud's most orthodox interpreters were not helped by Freud himself, who significantly altered his sexual theories at the end of his life to account for a competing death instinct. As well, Freud had spent the majority of his career articulating a psychology of primitive unconscious forces and the means by which instinctual impulses became socialized. Meanwhile, a succeeding generation of younger analysts in both England and America, the so-called object relations theorists, had already turned their attention to the adaptive functions of the ego and were pushing for an interpretation of psychoanalysis that was more cognitive in orientation.

Nevertheless, the dynasty was continued by Anna, Freud's daughter. As a woman and a child analyst, Anna added new dimensions to psychoanalytic discourse from the 1930s onward, yet her gender and her specialty also created a power vacuum in the psychoanalytic hierarchy as to who could take the master's place, who could out-Freud Freud, or, at best, who could ascend to the position of an American Freud and keep the theoretical formulations coming. Although various personalities began to jockey for the position, the man who accidentally donned that mantle by popular acclaim and who had not even intended to compete in such a race in the first place was Erik Erikson.[28]

At the same time, to the general and professional public, it appeared that orthodox psychoanalysis was fractionating into several streams. Three that were significant for what was to come included the work of Wilhelm Reich, who radicalized psychoanalysis by extending it into sexual politics;[29] the work of Victor Frankl, who, as a result of surviving the Nazi death camps, evolved into an existentialist;[30] and what appeared to be a revision of Jung's work by such neo-Jungians as Joseph Campbell and James Hillman, who, in the Jungian tradition, further spiritualized the unconscious and populated it with archetypal motifs drawn from a visionary map of the world's mythologies.[31]

In sum, it can be said that Freud's message was eminently suitable for the modern Judeo-Christian world, coming from a mix of religion and science and speaking directly to the needs of modern Protestant secular culture by adopting the language of the unconscious. The widespread dissemination of his ideas in America, however, required further modification, which took his ideas out of their original context and, by imbuing them with the elements of popular folk psychology, turned psychoanalysis into something uniquely American.

In the process, though the attempt to keep Freud's teachings pure has proved an impossible task, psychoanalysis has retained many of its variations within the original framework Freud established. It was inevitable, however, that at some point the seams would burst and the discipline would produce flagrant examples of ideology beyond anything

Freud could have imagined—ways of thinking that contained precisely those elements that he had tried to keep out.

Perhaps one of the most important realizations to come from this process is that the psychoanalytic frame of reference is built upon a set of assumptions historically relevant for the time in which it flourished but that is now seen in the tradition of contemporary folk psychology as totally insufficient for comprehending altered states of consciousness, the transcendent experience, and non-Western views of reality. The question of whether or not people trained in the psychoanalytic frame of reference can ever really, themselves, transcend the limits of Freud's system is an important one. Many schooled with an analytic background may see that there are other ways to approach these larger questions about consciousness, but they may not be able to access them without setting aside the very foundation upon which Freud's thought is based.

Why anyone would even contemplate transcending such limits is the real issue. One possible reason is that nothing less may be required if we are to grasp the direction of some new depth psychology to come. At the same time, it is also equally plausible that, given a new era beyond the present one in which we experience a cross-cultural exchange of ideas between East and West unprecedented in the history of Western thought, a new depth psychology of the future may look more Jungian than Freudian, although neither of these names will likely be associated with it.

Notes

1. Adapted from S. Rosenzweig, *Freud, Jung, and Hall the Kingmaker: The Expedition to America, 1909* (Seattle: Hogrefe & Huber, 1992).

2. See, for instance, Nigel Walker, *A Short History of Psychoanalysis in Theory and Practice* (New York: Noonday Press, 1957); D. Shakow and D. Rapaport, *The Influence of Freud on American Psychology* (Cleveland, OH: Meridian Books, 1968); J. Gach, "Culture and Complex: On the Early History of Psychoanalysis in America," in E. R. Wallace III and L. C. Pressley, eds., *Essays in the History of Psychiatry* (Columbia, SC: Wm. S. Hall Psychiatric Institute, 1980), pp. 135–160; J. C. Burn-

ham, "Psychoanalysis and American Medicine, 1894–1918: Medicine, Science, and Culture," *Psychological Issues Monograph,* 5:4 (1967): 1–249; Philip Rief, *The Triumph of the Therapeutic: Uses of Faith After Freud* (New York: Harper & Row, 1966); and J. M. Quen and E. T. Carlson, eds., *American Psychoanalysis: Origins and Development* (New York: Bruner/Mazel, 1978).

3. E. I. Taylor, "The New Jung Scholarship," special issue of *Psychoanalytic Review,* ed. Andrew Samuels, 83:4 (August 1996): 547–568.

4. E. I. Taylor, "Jung in His Intellectual Context: The Swedenborgian Connection," *Studia Swedenborgiana,* 7:2 (1991): 47–69.

5. E. I. Taylor, "Jung Before Freud, Not Freud Before Jung: Jung's Influence in American Psychotherapeutic Circles Before 1909," *Journal of Analytical Psychology,* 43:1 (January 1998): 97–114.

6. Auguste Forel, *Out of My Life and Work,* trans. Bernard Miall (New York: Norton, 1937).

7. William McGuire, ed., *The Freud/Jung Letters: The Correspondence Between Sigmund Freud and C. G. Jung,* trans. Ralph Manheim and R. F. C. Hull (Princeton, NJ: Princeton University Press, 1974).

8. Sabina Spielrein was considered a patient, not a younger colleague (see A. Caratenuto, *A Secret Symmetry: Sabina Spielrein Between Jung and Freud* [New York: Pantheon, 1982]), and the era of Anna Freud and Marie Bonaparte did not begin until the late 1920s (see Paul Roazen, *Freud and His Followers* [New York: New York University Press, 1984]).

9. William McGuire, "Jungian New York," *Quadrant,* 16:1 (1983): 39–44; and William McGuire, "Jung's Relation with Britain and the United States," *Journal of Analytic Psychology* (1995).

10. Emma Jung, *Animus and Anima* (New York: Spring Publications, 1978).

11. Nathan G. Hale Jr., *Freud and the Americans: The Beginnings of Psychoanalysis in the United States, 1876–1917* (New York: Oxford University Press, 1971), esp. pp. 397–433. See also Edwin Tenney Brewster, "Dreams and Forgetting," *McClure's Magazine,* 39 (October 1912): 714–719; Max Eastman, "Exploring the Soul and Healing the Body," *Everybody's Magazine,* 32 (June 1915): 741; Floyd Dell, "Speaking of Psychoanalysis: The New Boon at the Dinner Table," *Vanity Fair,* December 5, 1915, p. 53; Pearce Bailey, "The Wishful Self," *Scribner's Magazine,* 58 (July 1915): 115–121; and Peter Clark MacFarlane, "Diagnosis by Dreams," *Good Housekeeping,* 60 (February 1915): 132.

12. For the European counterpart to the American visionary tradition that purportedly contributed to the cultural atmosphere of the radical depth psychologists, see Martin Green, *Mountain of Truth: The Counter-Culture Begins, Ascona, 1900–1920* (Hanover, NH: University Press of New England, 1986).

13. The classic text in psychology is E. G. Boring's *History of Experimental Psychology* (New York: Century Co., 1929; rpt. 1950), whereas Franz Alexander and Sheldon Salesnick's *History of Psychiatry: An Evaluation of Psychiatric Thought and Practice from Prehistoric Times to the Present* (New York: Harper & Row, 1966) is more favorable to psychoanalysis, as is Gregory Zilboorg, in collaboration with George W. Henry, *A History of Medical Psychology* (New York: Norton, 1941) or Gardner Murphy, *Historical Introduction to Modern Psychology* (New York: Harcourt, Brace & Co., 1929).

14. Hale, *Freud and the Americans,* pp. 225–249.

15. *Boston Evening Transcript,* September 11, 1909, pt. 3, p. 3.

16. Nathan G. Hale Jr., *James Jackson Putnam and Psychoanalysis: Letters Between Putnam and Sigmund Freud, Ernest Jones, William James, Sandor Ferenczi, and Morton Prince, 1877–1917* (Cambridge, MA: Harvard University Press, 1971); and E. I. Taylor, "James Jackson Putnam's Fateful Meeting with Freud: The 1909 Clark University Conference," *Voices: The Art and Science of Psychotherapy,* 21:1 (1985): 78–89.

17. L. Eugene Emerson, "A Philosophy for Psychoanalysis," *Psychoanalytic Review,* 2 (1915): 422–427; and L. Eugene Emerson, "Emerson and Freud: A Study in Contrast," *Psychoanalytic Review,* 20 (1933): 208–214.

18. Herbert Silberer, *Problems of Mysticism and Its Symbolism,* trans. Smith Ely Jelliffe (New York: Moffat, Yard & Co., 1917).

19. Hale, *Freud and the Americans,* pp. 242–244.

20. Nathan G. Hale Jr., *The Rise and Crisis of Psychoanalysis in the United States: Freud and the Americans, 1917–1985* (New York: Oxford University Press, 1995), pp. 68–69.

21. Ibid.

22. Ibid, pp. 66–68.

23. Ibid., p. 72.

24. Ibid.

25. Thomas Martinez and Eugene Taylor, " 'Yes, in You the Tempest Rages': The Archetypal Significance of America in Jung's Own Individuation Process," *Spring: Annual of Archetypal Psychology,* 1999.

26. Helen Swick Perry, *Psychiatrist of America: The Life of Harry Stack Sullivan* (Cambridge, MA: Harvard University Press, 1982). See also Patrick Mullahy, *The Beginnings of Modern American Psychiatry: The Ideas of Harry Stack Sullivan* (Boston: Houghton Mifflin, 1973).

27. See, for instance, Joseph M. Natterson, "Karen Horney, 1885–1952," in Franz Alexander, Samuel Eisenstein, and Martin Grotjahn, *Psychoanalytic Pioneers* (New York: Basic Books, 1966), pp. 450–451; Susan Quinn, *A Mind of Her Own: The Life of Karen Horney* (New York: Addison-Wesley, 1988); and Daniel Burston, *Erich Fromm: The Man and His Work* (Cambridge, MA: Harvard University Press, 1991).

28. Robert Coles, *Erik Erikson: The Growth of His Work* (Boston: Little, Brown/Atlantic Monthly, 1970).

29. Myron Sharaf, *Fury on Earth: A Biography of Wilhelm Reich* (New York: St. Martin's Press, 1983).

30. Victor Frankl, *Man's Search for Meaning: An Introduction to Logotherapy,* 4th ed. (Boston: Beacon Press, 1992).

31. Joseph Campbell, *The Hero with a Thousand Faces* (New York: Pantheon, 1949); and James Hillman, *Archetypal Psychology: A Brief Account, Together with a Complete Checklist of Works* (Dallas: Spring Publications, 1983).

Chapter Eleven

Esalen and the Counterculture Movement of the 1960s

ON THE EVENING OF JANUARY 6, 1966, ESALEN INSTITUTE, AN educational center of the burgeoning cultural revolution in consciousness, launched its new San Francisco branch with a public lecture by Abraham Maslow, the humanistic psychologist famous for his ideas about the self-actualizing personality. Typifying the close interrelation between psychology and religion in the folk culture, the event was held at Grace Cathedral, the cavernous Episcopal church in the heart of the city that had long been associated with innovative programs, social activism, and ecumenical dialogue among religions.

To open the event, George Leonard, the West Coast editor of *Look* magazine and the man who had helped broadcast the Esalen message, rose before a standing-room-only audience and delivered a preliminary statement on behalf of the institute.[1] His speech was full of hope and high ideals, reflecting the expansiveness of unlimited possibilities that so many felt at the time. In fact, it was delivered in such a charismatic and oracular style that for some who were there, it made more of a lasting impression than the remarks of the main speaker.

This was the festival of the Epiphany, Leonard said, and all there had gathered to celebrate a new *kairos,* the awakening of a new intelligence, where every scientist would become a seer and every academic a prophet. He then proclaimed: "The atom's soul is nothing but energy. Spirit blazes in the dullest clay. The life of every man—the heart of it—is pure and holy joy."[2]

It is difficult to speak of joy, however, when so many people on the planet are suffering, Leonard continued, and although we now have the means at hand to alleviate it, all we hear are the same worn-out doctrines of original sin and market forces driving the world economy: "At a time when at last we have all the means at hand to end war, poverty, and racial insanity, the prophets of despair discover no vision large enough to lead men to the merely possible."

On that evening, Leonard assured the audience that those who spoke would also speak for everyone who cast their lot with the future. The means had to be found for all people to actualize their divine potentiality, not by denying the world, but by affirming every part of it. He believed, too, that if the divine is present in the individual soul, then it must also be present in our social institutions—in the interplay of the two together. He foresaw no violent revolution, but a transformation that would come through constant interplay. In any event, the revolution had already begun. Human life would be transformed. But how it would be transformed, Leonard declared, was up to us.

This all happened right before the media discovered San Francisco as a site for social revolution and remade the counterculture community that was flourishing there into a national icon. Grace Cathedral was not so much a singularly momentous event as it was an emblematic instance of the times. American folk psychology as it is known today has been defined in large part by the cultural events of the 1960s. Whether for it or against it, observers have examined that era from the inside out and from every angle imaginable—political, social, economic, religious, and scientific, not to mention the interpretations fielded by deconstructionists, feminists, Marxists, and the various players in the counterculture movement. George Leonard was just giving us his take on the era. But the 1960s have yet to be considered within the larger context of the American visionary tradition or as a benchmark in the larger alternative-reality tradition in the West.

That story reads in three historical segments. The first phase of the movement began in the early 1940s with the interface among psychology, religion, and psychotherapy; it became more highly visible in the 1950s and ended roughly in the late 1960s. The second phase began around 1967, at the height of the intensive media attention that elevated the fledgling counterculture movement to the level of national and then international attention. When the media blitz passed in the mid-1970s, however, the interpreters of high culture sounded their requiem for the period. Then a third stage emerged, somewhat unobtrusively in the late 1970s, giving us a hint of what the long-term effect of the counterculture movement might be—namely, a spiritual awakening in modern popular consciousness of unprecedented proportions. This is the story from then until now.

What before had been considered merely a part of the counterculture has since become a permanently embedded influence within American society informing lifestyles, living arrangements, child rearing, definitions of family, and the meaning of work. At the same time, within certain quarters of the science establishment, objective interest in the intuitive and visionary dimensions of consciousness began to define a number of new social institutions at the intersection between higher learning and popular culture. The physics and consciousness movement, holistic health, transpersonal psychology, energy medicine, and what has come to be called frontier science are but a few of the names associated with the new awakening. Simultaneously, what previously had been considered the unique province of denominational Christianity came to include innovative and cross-cultural forms of spirituality that have completely redefined the religious landscape for more than two generations.

Esalen: A Case Study

CONTEMPORARY INTERPRETERS DELIGHT in characterizing the counterculture movement of the 1960s as a temporary adolescent flight from responsibility originating with the Beat generation that had preceded it in the 1950s. But it was also the case that the sons and daughters of the educated middle class coming of age in the 1960s spontaneously chose to leave the expected track of social development defined for them by authority figures who morally and spiritually came to command less and less respect. Sometimes setting aside the mantle of affluence completely and at other times deftly exploiting it, millions of young people began creating alternative ways of living, thinking, and worshipping that now, at the end of the twentieth century, continue to set the agenda in popular culture and show every sign of continuing to transform many of the most staid and immovable institutions of American high culture. In every way, the emerging generation carried on the theme of dissatisfaction first sounded by the Beat poets, but this was no mere adolescent flight—it was a sea change of generational opinion. And just as it was the birth of a new mythology inspiring a different type of cultural consciousness, it was also a coming-of-age of the modern shadow culture.

One of the most overt examples of the new mythos was none other than the Esalen Institute. Founded by Michael Murphy and Richard Price in 1961, Esalen is located in the forested regions of Big Sur along Highway 1, three hours south of San Francisco.[3] It sits in the midst of natural hot sulfur springs and hangs over a dramatic cliff on just a few acres of land 100 feet above the sea. Located in these dramatic surroundings at the farthest western outpost of the continent, Esalen became known as the modern temple of the body, the growth center of the new millennium, and a mecca for the American counterculture movement. Its history since its inception represents the flourishing in miniature of the American visionary tradition in the modern period, although it by no means represents the exclusive history of the larger counterculture movement of which it was a part.

According to its most recent historian, Walter Truett Anderson, the area around Esalen had long been the haunt of literary bohemians. Jack London had once journeyed there. John Steinbeck had been born and raised in nearby Salinas. And Henry Miller, author of *The Tropic of Cancer,* whose books had been banned in the United States, lived there off and on beginning in the 1940s. As a result, the area was highlighted in *Harper's* magazine in 1947 and became known as the rural Greenwich Village of the West Coast. Even at the time Esalen was founded, the area's residents were devotees of D. H. Lawrence and read the various gospels of William Blake, Henri Bergson, and G. I. Gurdjieff, while subscribing to the astrology of Dane Rudhyar and the psychotherapy of Wilhelm Reich.

The grounds that eventually became the Esalen Institute had passed into the Murphy family in 1910, when Henry Murphy, a physician, purchased the property, intending to develop it as a Continental-style spa. It remained in a wild state because of poor access, however, until state convict labor built the first road into the area in the 1930s. It was then used as a tourist resort and summer vacation spot, and though it eventually became a spiritual growth center, it continues to blend these purposes. As Anderson has characterized the place, it remains part motel, part monastery.

Michael Murphy, the eldest son of an attorney in Salinas, was born in 1930.[4] He was studious, athletic, eager, open, and gregarious but with an inward bent. A local rumor has it that he may have been immortalized at an early age as one of the characters in Steinbeck's novel *East of Eden.* An altar boy in the Episcopal Church, he once thought of the ministry as a proper vocation, but as he grew older, he became attracted to the spiritual psychology of Carl Jung and the philosophy of Will Durant. These influences set him on a course to define a religious outlook of his own.

He went to Stanford University, joined a fraternity, attended football games, and began a premedical course, intending to go into psychiatry. An accident of scheduling, however, led him into the class of Frederick Spiegelberg, a professor of Asian studies and recent German refugee, one of Europe's leading scholars in oriental religions, and a friend of Martin Heidegger, Paul Tillich, and Alan Watts. Due to Spiegelberg's influence, Murphy turned his attention to the writings of the Hindu mystic Sri Aurobindo, and though he retained his interest in athletic activities such as golf, he soon became an intensive meditator, sometimes sitting for eight hours a day.

Murphy fell in with a study group discussing East-West philosophy and soon conceived a plan to quit the premedical program and embark upon a course of personal spiritual exploration. He left Stanford briefly to study with Spiegelberg at the newly founded American Academy of Asian Studies in San Francisco before returning to finish his degree in psychology in 1952. Meanwhile, he steeped himself in writings on American transcendentalism, German idealism, Christian mysticism, Theosophy, Buddhism, and Hindu philosophy.

After two years in the army, where he was stationed in Puerto Rico, Murphy returned to Stanford to begin graduate work in philosophy. But he found the analytic atmosphere too stifling, so he left to tour the golf courses of Scotland in 1956. He soon ended up in India. There he took up residence at the Sri Aurobindo Ashram in Pondicherry. He meditated, lived the life of a monk, and developed a fantastically successful sports program in that religious environment. After sixteen months, he returned to California, where he took a room in Palo Alto, worked as a part-time bellhop, and wrote his first book, *Golf in the Kingdom,* an imaginative tale about a mythical golf course in Scotland and the ability to play through to the end of what became a spiritual journey for the hero, Shivas Irons.

In 1960, Murphy moved to San Francisco and into a rooming house full of Aurobindo followers. It was here that he met Richard Price, a Stanford graduate in psychology whose father was a Sears Roebuck executive from Chicago. After Stanford, Price had gone to Harvard to do graduate work in the Department of Social Relations, but he had dropped out and joined the air force. While stationed in northern California, he once again took courses at Stanford and thus came under Spiegelberg's influence. Spiegelberg steered him toward Vedanta and introduced him to Alan Watts, Episcopal minister and student of Zen, and

Fritz Perls, the psychoanalyst who originated Gestalt therapy. Price began taking courses at the American Institute of Asian Studies and soon married a woman he met through his friend Gia-Fu Feng, who taught the Chinese discipline of tai chi.

Shortly afterward, however, Price had a major psychotic episode and underwent shock therapy and Thorazine treatments for three months. He was transferred against his wishes to a facility near his family home outside Chicago, and from there his father forced him to go to the Institute of Living in Connecticut, where he stayed for a year. At the institute, Price was subjected to extensive insulin-shock treatments in addition to the standard electroshock therapy. He returned home a changed and beaten man. After a short time working for one of his uncles, he learned of an Aurobindo house in San Francisco started by his friends. His introduction there to Murphy established what would become a lasting friendship.

Their first act, without telling anyone, was to move down to the cabins on the Murphy family's land at Big Sur, intending to meditate and read. In the middle of their first night, they were suddenly awakened by a shotgun-wielding Hunter Thompson, who at the time was working as a security guard for Murphy's grandmother. Although there were a few friendly people living in the cabins, among them the young Joan Baez, it turned out to be a rough-and-tumble place. Fights were common at the local bar. Henry Miller and his friends were still around to frequent the hot-spring baths. Members of the First Church of God of Prophesy ran the motel but looked the other way in the face of frequent salacious behavior, as groups of rowdy homosexuals from San Francisco would overrun the place on weekends.

Murphy and Price nevertheless hatched a plan to take over the property and turn the hot-springs resort into a center for spiritual development. With the Murphy family behind them, they turned for advice to Spiegelberg, Watts, Gregory Bateson, Aldous Huxley, and Gerald Heard, all of whom lent their support. It was agreed that Murphy would arrange the programs and Price would administrate the daily activities. The two of them negotiated a loan, erected a few metal fences, and let loose some Dobermans to chase away recalcitrant freeloaders.

The first seminar, an informal gathering of some two dozen people, was held at the lodge in the summer of 1962 and was led by Watts. A gaggle of Stanford students soon began to come down for weekend seminars. One session was eventually led by Joe K. Adams, a psychologist who had done research on LSD under grants from the National Institute of Mental Health and who had studied psychic phenomena at Stanford. Another seminar leader was Dell Carlson, a high school teacher associated with a Bay Area group called the Sequoia Seminars. Kenneth Rexroth, a noted poet of the San Francisco Beat scene, also held forth. Gia-Fu Feng, the tai chi teacher, came down and joined the staff, as did a number of other worthies attracted by the news that a vital seminar center was about to come into being. Huxley's apt phrase "human potentialities" came to formally describe the first of these fledgling efforts. Murphy and Price eventually named the place Esalen, after the Esalen Indians, an eccentric local tribe that worshipped at the hot springs, ate unusual foods, and often went without clothes.

Guided by a vision of cultural transformation, what Murphy and Price called the "Apollonian Age" soon began at Esalen. Huxley came to Big Sur to discuss it with them. So did Abraham Maslow, who happened to be driving down the coast with his wife one day and accidentally stopped in, looking for a motel for the night. He discovered instead a paradise where people were sitting around reading his books and where he was already considered one of the deities. And then still others came, such as Willis Harman, a Stanford professor of engineering, who contributed to Esalen by leading a seminar on the new conceptual revolution in psychology. Lofty ideals and large panoramas were discussed, and this continued over the opening months until it was shortly felt that something other than discussions had to happen if a transformation was to come about.

What happened next, of course, changed everything. LSD was becoming more widely known, and a host of new methods involving bodywork, sensory experience, and group dynamics was about to explode onto the scene. The formal policy at Esalen has always been no drugs, but on an informal basis, this standard was completely ignored. Psychedelic drugs, along with prayer, meditation, art, music, and poetry, became the early staples of the second human potential series, held in 1963.

At this point, according to Murphy, there occurred "an inflection into the experiential." Here the programs shifted away from discussion and plunged headfirst into deep exploration of the senses, the emotions, the body, and the hidden noncognitive springs of motivation. Some sessions emphasized contemplative practice or the shamanic trance in an attempt to achieve a transcendental reality. Others emphasized artistic, intuitive, and theatrical aspects of psychotherapy. In this context, Gestalt therapy and encounter techniques flourished. Still other sessions emphasized somatic therapies, intense bodywork, therapeutic massage, and physical development.

One of the first of the experiential approaches was Jacob Moreno's psychodrama. Moreno, an Austrian psychiatrist and friend of Martin Buber, had become involved early in his career with therapy done in groups, believing that neurosis is caused by spiritual alienation from others. He had worked with various avant-garde thinkers and was heavily influenced by a drama group called the Spontaneity Theater. His new form of therapy—part ritual, part religion, part psychology—crystallized in 1925 when he moved to New York and established the Moreno Institute for the study of psychodrama. His tack was to get each patient in a group to spontaneously act out past traumas in the manner of a play. As an extension of this work, Moreno invented sociometry, the charting of primary and secondary relationships around the individual, which soon became a standard part of social psychology.

Psychodrama was originally one of the key elements in sensitivity training. First launched in 1946 at a seminar in New Britain, Connecticut, by the Gestalt psychologist Kurt Lewin, sensitivity training used role-playing, confrontation, observation, feedback, and an exchange of honest perceptions to examine the relationships people had with one another in a variety of settings. It soon became formalized into the National Training Laboratory Workshops and found widespread application in the burgeoning field of business management in both industry and government. Sensitivity training first came to Esalen in 1963, the same year that Gestalt therapy and bodywork arrived.

T-groups, as they were called, were taught by many, but the leading figure at Esalen was the psychologist Will Schutz. A UCLA Ph.D.,

Schutz was a specialist in group dynamics and in the relationship between personality and compatibility. He had done group work in the navy and developed a number of tests to measure interpersonal relations in groups, which he later taught at Harvard for four years before going out to University of California at Berkeley.

Schutz nearly ended up at Esalen a few times in 1963 but instead went back East to the Albert Einstein School of Medicine in New York, where he also became associated with the National Training Laboratories in Bethel, Maine. While he was primarily associated with mainstream psychiatrists doing psychoanalysis at Albert Einstein, he also involved himself in the thriving New York psychotherapeutic underground, which included psychosynthesis, the bioenergetics therapy of Franz Alexander, Rolfing, Gestalt therapy, and Moreno's psychodrama. His own techniques changed drastically as a result, and he developed a system of group work that he called open encounter.

Moving westward, according to Anderson, Schutz gave up a career full of scholarly and academic prestige for the simpler things, such as fame, happiness, money, sex, and power. He ended up as a freelance workshop leader in the middle of the human potential movement and in residence at Esalen, just as the institute was about to gain international attention.

Schutz's book *Joy: Expanding Human Awareness,* which came out in 1967, became an immediate best-seller.[5] The system he came to promote fostered openness, honesty, a willingness to take risks, the full expression of human emotion, taking personal responsibility for one's acts, and an enhanced sense of the body—elements he believed were lacking in individual personalities, as well as in the national character. He went on television talk shows and lectured widely, carrying his message, and consequently Esalen's, to millions of Americans. Meanwhile, back at Esalen, the encounter-group techniques he developed became a major part of the next Esalen residential program. Schutz moved in and remained in residence for several years.

Gestalt therapy was another major experiential therapy at Esalen. It was based on a hybrid of ideas and techniques from psychoanalysis, Reichean bodywork, psychodrama, Gestalt psychology, and sensory awareness, but it was largely dominated by the whimsical, Zen-like rudeness of its co-founder, Fritz Perls.[6] Its methods sought to put patients in touch with repressed feelings in the here and now and to heal overloaded sensory apparatus that prevented them from being fully functional. It could be done in an individual setting between patient and therapist, but it was best suited as a technique of intensive group work.

The third experiential therapy at Esalen was bodywork. This encompassed, among other things, sensory awareness, a group of physical training techniques taught by Charlotte Selver and based on the work of Elsa Gindler, an early-twentieth-century calisthenics teacher from Berlin. Selver had learned from Gindler and had taught at the Bauhaus before moving to New York in the 1930s.[7] Erich Fromm and Fritz Perls studied with Selver in the 1940s. She attracted the attention of Alan Watts in the 1950s, who first brought her to the West Coast. She and her husband, Charles Brooks, taught at Esalen for many years.

Imagine the degree of trust you would need to extend to someone leading you around for an hour while you were blindfolded. Think of what you would have to overcome, eyes closed, in order to allow your body to fall backward into infinity, only to land in someone's arms. Conceptualize the feeling of ten people lightly massaging your entire body all at the same time. These were some of the simpler techniques that filtered out of the Esalen training and found their way into continuing education programs, weekend encounter groups, couples therapy sessions, and church retreats throughout the country.

Various forms of dance therapy and Asian disciplines such as yoga were of interest, but tai chi was the movement therapy that became most popular at Esalen, chiefly through Gia-Fu Feng. George Leonard was also influential in helping to shape the early programs. Among other endeavors, he first introduced the nonviolent Japanese martial art of aikido to Esalen. Instead of adhering to the traditional attacks and throws, Leonard adapted aikido to general audiences, with the liberal addition of sensory awareness, Gestalt, and other group-work techniques. Massage was also practiced in many varieties, the most well-known form of which was Rolfing. Developed by Ida Rolf, this technique attempts to work through every muscle of the body with excruciating thoroughness, separating the fascia all the way down to the bone. The general theory behind it is that experiences are stored in the muscles, which, when massaged deeply, liberate their contents in the form of cognitive and emotional material to be worked through. Massage was thus treated as a form of psychotherapy since it was an art of both the mind and the body.

What followed was an explosion of counterculture interest in what came to be called somatic therapies or somatic psychology. The massage training program at Esalen is famous and continues to this day. Graduates started their own practices, adding and dropping techniques, sometimes becoming patients to learn new techniques from other practitioners. Elderly matriarchs of European bodywork styles came into vogue. New schools of somatic therapy sprang up, such as postural integration, Lomi, Feldenkrais, shiatsu, and polarity therapy. Old schools such as the Alexander technique, which John Dewey and Aldous Huxley had practiced in the 1920s, were resurrected. Bodywork not only filled a void left by too great an emphasis on the merely talking cures of traditional psychotherapy, but, like many other psychotherapeutic innovations at the time, it also presented a significant new venue, especially for women, to make a living as mind-body healers.

The Patriarchy of Temporary Gurus

ALTHOUGH THERE WERE MANY STRONG PERSONALITIES who came and went at Esalen, none proved more problematic than Fritz Perls. Perls, who actually lived on the grounds as a full-time resident, was certainly one of Esalen's most influential and charismatic lights, but he was a controversial one as well. He was born in Berlin and received his doctorate in medicine from Friedrich Wilhelm University in 1921. After undergoing psychoanalysis, he went to Frankfurt briefly to work under the organismic and Gestalt theorist Kurt Lewin at the Institute for Brain Damaged Soldiers. He then vacillated between Berlin and Vienna; got married to Laura Posner, a graduate student in experimental Gestalt psychology; opened a practice; and eventually became a patient of the Freudian renegade and Marxist revisionist Wilhelm Reich, who taught

Perls how to lift the repressions surrounding his sexuality. In 1933, when Hitler came to power, Perls fled through Holland to England with his family and, with the help of Ernest Jones, landed a job teaching psychoanalysis in South Africa. He stayed there twelve years, founded the South African Institute for Psychoanalysis, rose to prominence, and became a financial success.

After an unpleasant encounter with Freud in 1936 and receiving the cold shoulder from the psychoanalysts, Perls turned to Zen and to European existentialism. The result was his try at a major revision of Freud's ideas, which Perls published as *Ego, Hunger, and Aggression.*[8]

In 1946, Perls moved to the United States by way of Canada and quickly established himself in New York. He set up an institute, took on patients, and became involved with Moreno's technique of psychodrama. Six years later, with Paul Goodman, a patient, and Ralph Hefferline, a professor of psychology at Columbia, Perls published *Gestalt Therapy* (1951). It was the first outline of a new therapeutic method that approached the neurotic patient as a whole person. The central idea for Perls was that health is the recovery of emotions and the reenlivening of sensory awareness.

In 1964, Perls was living by himself on the West Coast. By the time he was invited to come to Esalen, he was old, sick, and abrasive, and he dictated his wants in terms that left no doubt as to who was in charge. He set himself up at the institute, using its clientele as his own school to promote his own form of therapy. He found rejuvenation in the hot-spring baths, slept with the women, offended others with impunity as a therapeutic tool, and engaged in numerous boundary violations with people who might simultaneously be his lovers, friends, patients, and students. Nevertheless, he developed a large following and was soon a national figure in the human potential movement.

After several years, Perls left Esalen under a cloud because of the suicide of two of his followers. He moved his operations to Vancouver, where he continued to work. Diagnosed with cancer, he died in 1970 of an apparent heart attack. According to one account, in his last moment on Earth, he pulled all the tubes and needles from his body and, jumping from the bed, stood straight up. A nurse who had just entered the room screamed, "No! You can't do that!" His reply, before he dropped dead on the floor was, "I'll do it my way!" [9] Gestalt therapy remained a pervasive part of the counterculture landscape, not only in northern California, but across America, as it proliferated into many other mutations after its founder left the scene.

Another major influence to permeate the spiritual atmosphere at Esalen was Arica, based on the teachings of a Chilean Sufi named Oscar Ichazo. Arica came to Esalen through Claudio Naranjo, a Chilean psychiatrist who was trained in psychoanalysis. When Naranjo had first come to the United States in the early 1960s, he met Frank Barron, a psychologist associated with the Institute for Personality Assessment and Research in Berkeley who was then on a visiting professorship at Harvard. Naranjo later returned to the United States on a Guggenheim grant to spend a year working with Barron in Berkeley. While there, Naranjo was introduced to Carlos Castaneda, then a graduate student at UCLA. They ended up at a seminar together on shamanism at Esalen, after which Naranjo and Castaneda became close friends. Meanwhile, Naranjo became involved in Gestalt therapy and developed a continuing relationship with Esalen.

Naranjo's disciples in Chile notified him that a great teacher named Oscar Ichazo had appeared in Santiago.[10] Ichazo had as a young man been taken into a secret order of elderly men who had sent him abroad to learn the various esoteric traditions, especially the teachings of Gurdjieff. After a trip back to Chile to meet Ichazo, Naranjo returned to California, where he gathered together a band of some thirty others, largely from the Esalen community. They all returned to the seaport town of Arica in Chile. A center was founded and intensive classes began, led by Ichazo. Meditation, fasting, and bodywork, such as the warrior massage technique from Tibet called *Chua Ka,* were taught.

But after several months, Naranjo and Ichazo fell out, and Naranjo left. Nevertheless, from this brief experiment, Ichazo believed his own work had real potential, so he disbanded the group in Chile and moved to New York, where he set up the U.S. headquarters of the Arica movement. Centers eventually sprang up in cities across America and Canada.

Always a little unscrupulous and not a little devious, Ichazo lasted only a few years. A number of his centers later ran afoul of the Internal Revenue Service, and most were forced to close, but not before Arica had, along with other methods, entered the counterculture.

Another influence at Esalen during the early 1970s was psychosynthesis, a psychospiritual regime developed by the Italian psychiatrist Roberto Assagioli.[11] Assagioli was born in Venice in 1888 and had taken his medical degree from the University of Florence in neurology and psychiatry. Disenchanted with the prevailing attitudes of a strictly biological psychiatry, Assagioli read widely in the literature of the alternative-reality tradition and came to advocate a variety of different methods, from meditation to guided imagery, that he believed were designed to strengthen the will. From these researches, he developed a theory about psychological health based on realization of the higher self.

In 1926, Assagioli opened the Institute of Psychosynthesis in Florence, which operated for twelve years until it was closed down by the Fascists. It reopened after World War II, after which point his work became more well known, and in 1957, the Psychosynthesis Research Foundation was started in the United States. Assagioli's system was introduced to Esalen in the late 1960s, before Michael Murphy went to Florence in 1970 to meet the aging founder. Thereafter, psychosynthesis began to play an even greater role in Esalen programs. Like Arica, in the wider culture psychosynthesis institutes arose around the United States, and graduates went on to set up their own therapeutic practices, usually around some nucleus consisting of other trainers and graduates. While psychosynthesis expanded into the 1970s, its visibility also crested with the larger counterculture wave then passing out of public consciousness.

Psychosynthesis proved itself to be more enduring than the Arica training, likely due in no small part to the similarity between Assagioli's total program and Jung's analytical psychology of individuation. A younger contemporary of Jung's, Assagioli moved in many of the same European circles as the Jungians, even occasionally participating in the Eranos conferences at Ascona. Ichazo's schools, on the other hand, came and went as more of a temporary cultural phenomenon.

Other Influences

NUMEROUS ADDITIONAL INFLUENCES were in the air. Esalen participants brought all the new alternative spiritual trends in the door with them. The spiritual teachings of Bhagwan Sri Rajneesh or Guru Maharaj Ji, Jose Silva's mind control techniques, Scientology, Synanon, and many more "systems" were being practiced both separately and together in the eclectic psychotherapeutic and self-help environment that the counterculture movement engendered. None, however, seemed as popular as the Erhard Seminars Training, better known as est, started by Werner Erhard.[12]

Erhard was born Jack Rosenberg in Philadelphia, in September 1935, in the middle of the Depression. He was the oldest son of Joseph Rosenberg, a Jewish restaurant owner who had become a fundamentalist Christian, and Dorothy Clauson, an Episcopalian of English and Swedish extraction. Young Jack's early life appeared relatively normal in most respects, except that he was plagued with numerous accidents, the most serious of which was a fall from a second-story fire escape, which cracked his skull. He recovered. At age twelve, he discovered yoga, which he studied from books. He did the postures, tried the breathing techniques, and began what he later called an "interior dialogue" with himself about the process of self-knowledge.

Rosenberg became separated from his parents and spent the majority of his adolescence living with his Jewish grandparents in Germantown. During this time, he attended the Episcopal Church, learned its teachings, and was an altar boy for eight years. He graduated from Norristown High School and, at the age of eighteen, married his high school sweetheart, who was pregnant. He worked at various jobs until settling into a position as a used car salesman, then as the manager of an industrial equipment firm. Within a few years, he had two more children, but by then his marriage was falling apart.

Abandoning his wife and children in 1959, Rosenberg left Philadelphia clandestinely with another woman in a stolen car. The two of them made their way as far as St. Louis, where they settled in dingy circumstances under false names. The name Rosenberg chose came from an *Esquire* magazine article on West Germany—Werner Erhard, a fusion of the rocket scientist Wernher von Braun and the economics minister Ludwig Erhard. To get by, Rosenberg, now Erhard, sold used cars and gambled. He also began reading books, such as Maxwell Maltz's *Psycho-cybernetics* and Napoleon Hill's *Think and Grow Rich,* which taught him about physical relaxation, imagination, mental control of thoughts, will training, autohypnosis, and positive thinking. The key concepts he gleaned from them were "responsibility" and "internal self-image," which he took to imply that we are the unconscious creators of our own identity. To change who we are, we need to take responsibility not for the mere outward trappings of our experience, but for the internal images that we hold about ourselves that determine thoughts, words, and deeds. Through these sources, he became attracted to the popular movement of self-help psychology, which he soon adapted to the field of business motivation.

Erhard soon became a traveling salesman. He crisscrossed the United States, working first for a correspondence school by teaching the operation of construction equipment, then as an employee of the Great Books program, run by the producers of the *Encyclopedia Britannica*. He finally entered the child development publishing house that produced *Parents' Magazine*. In this last position, Erhard's rise was meteoric.

He taught classes on how to handle resistance and trained people to confront other people's constructed images of themselves. He also taught them how to sell products by communicating with buyers about their deepest needs and interests. He eventually established himself as a national manager capable of increasing sales dramatically with a team largely made up of sharp, aggressive women who were attracted to his style. Essentially, he was teaching his sales team to sell by being motivational psychotherapists.

The sales and training business became an umbrella under which Erhard continued to expand his own interests in self-development. Stationed in San Francisco, first in 1962 and again in 1964, he was introduced to the ideas of Abraham Maslow and Carl Rogers, two of the founders of humanistic psychology. He began to attend seminars at Esalen in sensitivity training and group awareness. Living in Sausalito with the woman who was now his wife, he had started another family and eventually fathered three children. There, he also made friends with his neighbor Alan Watts and, through him, broadened his interests in Zen.

In 1968, Erhard took a Dale Carnegie motivational course and drew many of his followers into it. He went on to study meditation briefly under the Indonesian Pak Subud, founder of Subud International Brotherhood; he also dabbled in the martial arts, became an initiate in L. Ron Hubbard's Scientology, and attained the rank of senior trainer in a system called "Mind Dynamics." After these experiences, he claimed to be a psychic who could see into his past lives, and he was able to extend his charismatic mastery over larger and larger crowds of people.

Finally, in 1971, Erhard launched est, his own self-development training program. Here, he combined all his skills in motivation and sales and applied them to the business of personal transformation. The time was right, just at the peak of the human potential movement, and the place was right, San Francisco, capital of the American counterculture.

At first, Erhard worked out of hotels, confining the training seminars to weekends, keeping the price at a reasonable rate, and setting attainment of high numbers of participants as his goal. His eventual aim was to attract extremely wealthy executives who might pay up to $10,000 for the initial two-weekend sessions. Meanwhile, for the working middle-class professionals who packed his seminars, he charged $150. A new, more mainstream audience thus began to participate in the counterculture movement and its ethic of self-realization.

Erhard was an instant success. In the first year alone, 6,000 people took the est training. In the first eight years, it was estimated that a quarter of a million people had gone through the program. Est was by then even being tried out in prison programs. Training centers existed all over the United States, and cadres of teachers were trained so they could take over the sessions from Erhard, who by then had gone on to initiate other projects. One of these, the Hunger Project, was founded in 1977 to end world hunger by 1997, and over 200,000 people enrolled in its first two years of operation. By this time, Erhard had built a far-reaching empire, flew everywhere in a large private jet, and was able to spread his message around the world.

Twelve years after leaving his hometown, he returned to Philadelphia and reconciled himself with his mother and father and his first wife, who had divorced him on grounds of desertion. He was also reunited with his children. He set up a palatial home in Philadelphia, and eventually his entire extended family took the est training. The picture of Erhard that the public received in the late 1970s was one of his old and his new family joined together. He was on good terms with his ex-wife (she worked as an assistant in the est office and picked out the clothes he would wear to his big events), and she became friends with his present wife, while all six children had gotten to know one another.

Whatever one's specific reaction to this particular circumstance, here we have the quintessential case study of how the counterculture movement of the 1960s began to radically alter the definition of the family. Old nuclear ties established by blood and marriage were broken as people entered into experimental lifestyles. The established customs of a patriarchal male who ruled the home, of a female confined to her activities of domestic servitude, and of children who did not speak until spoken to gave way as young people fled into the counterculture and mothers began to see new possibilities in the fledgling women's movement. The world of work and careers independent of the home; self-awareness classes with people who began as complete strangers; increased sexual experimentation; changes in social consciousness brought about by psychedelics—these were but some of the factors that contributed to new lifestyle changes, the long-run consequences of which remained unknown. Often, but not always, some of these experiments involved attempts to reconcile the old with the new, as exemplified by Erhard's very story. His devotees warmed to the tale of their hero's journey: Troubled youth makes good in a crazy world and returns to unite the various parts of his discontinuous past.

Erhard had a similar relationship to the larger spiritual community of the American shadow culture. Although he himself had taken seminars at Esalen to get started, est was never a formal program in Big Sur. Nevertheless, by the mid-1970s, est had been taken by most of the people in the human potential movement who were associated with the institute. In fact, the opening of the San Francisco branch of Esalen, celebrated at Grace Cathedral, occurred at the same time that est opened offices just down the street from Michael Murphy's, launching its own competing programs.

Est's success paralleled the explosive growth of the larger counterculture movement. Just as Esalen was becoming a national phenomenon, Erhard's operation was definitely assisted by what Murphy had already established. To the throngs who involved themselves in both programs, Esalen and est probably appeared largely the same. And although Erhard has been treated as an opportunist and a con man by mainstream observers, he is vigorously defended by a wide-ranging and diverse spiritual community, the members of which, numbering at least in the hundreds of thousands, believe that est was an important doorway through which they passed on a much longer and deeper journey of spiritual awakening.

Transformative Experiences at Esalen

MEANWHILE, ESALEN'S PROGRAMS CONTINUED to emphasize their own form of transformative practice. The idea that one could have a life-changing experience in Big Sur was practically Esalen's purpose for being. One example of the transformative moment has been recorded by the Harvard theologian Harvey Cox, a Baptist minister and author of such works as *The Secular City* and *Turning East*. In his autobiography, Cox recounts a succession of spiritual awakenings, one of which was a visionary experience at Esalen while taking a mineral bath accompanied by a candlelit group massage:

> Though the group massage sounds vaguely promiscuous, it is not. In fact after I'd enjoyed the sheer sensation of it for a while, I even began to have a vision. The candles seemed to expand and I caught a glimpse of Teilhard de Chardin's Omega Point, a supra-personal future in which individuals become joyous corpuscles in a more inclusive organism. . . . Then . . . I felt myself slipping back into childhood and infancy . . . that generalized form of sensual enjoyment children seem capable of but adults have lost. "Except ye become as little children," blended with "We are members one of another," in a shifting collage of faces, hands, candles, mandalas, omegas, and unending future vistas.
>
> Time, I have no idea how much, passed. Now all the candles were one flame and all the fingers were on one great hand. The combination

of water, chanting, body dissociation, and massage was moving me beyond a pleasantly sensuous swoon into something closer to what I could only imagine was either a fanciful reverie or a mystical trance. I could feel the hydrogen and oxygen molecules of the water seeping into the amino acids and carbohydrates and bone cells and nerve endings of my body. The hands touching me became mine, and my own hands slid off my wrists to fuse with the dampness in and around me. Again the vision faded. Now I felt something I had read about many times before but never understood, the underlying unity of Brahman and Atman, the oneness of self, other, and All. With an infinitesimal corner of critical consciousness still looking on, like that part of you that knows a dream is a dream, I thought about the fact that the modern Western convention which draws the border of "me" at my epidermis, and posits "you" and "me" as two entirely separate entities, is after all only one way of looking at things. We are all in some ways one with the water, the sky, the air, each other, and in the sulfur baths the reality of a collective self seems a little less bizarre than it does in the everyday world.[13]

Reflecting later about this experience, Cox noted that in the history of religions there are many examples of spirituality emerging out of the sensual, among them the myths of Lord Krishna and his gopis, who were the young women herding goats; the rituals of Indian and Tibetan Tantrism; and even one biblical allusion from the Song of Songs. So Cox asked affirmatively, why not, then, at Esalen?

Another example of the transformative moment at Esalen was the account written by Stewart Miller, an East Coast Jewish intellectual and college professor whose dean had sent him to Esalen as a part of an extended faculty training program. Miller became so changed by his experiences that he left his teaching job and stayed on to help run Esalen. He describes a moment following a day of intensive workshops:

I began to walk slowly across the property to my house. The moon had not yet risen, the path before me obscure, and I was filled, as I looked back on the day, with a sense of joy that brought me to tears as I walked. The stars were only beginning to come up, and, for some reason, there at Esalen, back in that magic landscape of Big Sur, a presence that had haunted my childhood, informed by so many nights when I was seven and eight years old, seemed to come back to me. The old God of childhood, that paternal deity, all-powerful, master of all events, final resort in trouble, a gigantic male presence that brooded over me, in the heavens, especially in the black heavens of nighttime. I had never entirely lost touch with Him, through all these years, for in my moments of special anguish or danger, all else failing, even though I knew better, I would call on Him. And that night in Big Sur, the ocean vast, with light still at the Western edge, and a few stars blue-white, here and there, I looked at the immense sky and felt his return. I felt his warmth, his breath overreaching the earth was on my shoulders and on my neck when I bent my head toward the ground. Or something at once more gigantic even than Him and less precise. I walked along the dark path, down towards the Hot Springs creek, my Bible in my hand, and felt the large and pleasing warm tears brimming in my eyes. How little I had deserved. And how much suddenly, for no sufficient reason, I had been given. Strange mixture of the Hebrew God of my childhood, that stern promulgator of rules which had to be exactly obeyed, and something else which was new, another intimation of Deity. Jews don't kneel; it is forbidden, but it seemed right to kneel, and my knees rested gratefully on the cold path. I was filled with a sense of my smallness. A mighty power was present to me, but it was full of love and I felt that if I merely did the humble thing, the little thing, without phoniness or selfishness, it would give me such Grace as would bring me again to tears of thanks.[14]

Miller recounts that afterward, he began to delight in even the most menial jobs. Whereas before he had remained aloof from the rest of the staff at Esalen, he now came around and, to everyone's surprise, offered his help, even making beds and cleaning the floor. His newfound awakening had many twists and turns, but it made a different person of him from then on.

According to Michael Murphy, ecstatic states, which were originally believed to be one of the goals that Esalen promoted, turned out not to be the end of the story after all. Peak experiences, encounter techniques, illuminating visions, and sudden breakthroughs all seemed completely new in the beginning. With the optimism typical of the American folk tradition and the pressure for instant results that modernism always demands, this group of seekers thought it had a program that would lead to instant awakening.

The first glimmer that there was more work to do came when the Esalen staff inaugurated the residential training program. Instead of attending a weekend encounter or a weeklong intensive workshop, students would come for an entire year. After several years had passed, a new realization set in. Simply helping to open the internal doors of perception was not enough. What the Esalen program needed was to harness its sights on the long term and to fashion its programs around helping individuals to embark upon a lifetime of spiritual practice.

Not only did the Esalen Institute reflect the larger counterculture movement as a whole, it was emblematic of many of the utopian experiments that had preceded it in the history of the American visionary tradition. The vestiges of Grahamism—pure water, coarse grains, and a vegetable diet—are still practiced there. Whether self-consciously following the transcendentalists or not, the Esalen practitioners have pursued the same ideals of personal self-expression and a spiritual reverence for the land. They have continually been a conduit for the dissemination of Asian ideas into the West. Like all heretics before them, they have had very liberal attitudes about the consecration of human relationships outside the control of the institutional church. They have always been seekers after visions. In all these ways, Esalen continues to be a case study of the alternative reality tradition in the West and the visionary tradition in America.

Notes

1. George Leonard, *Education and Ecstasy* (New York: Delacorte Press, 1968); George Leonard, *The Ultimate Athlete: Re-visioning Sports, Physical Education, and the Body* (New York: Viking Press, 1975); George Leonard, *The Transformation: A*

Guide to the Inevitable Changes in Humankind (New York: Delacorte Press, 1972); and George Leonard, *Mastery: The Keys to Long-Term Success and Fulfillment* (New York: Dutton, 1991).

2. Comments reprinted with the permission of George Leonard.

3. In this section, I have relied on personal interviews with Michael Murphy; on a reading of texts such as George Leonard's *Walking on the Edge of the World* (New York: Houghton Mifflin, 1988), Stuart Miller's *Hot Spring: The True Adventures of the First New York Jewish Literary Intellectual in the Human Potential Movement* (New York: Viking Press, 1971), and Walter Truett Anderson's *The Upstart Spring: Esalen and the American Awakening* (Reading, MA: Addison-Wesley, 1983); and on extensive interviews with various members of the unofficial permanent staff at Esalen.

4. Michael Murphy, *Golf in the Kingdom* (New York: Dell, 1972); Michael Murphy, *Jacob Atabet: A Speculative Fiction* (Millbrae, CA: Celestial Arts, 1977); Michael Murphy, *The Future of the Body: Explorations into the Further Evolution of Human Nature* (Los Angeles: J. P. Tarcher, 1992); Michael Murphy, *The Kingdom of Shivas Irons* (New York: Broadway Books, 1997); and George B. Leonard, *The Life We Are Given: A Long-Term Program for Realizing the Potential of Body, Mind, Heart, and Soul* (New York: G. P. Putnam's Sons, 1995).

5. Will Schutz, *Joy: Expanding Human Awareness* (New York: Grove Press, 1967).

6. Its other co-founder was Laura Posner Perls, Fritz's wife, who took her doctorate at Frankfurt in experimental Gestalt psychology of perception. Of the two, she is the real historical link between the laboratory-oriented Gestalt psychology of Wolfgang Köhler, Kurt Koffka, and Max Wertheimer and the Gestalt therapy movement of the American psychotherapeutic counterculture. See Joe Wysong, *An Oral History of Gestalt Therapy: Interviews with Laura Perls, Isadore From, Erving Polster, Miriam Polster* (Highland, NY: Gestalt Journal, 1982).

7. Charles C. W. Brooks, *Sensory Awareness: Rediscovery of Experience Through the Workshops of Charlotte Selver* (Great Neck, NY: Felix Morrow, 1986).

8. Perls's work includes *Ego, Hunger, and Aggression* (London: Allen & Unwin, 1947); with Ralph Hefferline and Paul Goodman, *Gestalt Therapy: Excitement and Growth in the Human Personality* (New York: Delta Books, 1951); and his autobiography, *In and Out of the Garbage Pail* (Lafayette, CA: Real People Press, 1969).

9. Dr. Madeline Nold, personal communication with the author.

10. Oscar Ichazo, *The Human Process for Enlightenment and Freedom: A Series of Five Lectures* (New York: Arica Institute Press, 1976); Oscar Ichazo, *Interviews with Oscar Ichazo* (New York: Arica Institute Press, 1982); and Oscar Ichazo, *Between Metaphysics and Protoanalysis: A Theory for Analyzing the Human Psyche* (New York: Arica Institute Press, 1982).

11. Roberto Assagioli, *Psychosynthesis: A Manual of Principles and Techniques* (New York: Hobbs, Dorman, 1965).

12. The following section is adapted from W. W. Bartley III, *Werner Erhard* (New York: Clarkson Potter, 1978).

13. Cox's account, which has been printed in many places, was taken from Jon Alexander, *American Personal Religious Accounts, 1600–1980: Toward an Inner History of America's Faiths* (New York: Edwin Mellen Press, 1983), pp. 428–429.

14. Stewart Miller, *Hot Springs: The True Adventures of the First New York Jewish Literary Intellectual in the Human Potential Movement* (New York: Viking Press, 1971), pp. 262–263.

Chapter Twelve

Humanistic and Transpersonal Psychology

The Humanistic Current

LIKE THE TRANSCENDENTALIST MOVEMENT A HUNDRED YEARS earlier, the humanistic revolution in American culture became the voice for a deep disquiet that had been building throughout the twentieth century. Soon, it pervaded everything and eventually provided the backdrop against which more specific events were allowed to come into being. Humanistic psychology, as it was properly called, was the name given to an intellectual and psychotherapeutic movement that began within American academic psychology in the 1940s, developing chiefly at the borders of personality theory, motivational psychology, and the counseling movement.

There were four principal players at the beginning: Carl Rogers, an innovative counseling psychologist from Ohio State University who pioneered client-centered therapy, the first indigenous American challenge to psychoanalysis; Rollo May, a Methodist minister turned clinical psychologist who first introduced European existentialism and phenomenology into American psychotherapy; Abraham Maslow, a comparative animal psychologist who became interested in motivation and personality theory and first introduced the concept of the self-actualizing personality into American psychology; and Anthony Sutich, a physically challenged social activist, ethicist, and psychotherapist who became the founding editor of the *Journal of Humanistic Psychology* and co-organizer with Maslow and others of the American Association for Humanistic Psychology. Between them, they fomented a professional revolution in the study of personality and in the practice of psychotherapy that promised to change academic psychology forever. But historical circumstances diverted their course. Drawn into the counterculture, they ended up as emissaries who introduced folk psychology into the institutions of American high culture, the effects of which continue to proliferate to this day.[1]

Rogers, a key figure from the very beginning, was an Illinois farm boy born in 1902 into a strict religious family.[2] He attended the University of Wisconsin in the 1920s, spent a year in China, and went on to Union Theological Seminary. He took courses at Teachers College, Columbia University, where he fell under the influence of John Dewey, the American pragmatist and former colleague of William James. Earning his doctorate in 1928, Rogers distinguished himself in the area of counseling with children before turning his attention to problems of psychotherapy. He was influenced, he later wrote, by students of the Freudian dissident Otto Rank, who believed that unresolved issues around the birth trauma were the source of neuroses. But Rogers turned out to be more interested in what Rank had to say about the dynamics of the patient-therapist relationship than what he said about psychoanalysis proper.

Rogers's psychotherapeutic work led him to Ohio State University, and after publishing a text, *Counseling and Psychotherapy,* he accepted a position at the University of Chicago, where he founded the university's counseling center. It was during this time, on a guest lecture tour at a

Midwestern college, that Rogers first introduced the idea of client-centered therapy.

Psychotherapy, Rogers thought, needed to be brought out of the realm of psychopathology and applied to understanding personal growth and the normal personality. He began by calling the people who came to see him "clients" instead of "patients." He believed that the client should be encouraged in the process of self-knowledge and inner exploration without undue control from the therapist, so he evolved a nondirective method where the patient's own associations and insights controlled the therapeutic hour and the course of treatment. The therapist's role was to encourage self-reflection, to empathize with the client's struggle to understand personal problems, and to extend to the client what Rogers came to refer to as "unconditional positive regard," creating an environment where self-disclosure could be carried on in complete confidence and safety.

These were innovative ideas. Therapeutic treatment had been almost completely dominated by the Freudian approach in which the patient free associated while the therapist analyzed, probed, and diagnosed, in an exchange designed to elicit feelings of intense love or hate in order for the analyst to access appropriate unconscious material with which to work. And although the approach of Harry Stack Sullivan and the neo-Freudians was gaining ground, casting therapy in the context of interpersonal relations, Rogers's conception of therapy not only put more of the active work in the hands of the client, but also was refreshingly free of any theoretical debt to psychoanalytic concepts.

These ideas culminated in Rogers's pioneering book, *Client-Centered Therapy: Its Current Practice, Implications, and Theory* (1951), a major challenge to both psychoanalysis, which controlled clinical teaching in psychology and psychiatry at the time, and animal behaviorism, which controlled academic teaching departments of psychology in American universities. As a measure of the importance of his work for defining a new direction in the field, the American Psychological Association gave Rogers its first Distinguished Contributions to Psychology Award in 1956. That year, Rogers also held the first of three historic debates with B. F. Skinner on the client-centered approach versus Skinner's theories of reductionistic behaviorism.

In 1957, probably at the height of his reputation in the academic world, Rogers went to the University of Wisconsin, where he held a joint professorship in psychology and psychiatry. It was during this period that he first became acquainted with Maslow. By the early 1960s, he was able to use his considerable influence to help Maslow and Sutich launch the new movement of humanistic psychology.

Meanwhile, another important figure was emerging on the scene: Rollo May.[3] Also a conservative Protestant Midwesterner, May was born in Ohio in 1908 and raised in Michigan. As a college student, he had to leave Michigan State because he edited a radical newspaper the authorities disliked. He graduated from Oberlin in 1930 and secured a teaching position in Greece, where he absorbed classical culture and traveled throughout Europe for three years. His interest in psychology was reinforced when he attended seminars in Vienna led by Alfred Adler, another Freudian dissident.

After his excursion abroad, May attempted to enroll in the Union Theological Seminary. Due to family problems, however, he went back to Michigan State College, where he worked as a counselor. He returned to Union Theological Seminary in 1936 and came under the influence of the great Lutheran theologian Paul Tillich, who had recently fled Nazi Germany. Above all others, it was Tillich who turned May's attention to existential philosophy. May graduated in 1939 with a bachelor's of divinity degree and, after ordination, took a Congregationalist parish in Verona, New Jersey. He worked at this post for a two-year period but soon became discouraged with the unsatisfactory answers that denominational religion provided for his parishioners' problems.

In 1941, he enrolled in the clinical psychology doctoral program at Teachers College, Columbia University. That same year, he also produced *Springs of Creative Living: A Study of Human Nature and God*. The book sold well, but May soon gave up completely on Christianity, now convinced that it was inadequate to address the most pressing life issues of hopelessness and anxiety. He stunned his publisher by canceling an expected second edition of the book and retracting it from the market.

Then, in 1942, May had a near-death experience when he contracted tuberculosis. He entered the Saranac Sanitarium in upstate New York and remained under treatment for eighteen months. At Saranac, he came to the realization that he alone was responsible for whether he would live or die. He believed his recovery depended not so much upon medical care as upon his own struggle against death, especially the personal sense of hopelessness that had befallen him over leaving the ministry.

May left the sanitarium in 1943, took a job as a student counselor at New York's City College, and reenrolled in the doctoral program at Columbia. In 1949, he was awarded the first doctorate in clinical psychology given by that school. His dissertation was eventually published as *The Meaning of Anxiety* (1950), a best-seller and the first postwar analysis of the despair that fell over Western civilization as a result of the threat of atomic annihilation. May's argument was that the impact of global problems on meaning and values led directly to the development of individual neuroses.

But there were many types of anxiety, he claimed. When met constructively, normal anxiety is a life stimulant that is an integral part of growth and vital for creative expression. Neurotic anxiety, however, results from normal anxieties with which one has not adequately dealt. The goal of psychotherapy, May argued, is not to free patients from anxiety but, rather, to help them accept, bear, and live constructively with it.

Shortly before completing his graduate work at Columbia University in 1948, May joined the faculty of the William Alanson White Institute of Psychiatry, Psychoanalysis, and Psychology in New York City. There he associated himself with the tradition of those neo-Freudians like Sullivan who were chiefly responsible for the Americanization of psychoanalysis. May later said that what he appreciated most about the institute was its broad-mindedness: It allowed existential, humanistic, and psychoanalytic perspectives to flourish all at the same time. In 1952, he became a fellow at the institute; in 1958, its president; and in 1959, a senior supervisory and training analyst.

In the years leading up to the early 1960s, May engaged in psychotherapy at the institute and, under its aegis, pioneered in the introduction of existential psychotherapy to American psychology. In 1958, in collaboration with the Swiss existential psychiatrist Henri Ellenberger, May edited *Existence: A New Dimension in Psychology and Psychiatry*. This book gave

American psychologists their first look at concepts such as the phenomenological life-world of the patient: despair as a deep, unending chasm experienced within the existential void and how we confront the unnameable within us. For the first time, European existential philosophy—known for its darkness, its pessimism, and its emphasis on angst, or suffering—was presented in a psychological language understandable to Americans.

May followed this work with another pioneering text, *Existential Psychology* (1960), to which American psychologists such as Carl Rogers and Gordon Allport contributed. Here, existential thought became truly Americanized; that is, it was adapted to the positive, optimistic worldview of the humanistic psychologists. Whereas it was chiefly through the older American personality psychologists that existential thought was first applied to understanding problems of neurosis, it was clearly through the newer humanistic psychologists that existential and phenomenological approaches found their way into the American psychotherapeutic movement. The predominant themes of psychotherapy quickly became those of choice, responsibility, meaning, awareness, development of the will, problems of intentionality and decision making, and self-realization.

May held no formal academic appointment, but he was associated with an independent, freestanding institute in New York. As well, through a number of his works that became best-sellers, such as *The Meaning of Anxiety* and *Love and Will,* he became best known as a writer on psychotherapeutic subjects that appealed to an educated but popular audience. He became the quintessential example of a psychotherapist in the tradition of American folk psychology. At the same time, his stature and importance elevated the visionary tradition to a level where it began to have an impact on high culture.

But May's work, although read by literary intellectuals, had very little impact on academic psychology or the profession of medical psychiatry, because most of what he broached was unacceptable to the psychoanalysts, behaviorists, and scientific psychiatrists and psychologists who defined these disciplines at the university level. In fact, May was part of an ever-growing number of educated people in the United States who were radically dissatisfied with the provincial and narrow limits set by disciplinary boundaries and reigning ideologies in the helping professions. The postwar revolution in thinking about personality and consciousness was already under way. It seemed that the merely rational Western academic disciplines that had for so long dictated acceptable definitions of the self would never again lead the way in defining the possibilities of human experience.

Another of the early figures responsible for catalyzing the new ideas about psychology was Abraham Maslow.[4] Maslow was born in Manhattan in 1908 into a working-class family of Russian Jews. He remembered a miserable, friendless childhood in which, to avoid contact with his mother, whom he thought intensely cruel, he spent most of his time in New York City libraries. He attended high school in Brooklyn and began studies at City College before switching briefly to Cornell University. Returning to City College, he became interested in the behaviorism of John Watson. This interest led him to transfer yet again, this time to the University of Wisconsin. There he fell under the influence of some of America's great psychologists of the time, including William Sheldon, originator of the classification of body types; Clark Hull, the learning theorist; and Harry Harlow, the comparative animal psychologist who studied infant attachment in monkeys. Maslow was Harlow's first doctoral student.

Maslow completed his doctorate in 1934 with a dissertation on power and sexual behavior in primates. He considered medical school but by chance was offered a position at Columbia University as scientific assistant under Edward L. Thorndike, a groundbreaking educational psychologist, a pragmatist, and one of William James's old students. At Columbia, Maslow continued to study dominance and sexuality, mainly interviewing women, whom he found more truthful than men when talking about their sex lives. After 1937, he taught at Brooklyn College and, while there, came into contact with anthropologists such as Ruth Benedict and Margaret Mead, psychoanalysts such as Karen Horney and Erich Fromm, and Gestalt psychologists such as Kurt Goldstein, the man from whom he would first hear about the self-actualizing personality. The influences Maslow drew upon were all cross-cultural, interdisciplinary, psychoanalytically inclined, and holistic. Through Benedict, for instance, he was led to do field research with the Northern Blackfoot tribe of Alberta, Canada, in the summer of 1938.

World War II soon changed Maslow's perception of psychology and its possibilities. Confronting the carnage and destruction, he began to feel strongly that psychology had important contributions to make not only in defining the democratic character, but also in fostering world peace. And he took these issues personally. He soon realized, however, that traditional theories in psychology completely neglected the higher aspects of personality involved in these issues.

Both behaviorism and psychoanalysis concentrated on a deficiency theory of motivation. Skinnerians, basing their conclusions on graphs from behavioral experiments in rat learning, maintained that people did things they were supposed to do to avoid punishment. Freudians, using the absence of psychopathology as their model, claimed that the normal person was basically neurotic but at least able to adjust to the norms of society. Maslow, seeking a growth-oriented standard, found the reigning models inadequate. He wanted to look at the highest and best examples that could be found of human functioning.

Consequently, Maslow spent the late 1940s and early 1950s developing his new theories, which he presented in 1954 in *Motivation and Personality*. Here was real heresy. One of the controversial ideas Maslow put forward was the hierarchy of needs. Maslow presented his model in the shape of a pyramid, in which he structured human needs on progressive, step-style levels: Food and shelter are the most basic, thus they occupied the foundational tier of his pyramid. The sense of safety comes next. When these are satisfied, then love and belongingness become the new emergent goals. And when these are all in place, then self-actualization becomes possible—the opportunity to achieve the highest and best of one's potential. Theoretically, people who are well educated and economically secure will be able to reach the higher levels. If they are not otherwise overcome by greed and avarice, wealthy nations should have more self-actualizers.

Maslow went on to analyze the characteristics of the self-actualizing personality. Self-actualizers are people who have better sex than others, who laugh more, and who are more philosophical because they are less emotionally hindered. Self-actualizers act out of moral codes defined by the depth and breadth of their inward experiences. The realization of these experiences puts them in touch with the spirit of the law from which the letter was derived; consequently, 98 percent of self-actualized people will behave in ways that correspond to the customs and mores of the society in which they live. As for the other 2 percent, these are the ones who stand up for what they believe in and move groups and nations to do the same. Such self-actualizers are prone to a love of poetry and to flights of mysticism; and if they do not seem like everyone else, it is because they are actually more like one another than like the members of their own respective cultures. On the other hand, they are not particularly special, in that such a one could be standing right next to you at any moment. They just do not make their differences apparent by readily talking about them.

In this paradox, Maslow saw the makings of a world personality, a personality that can adapt to a variety of different cultures but the essence of which transcends the limits of any given culture. He did believe, however, that self-actualizers are better able to flourish in a democratic environment, but the fact that their behavior is motivated by the depth and power of the transcendent experience suggested an altogether new standard for how people of different cultures might relate more harmoniously.

Of course, there were many theoretical problems with such an optimistic conceptualization of human functioning. Critics pointed out that Maslow provided no data to back up these claims. Therefore, the way he conceptualized these phenomena was unscientific. In addition, Maslow himself was a paradox in relation to the social movements of his time. He was a leader of the American counterculture movement, but he also supported U.S. involvement in the Vietnam War. He spearheaded humanistic psychology, which supported growth in all its highest aspects, but he was also a member of the American Humanist Association, which promoted atheism and helped ban prayer from schools. Nevertheless, educated intellectuals across the helping professions and the social sciences flocked to the newness of his ideas. They were a breath of fresh air after so many years of reductionistic thinking. Finally, they were the first modern, overt expression within the scientific professions of characteristics that had long been a part of American folk psychology.

This was all very radical for the times, when conformity was the rule. The McCarthy hearings were going full tilt. The purpose of universities was to produce competent, reliable, predictable, and efficient workers for the new postwar industrial society. The dominant social model defined strict family roles whereby the male of the household was "the Organization Man," while his dutiful wife stayed at home to cook and sew and their obedient children went to school, always did all their homework, and revered authority. Behaviorism, which manipulated all of the subject's rewards and punishments, was the ideal psychology for the control of such populations. Psychoanalysis gave credibility to the unconscious lurking below the surface, but it still tried to harness untamed sexual energies for purposes of adjustment to the norms of the new technological, modernist, and scientific society. The sexual urge could be redirected toward the building of bridges, the writing of books, or the production of art, since all culture was, at base, the result of sexual sublimation. Only its overt and unbridled expression was forbidden.

Maslow's type of psychology, in contrast, like that of William James before him, put too many wild cards in the deck. What could the new social order of the 1950s do with people who actually thought for themselves, whose self-actualization norms might be radically different from the required norms of mass society? The question applied likewise to Rogers's client-centered therapy. Let the client determine the course of treatment? Never! Existentialism, of course, was completely off the map, the preoccupation of beatniks and foreigners.

But a pivotal figure now stepped in to pull the new psychology together: Anthony Sutich was a Palo Alto psychotherapist, almost completely paralyzed, who had spent nearly his whole life confined to a prone position on a medical gurney. From this vantage point, thanks to his indomitable spirit, he was able to launch a major new movement in psychology.

At the age of twelve, Sutich had been severely injured when he had been hit on the head with a bat during a baseball game. This circumstance led to progressive arthritis. When he was eighteen, his condition started to deteriorate rapidly, and he was told he had only a few months to live. Sutich recovered but remained almost completely incapacitated. He could tilt his head to the side, talk through clenched teeth, and move one of his hands. All the rest was immobile. He remained in this condition for the next fifty years.

During Sutich's hospitalizations, he noticed that people kept coming to him to talk about their personal problems and to seek his advice. This moved him to persevere and inspired him to consider counseling as a profession. Although his formal education was cut off at the ninth grade, he continued to seek educational opportunities. The wife of the Stanford psychologist Lewis Terman helped provide tutors at his bedside. He read books from a contraption that hung upside down so he could see the pages. Later, when he met another Stanford psychologist, Ernest Hilgard, graduate students would carry Sutich in the gurney up numberless flights of stairs to attend Hilgard's classes. Sutich continued to see people and talk to them about their personal problems until 1938, when he formally became a group counselor for the Palo Alto Society for the Blind.

In between these activities, Sutich met many new people. He became involved as an organizer in the labor movement, he campaigned for various forms of social legislation, and during World War II, he acted as a Serbo-Croatian translator for the State Department. During this period, he also met Allport and published an influential article on ethics and disclosure in psychotherapy in Allport's publication, the *Journal of Abnormal and Social Psychology*. Although he had no Ph.D., Sutich was grandfathered into the American Psychological Association and also became a licensed psychotherapist in the state of California.

Then, in 1949, at the suggestion of a grateful patient, Sutich met Maslow, and a lifelong friendship began. They shared a mutual interest in growth-oriented psychology and both had wide networks of colleagues similarly inclined, including Rollo May, Carl Rogers, Clark Moustakas, James Bugental, Margaret Mead, Ashley Montague, and Gregory Bateson. In 1961, Sutich and Maslow combined mailing lists and together launched the *Journal of Humanistic Psychology*. Sutich became the prime organizer and editor, while Maslow was the point man who traveled around the country lecturing on the new psychology. Ernest Hilgard paid their phone bills so they could keep in constant touch.

An important historical incident that, among many, pushed events in the direction of a new spiritual psychology within the American counterculture movement occurred in 1966 at Esalen, during meetings that Sutich attended with Maslow and others on the theme of humanistic theology. Maslow and Sutich had been talking for some time about psychologists' lack of understanding of spiritual experience. Humanistic psychology was definitely person-centered; it emphasized values and emotional development, it focused on the experiential. But it seemed to focus too much on bodily awareness. Its tendency had become anti-intellectual. And although its stated goal of character development inferred a spiritual dimension to personality, humanistic psychologists seemed incapable of discussing it directly, lacking a consensually validated language to describe it. Was a dialogue between the theologian and the psychologist about the nature of reality and the spiritual evolution of consciousness even possible? The Humanistic Theology Conference at Esalen, it was believed, was a way to begin such a discourse.

Sutich later recounted two disturbing incidents at the conference that proved to be pivotal moments in his career.[5] The first involved one of the sessions he attended with a group of Jesuits. A participant asked them if any in the group had ever had a mystical experience of any kind. The answer from each one was a blank "no." The questioner then felt impelled to ask further if it was official policy on the part of their church to systematically foster the attainment of mystical experiences among the lay members. Again the answer was a unanimous "no." Sutich was surprised. After all his years as a therapist and all the peak experiences he had heard people tell him about, combined with a few of his own, he naturally had come to believe that the profoundly transforming spiritual experience was at the root of all religious life. His conclusion was that if churches did not teach it, then some kind of new transformative psychology should.

The second incident proved to be even more shocking to him. This occurred during a seminar on the new language needed for such a transformative psychology. The group that gathered for an intellectual brainstorming session included a small number of invited participants, including Maslow, Sutich, and a man named Hobart Thomas, who was sitting next to Sutich when the session began. Suddenly, however, there was an invasion of about a dozen people who appeared to be part of the Esalen residential program, one of whom was Fritz Perls.

As the discussion began, Perls threw the session into complete disorganization by getting down on the floor. Spread out on all fours, he started slowly slithering across the room toward Thomas. As Perls passed by his chair, Sutich could hear him muttering over and over, "You are my daddy. I am coming to you." Eventually, Perls got to Thomas's chair and wrapped his arms around the man's legs, all the while continuing to mutter over and over this same chant. Thomas appeared quite embarrassed and at first could not shake off Perls. He finally succeeded, but by then complete chaos had developed. As groups at Esalen are traditionally leaderless, except when someone chooses to exert themselves, no one was in charge during this episode; no one took over the reins of command. Nevertheless, everyone was shocked, angry, and outraged.

The session broke down at that point, and Maslow left immediately. He stayed up late that night typing a letter in a white heat about the need for balance between the experiential and the intellectual, and he read it the next day when the group met again, this time without the uninvited guests. For Sutich, the episode decisively challenged his primary commitment to humanistic psychology.

It was only a short time later that he and Maslow began to formulate a new psychological movement directed toward inner exploration, self-transformation, and the spiritual aspects of personality. They would christen this movement transpersonal psychology, and what they would study would transcend the confines of the merely individual self. But as this new psychology got under way, the counterculture was emerging, largely driven by the psychedelic revolution. Maslow and Sutich's new ideas were to be engulfed by this larger social movement, which served to shape the contours of spirituality now flourishing in modern popular psychology.

The Transpersonal Orientation in American Folk Psychology

BETWEEN 1941 AND 1969, humanistic psychology thrived as an alternative within the academic university community. It proved itself capable of attracting an interdisciplinary core of scholars and administrators in the humanities and social sciences, as well as practitioners from various helping professions. But the ascent of the humanistic orientation in psychology as an intellectual discussion was soon overshadowed by the surge of social and political upheavals.

Within this flood tide, between 1967 and 1969, humanistic psychology split into at least three parts: The first was transpersonal psychology, with its emphasis on spiritual practice, meditation, and higher states of consciousness. The second was experiential encounter, which emphasized emotional relationships, cultivation of sensory experience, and a greater awareness of the body. Finally, there was radical therapy, a catchall term referring to the marriage of psychology and radical political action in such divergent areas as militant feminism, the antipsychiatry movement, critical thinking, and what has come to be called human science.

As these offshoots developed, humanistic psychology quickly became absorbed into the larger torrent of sociocultural events and lost its distinct identity. But what had before been an intellectual discussion at the periphery of high culture now moved to the forefront of the newly reemerging folk psychology.

Transpersonal psychology, as Maslow and Sutich conceived of it, claimed numerous godfathers. They recognized William James because of his emphasis on mystical consciousness in *The Varieties of Religious Experience* (1902). James had used the term "transpersonal" in a course description at Harvard in 1905–1906 to describe the concept of "outside of" or "beyond" in relation to how humans experience the world. They also recognized certain elements of transpersonal psychology in the work of C. G. Jung, because of Jung's emphasis on archetypes and the transcendent function. Jung had used the word *ueberpersonlich,* which was translated in 1914 as "superpersonal" but which he later rendered as "transpersonal" in 1942.

The transpersonalists themselves quibble over other predecessors. Some cite Aldous Huxley, whose work *The Perennial Philosophy* (1945) defined the monistic emphasis on higher consciousness that became so prevalent in the implicit assumptions about higher consciousness in the transpersonal literature. Further, there was Huxley's *Doors of Perception*

(1954), a work that helped launched the psychedelic revolution. Then there was Alan Watts, whose *Way of Zen, Joyous Cosmology,* and *Psychotherapy East and West* became bibles of the consciousness movement. There were also scientists like John Cunningham Lilly, whose *Center of the Cyclone* fused psychedelic experience with sensory isolation experiments and man-dolphin communication, and Elmer and Alyce Green of the Menninger Foundation, whose work *Beyond Biofeedback* helped launch the study of the voluntary control of internal states.

The year 1969 marks the birth of the transpersonal movement as an identifiable phenomenon, emanating largely from northern California, where Sutich maintained his home base. That year, Sutich turned over the editorial work of the *Journal of Humanistic Psychology* to Miles Vich, a young psychologist from San Jose. At the same time, from the very same office in Palo Alto, Sutich launched the *Journal of Transpersonal Psychology.* According to his introduction, the new movement would emphasize unitive consciousness, peak experiences, and mystical awakening. It would investigate states of bliss, awe, and wonder. It would study self-actualization and transcendence, and it would look for these phenomena everywhere they occurred, in the individual as well as in the group. Maslow submitted the opening article, titled "The Farther Reaches of Human Nature." It was an edited version of a lecture he had given for Esalen in San Francisco in 1967, during which he had first made the announcement that a "fourth force" was about to emerge in American psychology.

Also in 1969, Charles Tart, then a psychologist at the University of California at Davis, published his pioneering textbook, *Altered States of Consciousness,* a collection of papers on everything from the experimental study of meditation to dream psychology among the aboriginal Senoi of Malaysia. Tart's main message was that consciousness was not a single unitary state, but a plurality of continually altering conditions. As a result of this book, transpersonal themes were able to reach a vast popular audience, for it was widely available in bookstores and was adopted as a text for numerous college courses on the subject that were suddenly offered all over the country. Tart's book was the first to deal with a large cross section of topics normally banned from discussion in psychoanalytic or behavioral psychology. At the same time, it led to the development of what Tart has called "state-specific sciences"—the idea that different states of consciousness are enclosed coherent systems unto themselves and can be understood only by constructing a different science for each unique state. Tart maintained that normative science deals exclusively with phenomena in the waking rational state. According to this kind of science, dreams mean nothing or, at best, are only expressions of an unfulfilled wish; psychic phenomena (i.e., communications independent of the senses) do not exist; and religious ecstasy is a form of abnormal psychopathology. Tart claimed that, if there is more than one state, objective sciences unlike any yet known would need to be developed to understand them.

The year 1969 was also notable for the first Voluntary Control of Internal States Conference, held at a church camp forty miles from Topeka, Kansas. The gathering was sponsored by the American Association for Humanistic Psychology in conjunction with the Menninger Foundation. Eighty people from a variety of disciplines came to exchange ideas, and out of their interaction a science of altered states of consciousness began to develop that soon had a wide counterculture audience. When the second conference was held a year later, it deliberately had fewer people but led to more intense interaction. Presenters included Swami Rama, a yoga adept from India who was able to demonstrate extreme control of his physiological functions; Arthur Deikman, psychoanalyst and meditation researcher; and Stanislav Grof, a Czechoslovakian-born psychiatrist who had been a leader in the development of LSD-assisted psychotherapy at the Maryland Psychiatric Institute. Tart's theories were discussed, and Stanley Krippner, parapsychologist and psychedelic researcher, introduced the group to Rolling Thunder, a Native American medicine man who effectively melded the topics of shamanism and transpersonal psychology together for the first time. Maslow was there, apparently in good health, although still recovering from a recent heart attack. He had been elected president of the American Psychological Association in 1969, the pinnacle of recognition by the mainstream and an unprecedented opportunity for the ideas behind humanistic and transpersonal psychology to assert themselves throughout the discipline, but he had been unable to govern the 70,000-member organization because of heart trouble. He died eight weeks after the second conference in June 1970.

Maslow's death effectively ended one era and launched another. The pioneers were passing from the scene, and the fledgling institutions they had put in place were taken over by their less well-known disciples. But the significance of this power shift should not be underestimated. Basically, it represented the institutionalization of American folk psychology and a power base for the visionary tradition that would assure its continuity beyond the era of the founders. The *Journal of Transpersonal Psychology* was carried on by Sutich, who organized the American Association for Transpersonal Psychology in 1971. This new association held its first conference in 1973, which included many of those who had attended the Voluntary Control of Internal States Conferences. Also in 1973, Grof launched the International Transpersonal Association (ITA), which held its first meeting in Iceland. The event marked the opening of two different power centers in the formalized transpersonal movement, as the ITA allowed Grof the leeway to develop his own network somewhat independently of the Palo Alto–based organization. Since then, Grof has held international transpersonal meetings in such exotic places as India and South America, with sometimes surprising results for the kinds of programs that would not otherwise be possible in the United States.

Other related centers were also born around this time. In 1975, for instance, Robert Frager, a Harvard graduate in social relations, a Japan scholar, and a black belt in aikido, launched the California Institute of Transpersonal Psychology, the now-accredited doctoral-level granting wing of the formal California transpersonal movement. The American Association of Humanistic Psychology had begun to organize a graduate program in humanistic psychology by the late 1960s and, in 1970, formally established the Humanistic Psychology Institute, which soon became accredited to grant master's and doctoral degrees in California. Numerous lights such as Rollo May, Krippner, and later Amedeo Giorgi, the phenomenological psychologist, joined the faculty. Renamed the Saybrook Institute in 1981, after the historic Old Saybrook Conference of 1964, the graduate program in humanistic psychology, originally grounded in humanistically oriented psychotherapy, soon became a haven for transpersonal psychologists, as well as for political psychologists interested in deconstructionism, critical thinking, and the human sciences. With the advent of these accredited graduate programs, humanistic and transpersonal psychology continued to reshape the landscape of contemporary psychology by infusing the mainstream of professional doctorates with recognized voices from the shadow culture.[6]

The burgeoning influence of the California transpersonal orientation rippled through the counterculture, as psychotherapists, doctors, psychiatrists, psychologists, and others sympathetic to the transpersonal cause within the helping professions now had the beginnings of a science of consciousness to explain what they were doing. Publishers flocked around the new psychologists, each looking for the next best-selling New Age book. Soon, humanistic and transpersonal psychologists were commanding the attention of the American public through the popular media of lectures, weekend workshops, paperback books, and audiotapes, successfully circumventing automatic rejection by the science establishment, the medical editors, and the assembled rationalists who sat on the boards of academic journals and presses. The transpersonal orientation was even gradually infiltrating the academic establishment: In 1976, James Fadiman and Robert Frager published *Personality and Personal Growth,* the first college text in the English language to include chapters on non-Western psychology.

Also in 1976, after struggling to complete the only collegiate degree he ever earned, Anthony Sutich, at the age of seventy-three, was awarded a Ph.D. for his dissertation, "The Founding of Humanistic and Transpersonal Psychology: A Personal Account." Granted by the Humanistic Psychology Institute, a graduate program he had indirectly helped to found, the degree was conferred at his bedside. He died peacefully one day later.

With Sutich's death, a tight-knit group of younger transpersonal psychologists emerged, all of whom had associated their professional careers with the movement. Sutich's passing also brought a more conservative retrenchment of the movement, as its characteristics of explosive ideas and unlimited possibilities were replaced by pragmatic realities like running a professional journal and supporting a formal association of 3,000–4,000 members committed for the long term. Miles Vich took over as full-time editor of the *Journal of Transpersonal Psychology,* and the Association for Transpersonal Psychology rallied around the younger professionals. Along with Fadiman, Frager, and Grof, these included Daniel Goleman, a Buddhist meditator and writer for the *New York Times;* Francis Vaughn, a psychotherapist in private practice who wrote on intuition; Roger Walsh, a psychiatrist and Zen meditator; John Welwood, a psychotherapist interested in Buddhism; and Ram Das, formerly the Harvard psychologist Richard Alpert. Eventually, the association attracted into its fold Ken Wilber, who would come to be thought of as the Einstein of consciousness. A master's-level graduate student in chemistry and an eclectic meditator who had published his first book, *The Spectrum of Consciousness,* through the Theosophical Society, Wilber soon emerged as the spokesperson for the consciousness paradigm within the group most closely associated with Sutich's journal.[7] Thereafter, he began jockeying for public recognition as the "leader" of the transpersonal movement.

Actually, since the 1970s, transpersonal psychology, like the humanistic movement that preceded it, has splintered into three different groups. One, represented by Grof's ideas, believes that transcendence can occur only in the presence of an altered state of consciousness. This group generates conceptual models of nonordinary states of consciousness that they believe will help explain shamanic healing trances, psychedelic states, visionary experiences, psychotic episodes, and the dynamics of a variety of human conditions, from the experiential psychotherapies to the reasoning behind waging wars and revolutions.

The second group, led by Wilber, includes those who attempt to map inner states of consciousness. Self-consciously identifying himself with the monistic and perennial philosophy of Aldous Huxley, Wilber looks into the English-language rendering of non-Western religions and finds that all expressions of the highest state of consciousness in each tradition are the same. In the eclectic fashion of so many self-taught American folk psychologists who have come before him, he picks and chooses terms and concepts from various traditions to weave a large illustrated tapestry in which psychopathic states occur at the bottom, normal waking realities in the middle, and meditative states of higher consciousness at the top.

The gradations in between are the subject of Wilber's numerous books and articles, which attempt to make finer and finer discriminations among states with names borrowed from many traditions. The result is a chart of Wilber's inner universe showing the fixed location of specific states, as well as how to get in and out of them.

The third and, by far, the largest segment of the transpersonal movement has no identifiable standard-bearer, which is perhaps appropriate to its inherent metaphysics. This is the group that sees self-actualization as getting up and going to work in the morning and coming home to experience a normal life. Higher consciousness consists of sweeping the floor, doing the dishes, and raking the leaves. Enlightenment is doing whatever we are supposed to be doing at this minute. It is not a preconceived thing; it is not an altered state of consciousness; it is not a site distinct from the one we inhabit now. Rather, it is simply the philosophy of the profound, which is to be discovered most clearly in the mundane.

Leaderless, pervasive, yet unnamed, seemingly everywhere and yet without a center anywhere—these are the essential traits of the widespread psychospiritual revolution now in progress in modern culture. And if this all sounds a little too existential to some, it is because this offshoot of the shadow culture is precisely where all the existentialists have gone. In the 1950s, they went to the coffee houses, read poetry, and sang folk songs protesting the prevailing conservative influences of the times. In the 1960s, existentialism and psychoanalysis gave way to humanistic psychology, Jungian thought, and Asian ideas about consciousness. A large segment of an entire generation began to experiment with mind-altering drugs, to read Alan Watts, Abraham Maslow, and Timothy Leary, and to join the counterculture. In the 1970s, humanistic psychology graduated to transpersonal psychology, people suddenly became vegetarians and adopted lifelong spiritual disciplines. Assimilating themselves back into mainstream culture, hundreds of thousands of visionaries thereafter began a cultural revolution from the bottom up. They started new kinds of families, went back to school, and entered the professions with new questions. They started their own companies, they launched their own research projects, they began spending their money only on what they deemed most important, and they expressed their newfound spiritual ideals in myriad ways that are now completely trans-forming modern culture. And while we may see evidence of these changes everywhere in popular culture, the transformation in American social consciousness that these changes represent has now also reached the door of mainstream science and traditional medicine in the form of human science and alternative or complementary therapies.

Notes

1. Material in this section is adapted from the Saybrook Institute Oral History Project in Humanistic and Transpersonal Psychology, Saybrook Graduate School and Research Institute, San Francisco, CA. See also E. I. Taylor, "Review of Richard Katz's *Boiling Energy,*" *Journal of Transpersonal Psychology,* 14:2 (1982): 188–190; E. I. Taylor, "William James and the Humanistic Tradition," *Journal of Humanistic Psychology,* 31:1 (1982); E. I. Taylor, "Transpersonal Psychology: Its Several Virtues," in F. Wertz, ed., *The Humanistic Movement in Psychology: History, Celebration, and Prospects,* special issue of *Humanistic Psychologist,* 20:2–3 (1992): 285–300; E. I. Taylor, "William James and Transpersonal Psychiatry," in B. W. Scotton, A. Chinen, and J. R. Battista, eds., *Textbook of Transpersonal Psychiatry and Psychology* (New York: Basic Books, 1996), pp. 21–28; E. I. Taylor, "Psychology as a Person-Centered Science: William James's Relation to the Humanistic Tradition," in D. Moss, ed., *Handbook of the History of Humanistic and Transpersonal Psychology* (Westport, CT: Greenwood, 1999); and E. I. Taylor, "An Intellectual Renaissance of Humanistic Psychology?" *Journal of Humanistic Psychology* (forthcoming).

2. For a biographical statement, see Howard Kirschenbaum, *On Becoming Carl Rogers* (New York: Delacorte Press, 1979). Rogers's chronological bibliography can be found in an appendix to Roy DeCarvalho, *The Founders of Humanistic Psychology* (New York: Praeger, 1981).

3. A definitive biography of May is in preparation by Robert Abzug.

4. The most useful biography of Maslow is by Edward Hoffman, *The Right to Be Human: A Biography of Abraham Maslow* (Los Angeles: J. P. Tarcher, 1988). See also Richard J. Lowry, ed., *The Journals of A. H. Maslow,* commissioned by the International Study Project, Inc., in cooperation with Bertha G. Maslow (Monterey, CA: Brooks/Cole Publishing Co., 1979).

5. Anthony Sutich, "The Founding of Humanistic and Transpersonal Psychology: A Personal Account," unpublished Ph.D. diss., Humanistic Psychology Institute, San Francisco, CA, 1976.

6. Transpersonal psychologists and human science scholars also found a place among other independent northern California institutes, such as Alan Watts's California Institute for Integral Studies in San Francisco, the Wright Institute in Berkeley, the Pacific Graduate School, and the History of Consciousness Program at the University of California at Santa Cruz.

7. Ken Wilber, *The Spectrum of Consciousness* (Wheaton, IL: Theosophical Publishing House, 1977).

Chapter Thirteen

Psychology and Spirituality: Another Great Awakening?

OUR FINAL THOUGHT COMES FROM THE *APOLLO 14* ASTRONAUT Edgar Mitchell, who walked on the moon with Alan Shepard in 1972 and who, while there, performed some controversial and unauthorized experiments in telepathy with colleagues on Earth. In a recent interview, Mitchell described what he has since called an epiphany experience, which, he said, became the high point of his trip, as well as the high point of his life.[1]

At the time of this experience, Mitchell was 124,000 miles in the air. From his seat, he could look out the spacecraft's window and see a vast universe in front of him. The crew had just passed out of the moon's orbit, and the giant burning furnace of the bright sun was at their back. All around them, everywhere, were billions of stars and galactic clusters, ten times more than one can normally see from the ground of the planet. In front of him, and set against this backdrop, was Earth. She hung there in space and appeared to him as a gigantic, round, living organism. Some of the oceans and the continents were visible through the swirling patterns of clouds—colors of blue, green, brown, and white were all intermingled. Here was our Earth—the mother that sustains us, our birthplace, our home, teeming with both life and death, growth and decay, ever active, never sleeping, always changing, hurtling through space at a terrific speed. He proclaimed that it was like nothing he had ever seen before.

Then, suddenly, Mitchell had what he has since called an epiphany. He became one with the universe. His identity, he said, fused with all that was around him. He saw that he, too, was an active part of the very process he was viewing. Just as he was a living intelligent being, so, too, was the universe. Instantly, everything around him he saw as alive and infused with intelligence. Consciousness appeared to be everywhere, not just confined to human beings. And it seemed like a wider and deeper consciousness than merely rational human beings can know. At that moment, virtually everything that he believed was completely tossed up in the air. It was a euphoric experience.

Afterward, in reflecting on what he had seen, Mitchell concluded that, coming from a background in fundamentalist Christianity and physical science, he was completely unprepared for what he had seen up there in space about the relationship between himself and the universe. He was now certain that the possibilities of consciousness are far greater than we realize. At the same time, it became obvious to him that nothing in present-day science or in the religions of the past is sufficient to grasp this intelligence.

Mitchell has further come to believe that the knowledge base of the twenty-first century will be entirely different than that of the ancients 2,500 or 3,000 years ago, when most of our belief systems about the nature of divinity were created. The gap between what we are now experiencing and the traditional language we use to describe the world around us is rapidly becoming unbridgeable. This means that new structures for comprehending reality and understanding consciousness, he says, will have to emerge if we are to intelligently grasp what lies ahead of us in the future.

This is to say that the situation at the end of the twentieth century with regard to psychology and spirituality is not entirely unlike that at the end of the nineteenth—spectacular advances in the basic sciences accompanied by significantly more philosophical questions concerning the relation of consciousness to the physical world that have been left unanswered. Perhaps in the same way that the fusion of physiological psychology and psychical research led to major advances in psychotherapeutics 100 years ago, we may expect such presently opposing forces as mainstream science and complementary or alternative medicine, or neuroscience brain mapping and the self-induction of spiritual states of consciousness, to produce altogether new approaches to understanding the interaction of mind and body. It would not be unlikely, for instance, that deep states of prolonged, quiet meditation will become a standard procedure in extended space-flight to Mars or to destinations beyond our galaxy.

With regard to basic science, two options seem perfectly clear. Either science as it now exists will have to evolve into something else in order to accommodate psychological phenomena across a larger spectrum of human experience than it now does, or else scientists will have to accommodate themselves to the idea that science as we now define it is not all-encompassing and, in fact, may be only one more form of useful knowledge in modern culture next to political, economic, social, or religious forms, or even more internal frames of reference.

Foremost among the contributions of a modern, humanistic, and transpersonally oriented depth psychology to this discussion is an exploration of the phenomenology of the science-making process itself. Science, perhaps the greatest contribution to world knowledge that Western civilization has produced, will now permanently outlive the culture that has produced it. This has occurred not only because different forms of science have been adapted to nearly all cultures throughout the world, but also because science itself has matured beyond its original roots.

In the early history of Western science, the primary focus was mastery of the inorganic world of rocks and minerals. Throughout the eighteenth and nineteenth centuries, the sciences then progressed into the realm of the organic, encompassing not only geology and astronomy, but the biology of the plant and animal kingdoms as well. Rocks and stars were far enough away from human beings that their study was cause for only abstract theological and intellectual debates about different models of the universe. But when science encroached upon the level of the organic, a human being's place in nature became the new issue, and moral questions regarding the use of dead bodies for autopsies or the objective manipulation of body parts in a live physical examination became more rigorous and heated.

We have lived in our own time to see science make its way into the domain of psychology, into the study of the emotions, into neuronal patterns of our thought processes, and into the manipulation of traits of character and temperament once thought to be fixed by heredity or shaped only at the caprice of the environment. But the new biology of consciousness has also brought with it a host of philosophical questions about the relation of the brain to experience and about the very methods used to study physical phenomena. For the closer we get to the objective study of consciousness, the closer we get to the very mind that is studying the object—to the very consciousness that is generating the scientific knowledge. And as everyone knows, here is the great limitation of that extraordinary enterprise—its fatal flaw—namely, that science cannot objectively study itself. And when it does, at that precise point, it becomes something else—philosophy, metaphysics, religion, or whatever name we give to the process of the unconscious becoming an object of consciousness; whatever it is, the object is always transformed. This is what is meant by the phenomenology of the science-making process: Self-observation always leads us to an existential point about the metaphysics of experience, and it is almost always a transforming moment.

The inability of contemporary science as it is presently constituted to accommodate such phenomena, however, means that educated and thinking individuals who do not find adequate meaning in contemporary scientific explanations will look elsewhere for ways to understand their personal reality. Scientific knowledge will then take second place to other forms of knowing, such as the poetic, the numinous, or the visionary. This has, in fact, historically been the case with individuals who have crossed over into the shadow culture. Their skepticism of contemporary science and medicine may be extreme.

And though it is true that when serious illness threatens, they will likely seek out the mainstream medical solutions of Big Science, it is also true that we continue to negotiate both worlds simultaneously. David Eisenberg and colleagues at Harvard sent significant shock waves through the traditional scientific community in 1993 when they published an epidemiologic survey in the *New England Journal of Medicine* on unconventional medicine in the United States, couched in terms of prevalence, cost, and patterns of use.[2] The results of this study showed that over the period of one year, 34 percent of the population sampled had used alternative methods of treatment, the highest rate of use being among nonblacks between the ages of twenty-five and forty-nine with relatively good educational backgrounds and high incomes. Whereas the majority of visits were for chronic rather than life-threatening conditions, there were still visits made by those seeking treatment for the most serious medical disorders, such as cancer and AIDS, although these patients were simultaneously under the care of a Western scientifically trained physician; but most had not informed this physician of their dual treatment regime.

By applying their findings to the American population at large, Eisenberg and his associates estimated that unconventional therapies amounted to a $13.7 billion a year industry, much of it in cash transactions as the patient was also paying for regular monthly insurance premiums to cover traditional scientific medical treatment. They also estimated that, in all likelihood, the total number of patient visits to nonconventional healers exceeded the total number of visits to primary care physicians and that the money changing hands was roughly equivalent to the total amount spent yearly out-of-pocket for all hospitalizations in the United States.

Eisenberg and his co-workers then conducted a follow-up study analyzing patterns of usage for the 1990 to 1996 time period.[3] Surveying over 2,000 subjects, the team found that usage of at least one of sixteen alternative therapies increased from 33.8 percent in 1990 to 42.1 percent in 1997. The therapies for which use escalated the most included herbal medicine, massage, megavitamins, self-help groups, folk remedies, energy healing, and homeopathy. The probability of users visiting an alternative medicine practitioner also increased from 36.3 percent to 46.3 percent. Extrapolations to the U.S. population suggest a 47.3 percent increase in total visits to alternative medicine practitioners, from 427 million in 1990 to 629 million in 1997, thereby exceeding total visits to all U.S. primary care physicians. An estimated 15 million adults in 1997 took prescription medications concurrently with herbal remedies and/or high-dose vitamins (18.4 percent of all prescription users). Estimated expenditures for alternative medicine professional services increased 45.2 percent between 1990 and 1997 and were conservatively estimated at $21.2 billion in 1997, with at least $12.2 billion paid out-of-pocket. This exceeds the 1997 out-of-pocket expenditures for all U.S. hospitalizations. Total 1997 out-of-pocket expenditures relating to alternative therapies were conservatively estimated at $27.0 billion, which is comparable with the projected 1997 out-of-pocket expenditures for all U.S. physician services.

While scientists like Eisenberg are just beginning to study empirically how complementary and alternative medicine continues to overtake traditional medical practice, other investigators have been attempting to get at the root of these new trends by reexamining the very presuppositions of the scientific method. One example is the late Willis Harman's Causality Project, co-sponsored by the John E. Fetzer Foundation of Kalamazoo, Michigan, and the Institute of Noetic Sciences in Sausalito, California. Harman, who had also been an engineer by training, had embarked on a scientific career studying consciousness more than a half century ago. He eventually came to the conclusion that the basic foundations of science had to be overhauled first if an adequate science of consciousness was to develop. On this basis, funds were gathered to underwrite Harman's effort to convene a battery of scholars, historians, and scientists to address this question. Their research eventually produced a groundbreaking text, *The New Metaphysical Foundations of Modern Science,* which attempted to summarize the scope of newly emerging kinds of science in physics, engineering, medicine, sociology, anthropology, philosophy, and psychology.[4]

Simultaneously, we may ask similar questions of organized religion. What happens when traditional religious institutions fail to address the depth and breadth of an individual's contemporary experience? History has shown us that an entire generation has gone elsewhere and entered into unique and altogether unprecedented experiments in personal spirituality. Moreover, it is not an insignificant number we are talking about. Nevertheless, and most significantly, the modern psychospiritual revolution that forms the central thesis of the present work is not taken up in the very places where we would expect to see it—in the objective study of religions, such as the Harvard Pluralism Project.

Paul Tillich, probably the most influential force in Protestant theology in the twentieth century, called for Protestantism to abandon the old creedal apologies in favor of a new theology of culture, such as that reflected in the contemporary attempts to link theology and experience through existentially oriented depth psychology or through current endeavors to generate a science of the spirit. We should at least, he said, find the relevance of religious experience in the midst of contemporary culture. That traditional institutions of religious expression either have failed to address the new scope of people's experience or have even become hostile toward acknowledging the validity of it is reason enough for the flourishing of alternative and nonconventional forms of spirituality.

A more positive interpretation of historic events is that we are experiencing a period of collective opening of the doors of perception, the scope of which, of course, far exceeds the bounds of our present conceptual abilities as a culture. Nevertheless the traditional forms of religion are the direct beneficiaries. Evangelical Christianity has already begun to experience a resurgence in response to these larger developments. My prediction is that, following this lead, we may see a swelling of the ranks of not only the Protestant denominational churches, but also all forms of institutional religion. Tens of thousands of people will complete the cycle of the inward "hero's journey." They will return again to their roots and be changed entirely. The question is, will the old religious institutions of modernism be ready to receive them?

Two Prophesies

I WOULD LIKE TO MAKE TWO PROPHESIES in this regard. The first is that, based on the present historical analysis of an American visionary psychology and its contributions to the larger context of an alternative reality tradition in the West, we may be destined to see, possibly even within our own time, a cross-cultural exchange of ideas between East and West unprecedented in the history of Western thought.

I say this, first, because the alternative reality tradition has always functioned as a conduit for Asian ideas into the West, and there is no reason to believe that it will cease functioning to do so. Second, the reality is that man-made technological innovations of the most materialistic type have brought all parts of the world closer together and have, in fact, inadvertently created the conditions upon which an encounter with others no longer occurs impersonally, but now represents a face-to-face encounter on the most basic level of our humanity. The enemy is no longer faceless. The starving actually have names. One culture's values are now beginning to more and more affect the different values of another. Third is the observation that current trends toward multiculturalism may only be the first blush of a more pervasive opening up of the West to non-Western epistemologies, or ways of knowing, in a way that we see for the first time in our history the very contextual frame of reference upon which our own cultural presuppositions of reality are based. This can come about, however, only when we acknowledge these non-Western frames of reference as having some kind of parity to our own.

In any event, such a change in contextual frame of reference means that each object previously defined by the embedding process of our own exclusive way of looking at things will have to be reevaluated. A toaster may represent technological innovation at the same time that it represents the price we paid for extracting its metal from the Earth. Education may mean inward character development as much as it means the development of outward skills for a vocation. Science may mean both the inner and the outer sciences. Consciousness may refer to waking rational consciousness as well as to other more subtle states of consciousness beyond the mere rational attachment of the senses to external material reality. There will be a historic change in the very context in which reality is defined.

A second prophesy is that, with this change in contextual frame of reference, the status of psychology in Western culture may dramatically change. Technically, instead of seeing psychology as just another category in the school of arts and sciences next to that of sociology and anthropology, we may see it as the foundation of all knowledge accumulation. Instead of psychology being defined as the rational ordering of sense data, following the lead of such natural sciences as physics, chemistry, and biology, this kind of psychology is more personal, more immediate, and more phenomenological.

Instead of something mental that we cannot easily measure that is opposed to something physical, which is easy to measure, such a psychology may become the way we understand the interaction of the mind and the body. A psychology in this sense, following William James, I equate not with the modeling of reality as we do now, but with immediate experience—what is happening to us in the here and now. This is psychology as *erkenntnisstheorie,* meaning psychology as epistemology.

Such a psychology, I maintain, brings us closer to understanding the meaning of personal experience, which is the kind of spiritual psychology at the heart of the American visionary tradition. And here we have our most important clue as to the role of the shadow culture in the present unprecedented era of cultural transformation. Visionaries are already our most valuable translators of the changes to come. They are already prepared to understand non-Western epistemologies; they are already in touch with the context of the inward sciences; their outlook is already mythic and numinous.

The Enduring Importance of the Visionary Tradition

WHAT THIS VISIONARY PERSPECTIVE might have to contribute to modern culture in the long run, then, is worth examining. In the first place, psychologically, it represents a widening of our contextual frame of reference. Folk psychology readily acknowledges, for instance, the reality of the unconscious—what is in front of us is merely on the surface, while surrounding the present waking field is a vast inward domain normally hidden from view that operates according to its own dynamic processes. This seems simple enough, but the acknowledgment of this reality is not a part of the conscious lore of contemporary society. We do not teach this view to children in schools. We do not consciously or systematically appeal to this understanding in the treatment of physical illnesses or in our approach to crime, violence, or prejudice. And no language acknowledging the reality of the unconscious is a part of news reporting or documentary filmmaking. We do find it suggested in art, literature, and religion, but these have been relegated to the status of mere taste and opinion in modern culture, not what we teach as truth or reality. Such endeavors are what the realist used to pursue on weekends, before, when the old way of living was still intact.

By failing to collectively acknowledge the reality of the unconscious, we have no access to an understanding of the hidden springs of motivation. Most people, for instance, do not understand the subtleties of suggestion and the effects of propaganda. Most of us cannot clearly distinguish when we are truly learning from when we are being manipulated by outright brainwashing. Meanwhile, we are subject to the systematic application of just these principles on a daily basis through the mass media, particularly through advertising.

Advertisers, however, are well aware of the psychology of motivation, which requires that the person being motivated remains himself unaware of these processes in order to be successfully influenced. Products are, after all, displayed not by telling you exactly what is in them or how they are made, but by associating them with wonderful colors, soothing music, and beautiful-looking people, as well as by appealing indirectly to our unconscious needs and desires.

A century ago, our collective attention was dominated by the telegraph, the telephone, and the newspapers. This was followed by the age of radio. Then we became transfixed with television and now with computers. The leap from audio to video was tremendously significant for the increased manipulation of unconscious processes it brought in its wake. In the hypnotic effect created by the technology of the cathode-ray tube, we have the most pervasive example of how a true state change can be brought on just by flipping a switch and focusing our attention on the screen. The effect is intensified by the content of the medium, which is self-consciously designed largely to entertain by sensual arousal, to in-form by voyeuristic sound bites, and to sell by stimulating artificially induced compulsions.

But to have collective access to a dynamic understanding of the unconscious could possibly transform what we will allow to influence us. First, it would demystify psychotherapy, potentially enliven education, and open the way for a more in-depth and systematic understanding of how to develop character. The psychogenic hypothesis, the mechanism by which traumatic events and intrapsychic conflict are converted into physical symptoms, is already an established idea within American folk psychology and certain aspects of clinical psychotherapy, although it continues to remain a complete mystery even to the common college graduate. Rote learning, skills in analytic thinking, and the Western rational tradition still comprise the main focus of education. Meanwhile, alternative educational opportunities for the development of experiential, intuitive, and emotional capacities abound in the culture, beyond the repressive control of outmoded definitions of education put forth by many colleges and universities, while ethnographic interest in the experiential roots of non-Western cultures continues to exist wherever folk psychology has flourished in America.

Second, the cultural awakening presently under way requires a more acute understanding of how to develop the faculties of intuition and insight, dimensions of personality presently being sorely neglected. We hear all about the importance of repeating a scientific experiment but nothing about creative hypothesis formulation. Writing courses are full of instructions on grammar and syntax and how to edit but never on how to generate a good idea worth writing about in the first place. Self-defense instruction explains what to do after you are attacked but says very little about how to systematically develop those capacities that help you to avoid or diffuse the threatening situation before it can ever develop. And when budget cuts threaten the high school curricula, art and music courses are the first to go, while science and mathematics are always allotted more money.

Where are we as a modern civilization if our educational institutions conspire to train only a fraction of our capacities? And if this is all they can really do, then why not acknowledge that fact openly and give legitimacy to the other alternative forms of education that do cultivate those neglected dimensions of personality, instead of pretending that anything lying outside the standards set by the Western analytic tradition is either inferior, anti-intellectual, or diabolic?

Third, a widening of our collective cultural frame of reference to acknowledge the visionary dimension of our collective history would permit the freer discussion of what it means to embark upon a confrontation with the unconscious as a means of inward growth and transformation. We might develop a more systematic understanding of how to cultivate willpower and come to fathom that self-realization as a deeply inward phenomenological experience, though it takes place in a physical body, nevertheless occurs in a distinctly different epistemological domain than the physical world of objects. We might adopt a slightly different attitude toward our sexuality, thereby recognizing that repression may be a long-overlooked source of both neurosis and violent aggression.

Furthermore, we may adopt a somewhat more realistic attitude toward drugs. Instead of pretending that there are only two types—legal and illegal—or that the only way to cure drug addiction is through the administration of more drugs, we might finally acknowledge the extent to which we are a drug-oriented culture and in need of a completely different standard for judging how we will use these substances to better advantage. At the very least, conservative fundamentalists should realize that the psychedelic generation of the 1960s has moved quickly into a permanent lifestyle spiritual practice that is in many ways as fervent and committed as their own and that drug policy in America might take a page from the counterculture. Voluntarily accepted purification of mind and body in preparation for transcendence, the very element the scientific approach cannot teach us, has already been successfully employed in the amelioration of drug-taking behavior but by a new and younger generation whose values the older generation may not always comprehend.

To take seriously the claims of a visionary psychology would also entail a transformation of our attitudes regarding the mythic nature of symbols. In the context of a dynamic psychology of the unconscious, more empirical research in the future may focus on guided mental imagery as the most appropriate language by which consciousness communicates with normally involuntary processes of the physical body. This may have significant implications for healing and illness, as psychology comes to play a more central role in the delivery of physical medicine. It may also be that scientists will find all the empirical verification they need to show that imagery is the doorway into different interior states of consciousness. Or by gaining access to these states through cognitive means, it may be possible to enhance learning, an ability that would certainly have large implications for the way our educational system is presently structured.

An appreciation for the dynamics of mental imagery might also transform our attitudes toward nontechnological cultures that have what some deem a well-developed science of inner experience. The traditions of yoga and meditation in India, the philosophy of consciousness in the various schools of Asian Buddhism, the ethical psychology of the Confucianists—these are all much more than simply inner technologies. They suggest that different cultures operate from radically different conceptions of personality and consciousness and that these conceptions are collectively stored in the respective mythic images of those cultures. One could conceive, in this regard, of creating a much larger picture that might show the entire infrastructure of world mythologies, and this map would be useful in piecing together the contribution that uniquely distinct cultures have to make toward a definition of world mental health.

Finally, the extent to which the iconography of the transcendent will play a major role in the development of a science of consciousness or some form of depth psychology of the future must remain open. There can be little doubt that professionals in normative science, allopathic medicine, and present-day academic psychology reject categorically any attempt to reintroduce what they feel is the language of religious superstition back into scientific discussions about the relation between the mind and the body. To the extent that there remains a widespread belief in the possibility of the transcendent, to the extent that transcendence forms the basis for an awakened spirituality that has concrete effects now largely flourishing outside of the language of denominational Christianity, and to the extent that it can be buttressed by even the smallest shred of empirical evidence showing that true state changes in consciousness do occur (as in studies of hypnosis and meditation), the iconography of the transcendent cannot simply be waved away with some self-appointed authoritative hand.

Rather, conceptions of higher consciousness represent the core of present-day folk psychology. And however superficial and benign these conceptions may at first appear, detractors as well as adherents would do well to recognize that the American visionary tradition did not just come on to the scene yesterday, that it has a substantial history and a not inconsequential lineage. Moreover, to understand it, one must not get bogged down in minute details. Instead, the visionary tradition must be read largely and not pedantically. In any event, it remains, as William James once said of it, "a true religious power yet to be reckoned with." [5]

Notes

1. Adapted from Edie Weinstein-Moser, "Interview with Edgar Mitchell," *Visions,* Southeast regional ed. (July 1992): 6, and from my own interview with Edgar Mitchell, January 28, 1995.

2. D. M. Eisenberg, R. C. Kessler, C. Foster, F. E. Norlock, D. R. Calkins, and T. L. Delbenco, "Unconventional Medicine in the United States: Prevalence, Costs, and Patterns of Use," *New England Journal of Medicine,* 328 (1993): 246.

3. David M. Eisenberg, Roger B. Davis, Susan L. Ettner, Scott Appel, Sonja Wilkey, Maria Van Rompay, and Ronald C. Kessler, "Results of a Follow-up National Survey of Trends in Alternative Medicine Use in the United States, 1990–1997," *Journal of the American Medical Association,* 280 (1998): 1569–1575.

4. W. Harman and J. Clark, eds., The *New Metaphysical Foundations of Modern Science* (Sausalito, CA: Institute of Noetic Sciences, 1994).

5. William James, *The Varieties of Religious Experience* (New York: Longmans, 1902).